Teacher Education Yearbook XIX

EDITORS

Cheryl J. Craig, University of Houston
Louise F. Deretchin, Educational Consultant

EDITORIAL ADVISORY BOARD

EDITORIAL SUPPORT BOARD

EXECUTIVE DIRECTOR

Cultivating Curious and Creative Minds

The Role of Teachers and Teacher Educators: Part II

Teacher Education Yearbook XIX

EDITED BY CHERYL J. CRAIG
AND LOUISE F. DERETCHIN

Published in partnership with the
Association of Teacher Educators
ROWMAN & LITTLEFIELD EDUCATION
Lanham, Maryland • Toronto • Plymouth, UK
2011

Published in partnership with the
Association of Teacher Educators

Published in the United States of America
by Rowman & Littlefield Education
A Division of Rowman & Littlefield Publishers, Inc.
A wholly owned subsidary of The Rowman & Littlefield Publishing Group, Inc.
4501 Forbes Boulevard, Suite 200, Lanham, Maryland 20706
www.rowmaneducation.com

Estover Road
Plymouth PL6 7PY
United Kingdom

ISSN: 1078-2265
ISBN: 978-1-61048-113-7 (cloth: alk. paper)
ISBN: 978-1-61048-114-4 (pbk.: alk. paper)
ISBN: 978-1-61048-115-1 (e-book)

∞™ The paper used in this publication meets the minimum requirements of American National Standard for Information Sciences—Permanence of Paper for Printed Library Materials, ANSI/NISO Z39.48-1992.
Manufactured in the United States of America.

Contents

Illustrations

Tables

Figures

Foreword

Terrell M. Peace
Huntington University

Terrell Peace, Ph.D., is chair of the Education Department and director of Undergraduate Teacher Education at Huntington University, Huntington, Indiana. He has been involved in the Association of Teacher Educators (ATE) for more than twenty years and has served on numerous national committees and commissions. He was on the ATE Board of Directors from 2001 to 2004. Dr. Peace has been active in the ATE Indiana Unit since moving to the state in 1998 and received the ATE-I Distinguished Service Award in 2003. He is a member of Kappa Delta Pi and has served as a chapter counselor for ten years. Recent publications include contributions to *Affective Teacher Education: Exploring Connections among Knowledge, Skills, and Dispositions* (Rowman & Littlefield, 2009) and *Racism in the Classroom* (ATE/ACEI, 2002).

It is my distinct pleasure as president of ATE to invite you to search this engaging volume: *Cultivating Curious and Creative Minds, Part II.* It is an invitation to move beyond the trivial and mundane to that which can be and should be essential to our vision for teaching and for teacher education.

One of my first responsibilities as ATE president was to select a theme for the year that would be professionally relevant and would establish parameters for the call for proposals for the two ATE national conferences, and for other research possibilities as well. The theme for my presidency has been "Re-Igniting the Passion and Purpose for Teaching" and I have spoken in several settings about a number of the factors that, over the past several years, have worked together to rob many teachers and teacher educators of their passion for the profession. I believe that one contributing factor is the utilitarian, lock-step, *overly* standardized view of education that seems to permeate every level of the political landscape. As a society, we seem to have lost any sense of education as an opportunity to expand and develop minds. In our head-long rush to prepare students for work, I fear that we have lost sight of preparing them for life. The popularized notion seems to be that the teaching and learning process can be either practical or creative, but it cannot be both. While few would accept this false dichotomy as valid, teachers and teacher educators alike feel pressure to act as if it were.

I could not be more pleased with the focus of this ATE Teacher Education Yearbook because I believe that editors Cheryl Craig and Louise Deretchin have assembled a collection of articles that will challenge this bifurcated view of education by challenging our thinking about not only *how* we teach and prepare teachers but also *why*. The articles that focus more on tying the cultivation of creativity to the *how* of teaching can help reignite the passion that we have for the process of teaching by establishing the connection between creative learning and real, concrete, measurable results. The solid research and documented experience show that teaching can be, and should be, both creative and practical. The authors who focus more on the connection between creativity and the *why* of teaching remind us of the passion that drives so many teachers and teacher educators, the chance to make a difference in the lives of students. What a grand opportunity we have, as we engage students in the enterprise of learning! What an opportunity to impact students for the rest of their lives, as we teach and model a thirst for creative and curious knowing!

Introduction

Cheryl J. Craig
University of Houston

Louise F. Deretchin
Educational Consultant

Cheryl J. Craig is a professor at the University of Houston, where she serves as coordinator of the Teaching and Teacher Education Program Area and director of elementary education. She was recently elected secretary of the International Study Association of Teachers and Teaching. Craig's scholarship is published in such journals as *Teachers College Record, Teaching and Teacher Education, American Educational Research Journal,* and *Journal of Curriculum Studies.* Her book, *Narrative Inquiries of School Reform: Storied Lives, Storied Landscapes, Storied Metaphors,* was published in 2003.

Louise F. Deretchin, Ph.D., is an educational consultant, former director of Higher Education for the Houston A+ Challenge (formerly the Houston Annenberg Challenge), former director of Medical Informatics Education Center at Baylor College of Medicine, a fellow in the Association of Teacher Educators (ATE) Leadership Academy, founding member of the Texas Higher Education Coordinating Board Houston P–16+ Council, and cofounder of the Regional Faculty whose purpose is to take a regional approach to directing the growth of educational systems. She has been coeditor of the Association of Teacher Educators Yearbook since 2006. Her work focuses on creating collaborations among colleges, the business community, and school districts to improve teacher education, teaching, and learning.

When we circulated the call for chapters on "cultivating curious and creative minds in teaching education," we could not have predicted the kind of response our invitation would receive. Clearly, we struck a rich vein of intellectual interest.

In fact, so many educators responded to the call that what we initially imagined would be a single volume of the ATE Yearbook morphed into two volumes: *Cultivating Curious and Creative Minds: The Role of Teachers and Teacher Educators, Part I* (ATE Yearbook XVIII) and *Cultivating Curious and Creative Minds: The Role of Teachers and Teacher Educators, Part II* (ATE Yearbook XIX). In part I, published in 2010, we focused exclusively on teaching. In part II (published in 2011), we center on teacher education and students, programs, and schools. But make no mistake: the two volumes are pieces of the same cloth. Themes that began to unfold in part I reappear in part II; narratives shared in part II resonate with those in part I; and the reference lists of the chapters in parts I and II are near carbon copies of one another. As editors, we are delighted to present this volume to the ATE membership and the general readership. We also sincerely thank the many authors who made the publication of, not one, but two volumes on "cultivating curious and creative minds" possible.

Cultivating Curious and Creative Minds: The Role of Teachers and Teacher Educators, Parts I and II presents a plethora of approaches to developing human potential in areas not conventionally addressed. Organized around divisions—teaching (the sole division in part I), then teacher education (division 1) and students, programs, and schools (division 2) in part II—this international collection of essays provides viable educational alternatives to those currently holding sway in this era of high stakes accountability. We feel certain that readers will find this volume a refreshing change to the typical approaches that have dominated how students are characteristically taught in schools and colleges of education.

TEACHER EDUCATION

Overview and Framework

Cheryl J. Craig

Louise F. Deretchin

In this Yearbook, we focus full attention on "cultivating curious and creative minds" in teacher education and through various approaches and programs in the schools. In division 1, we shine the spotlight on teacher education and the five chapters having to do with it.

Division 1 begins with chapter 1, which is Anne Chodakowski, Kieran Egan, Gillian Judson, and Kym Stewart's essay on "Some Neglected Components of Teacher Education Programs." The team of authors argues persuasively that the potential of the following elements are not being adequately addressed in teacher education: engaging imagination through metaphor; story-shaping the curriculum; affective images in curriculum content; and humor in the classroom.

Donald Blumenfeld-Jone's chapter, "Fostering Creativity and Aesthetic Consciousness in Teachers: Theory and Practice," focuses on the development of aesthetic consciousness and creativity in a teacher education program. Using his "Teaching for the Aesthetic Life" course as a model, he illustrates how art (pop art and high art) is a mode of living.

"Sunshine and Shadows: Opening Spaces for Creativity, Metaphor, and Paradox in Teaching and Teacher Education" is the title of chapter 3, which is authored by Dixie Keyes. The work centers on metaphorical and narrative ways of knowing, through using William Gordon's Synectics to spur teachers to embrace metaphors and paradox in order to generate new ideas.

Chris Lasher-Zwerling and Kip Téllez contributed chapter 4, "No Less 'Real' in My Mind: Using Fiction as Creative Curriculum in an Undergraduate Teacher Education Course." In it, they present a study they undertook where fiction was used to help broaden preservice teachers' reflective understandings of teachers and teaching.

3

In chapter 5, "The Power of Art in Observation," Kathryn Jenkins and Joyce Dutcher use the visual thinking strategy to help preservice teachers view museum art for the purpose of developing their observational skills. In the authors' words, they are using "aesthetic experience to enhance . . . teaching."

Combined, the chapters call attention to overlooked components in teacher education programs and provide concrete ways that identified absences can be ameliorated.

CHAPTER 1

Some Neglected Components of Teacher Education Programs

Anne Chodakowski
Simon Fraser University

Kieran Egan
Simon Fraser University

Gillian C. Judson
Simon Fraser University

Kym Stewart
Simon Fraser University

Dr. Anne Chodakowski has recently completed her Ph.D. in education at Simon Fraser University. Her thesis explored the possibility of using the principles and practices of imaginative education in the context of teacher education. Her work includes an exploration of how the theory of imaginative education needs to be further expanded for use in teacher education programs.

Dr. Kieran Egan, Ph.D., is a professor in the Faculty of Education, Simon Fraser University. His most recent book is *The Future of Education: Reimagining Our Schools from the Ground Up* (2008).

Dr. Gillian Judson, Ph.D., is a postdoctoral fellow attached to the Imaginative Education Research group (www.ierg.net/) of Simon Fraser University, Burnaby, B.C. She is currently engaged in exploring ways to expand uses of imaginative education in schools around the world. She is interested in blending features of imaginative education with ecological education.

Ms. Kym Stewart is a Ph.D. student in the Faculty of Education, Simon Fraser University. Her thesis aims to contribute to research on the role of imagination in teaching and learning in different cultural and social contexts, the role of imaginative education on the development of media education lessons, and the role of imaginative media education's influence on reawakening elementary students and teachers to the impact of media in our everyday lives.

ABSTRACT

Teacher education programs attend relatively little to some areas that are crucial to an adequate education. Such programs tend to provide preservice teachers with inadequate opportunities to develop skills in how to develop students' imaginative engagement in learning, skills of story-shaping curriculum content, locating affective images in curriculum content, and deploying humor in the classroom. The skills, each tied in with emotions in some degree, are related to each other in their concern to enrich students' learning. This article argues for the importance of this set of skills becoming a routine part of teacher education programs and explores how their development can be brought into the regular curriculum of such programs.

If we try to stand back and look at the various components of typical teacher education programs,[1] it is not altogether clear that they are well attuned to the importance of the various aspects of the job teachers are to perform. In this chapter, we consider important components of the educational job of teaching that are somewhat neglected in typical teacher education programs. These components are engaging students' imaginations in learning; learning the skills of story-shaping curriculum content; locating affective images in curriculum content; and deploying humor in the classroom.

Our aim is to show that this perhaps unusual set of components should be given a much higher profile in teacher education programs. We will discuss each of them, making a case for their importance as part of the skill set preservice teachers should develop. We will discuss how it is not especially difficult to do this and to achieve considerable educational benefits for teachers and students in the process. What may seem more difficult is dealing with the conflict between these relatively neglected items and those that currently fill, and overfill, typical programs. Just mentioning that we want to add a series of further topics to the curriculum of teacher education will surely lead to skepticism about the possibility of accommodating yet more material into already crowded coursework.

Each of the items we will discuss might be seen as tied, even if only in a small way, to our emotions. Each also deal with our intellects, of course, but it is useful to emphasize that one general concern we have about teacher education programs is that they have tended to neglect the roles of the emotions in learning. As L. S. Vygotsky put it, referring to a different time and place but seemingly prophetic of our time and place:

> Somehow our society has formed a one-sided view of the human personality, and for some reason everyone understood giftedness and talent only as it applied to the intellect. But it is possible not only to be talented in one's thoughts but also to be talented in one's feelings as well. The emotional part of the personality has no less value, than the other sides, and it also should be the object and concern of education, as well as intellect and will. (Vygotsky, 1997, p. 57)

So let us consider a few possible components of a teacher education program that might give more balanced attention to the human personality, of both teachers and students.

Engaging the Imagination

It may seem a little odd to claim that engaging the imagination has too small a profile in typical teacher education programs. Nearly all programs, after all, involve attempts to show preservice teachers how to make what they are to teach interesting and engaging to students' imaginations. Mostly, this involves showing how one can locate in a subject some "hook" that will catch students' interest in a topic. And, in turn, this usually involves finding something connected with what students already know or with something relevant to their experience from their environment. Enabling preservice teachers to look for ways of making their topics more interesting to students constitutes a useful skill any teacher can benefit from. Too often, though, this skill is taught as a limited and fairly trivial way of introducing a topic. Also, even though engaging students' imaginations might be the stated aim, it is usually far from clear what the imagination is. Often, it is only too clear that the imagination is considered to be a relatively trivial capacity for use in learning, rather than as one of the great workhorses of human understanding.

Perhaps it might be best to begin with a summary definition of what we mean by imagination; it isn't a particularly contested term, though it suffers from a significant degree of vagueness in its usual uses in education. One might begin with Alan White's (1990) conclusion that imagination is the ability to think of the *possible*, not just the actual, or, as Brian Sutton-Smith (1988) put it, the imagination is tied into our ability to use the subjunctive mood. In general, it indicates a degree of richness and variety in our ability to think of the possible and is the source of creativity and generativity in human thinking.

Robin Barrow (1988) describes imaginativeness as evident in thinking that is a combination of the unusual and the effective. That is, simply being able to generate unusual ideas or images is not an indication of imagination at work unless the ideas and images are effective for achieving some end. It is good to have that sense of imagination underlined, as imagination is too often thought of as some fluffy kind of thinking that is often a bit weird or wacko, perhaps engaging but also fruitless and not useful in the hard lifting of learning important curriculum content. It is also generally assumed to be something to do with the arts and is not seen as equally important in teaching math and sciences. (As one teacher said in response to our question about imagination in her classes, "Oh, yes, we let their imaginations go wild in arts projects on Friday afternoons.") But, in the sense derived from the scholars referred to above, and in the sense used in this article, imagination is one of the crucial hardworking tools of our intellects and is especially important in meaningful learning.

Given Mary Warnock's claim that deploying the imagination always involves some emotional engagement (Warnock, 1976), our opening claim from Vygotsky that typical educational practice has significantly neglected our emotional lives highlights again the importance of imagination to teacher education programs (Gajdamaschko, 2007). "Emotion" should be read here as not needing wild tears and flaming passions but rather simply bringing to learning some elements of the emotions that have been involved in one way or another in the creation of all the knowledge specified in the curriculum. That is, all knowledge is human knowledge and it is all a product of human hopes, fears, and other emotions, as well as the more usually recognized features of our intellectual lives. To make knowledge imaginatively engaging to students, then, it seems sensible to explore how we can bring it to them in the context of the hopes, fears, and other emotions in which knowledge was created in the first place or in the context of meaningfulness to current life.

The relative neglect of the emotions and imagination in teacher education programs is understandable given that, in our cultural history, both emotions and imagination have tended to be seen as dangerous features of our minds and as subversive of order (Egan, 1992, Ch. 1). The classroom is a society in which order is important for learning to take place, and it has consequently been typically a place in which disruptive capacities have been discouraged. But we think this general distrust of emotions and the imagination has had something of the effect of throwing babies out with bathwater in education. We need to be wary about how emotions and imagination are used in classrooms, of course, but that wariness should not lead us to neglect crucial features of human life and intellectual activity.

How can preservice teachers learn to engage students' imaginations in learning? If the imagination involves thinking of the possible, and always has some, even if small, emotional component, it might help to constantly search below the literal surface of things, looking for a more important grasp of knowledge.

Language and Imagination

Each of the following sections of this article explores the ubiquitous example of language and ways we can use it to stir imagination, engage students, and build bridges to new knowledge in regular teaching. We can begin here by considering how we tend to use it constantly without much reflection on how it is working its magic for us.

METAPHORS AND IMAGINATIVE UNDERSTANDING

We can engage students' imaginations with language by constantly drawing their attention to its underlying features. One somewhat mysterious component of language is metaphor—seeing one thing in terms derived from something quite different: "couch potato" describes a person who stays home sitting on a couch, probably watching TV a lot, who is like a potato lodged in the soil, and gradually looks increasingly like a potato in shape. Metaphor nearly always entails, in greater or lesser degree, the emotion of humor.

When used with wit, metaphor can help to enlarge our understanding of the new process or knowledge it is referring to. We easily forget that our language is very largely metaphoric, even though there is something decidedly odd about metaphor (Lakoff & Johnson, 1980). Its enormous fluidity enables us to see almost anything in terms of almost anything else. Being able to use metaphor flexibly, fluently, and in a controlled way is crucial to being able to use language well and, thereby, being able to think well. Children have no difficulty grasping metaphoric meanings; indeed, there is some evidence that they can manage such tasks better than adults (Gardner & Winner, 1979). The child seeing her first Western movie at about five might hear for the first time someone say, "He bit the dust!" She will have no problem at all understanding what it meant, even though the literal meaning would give no clue to the metaphor-driven real meaning.

We have sometimes recommended to preservice teachers that they try instituting in their classroom a "metaphor of the week" prize. A large piece of paper can be stuck on the wall, and each time a student uses or recognizes in someone else's language a good metaphor, they can add it to the sheet. At the end of the week, there are votes for the best metaphor. The preservice teachers who are usually anxious about how to teach something as difficult as the nature of metaphors find their main problem is adding extra sheets of paper to their classroom walls as the students become enthusiastically engaged with the activity.

This activity can be augmented by having, maybe two or three times a week, a ten- or fifteen-minute "metaphor time," in which students are given such tasks as completing a sentence like, "My heart is . . ." Students commonly give answers like "a house," "a thorn," "a bird," "an ocean," and one, for whatever reason, "a potato." Sometimes, the teacher can give a simple descriptive sentence and ask the students to substitute metaphors for every word possible while retaining the original meaning. "The dog ran along the street" becomes "The paws padded along the tarmac"; "Fido legged it along the blacktop"; "The canine galloped along the dead earth," and so forth.

Students can also be asked to explain such metaphors as "road hog," "feeling blue," "boiling mad," "deep secret," and so on. An activity students typically enjoy most in these brief sessions is the deliberate mixing of metaphors: "He stepped up to the plate and grabbed the bull by the horns"; "That wet blanket is a loose canon"; "Strike when the iron is in the fire"; and (quoted from a school administrator) "Now we can just kiss that program right down the drain" (for further examples, see Judson, 2006).

When a cat runs through the garden on a windy day, it is unlikely that it sees the waving flowers and falling leaves as like the turmoil in its soul about its relationship with a prospective mate. But the great tool-kit we acquire with language involves precisely this odd ability to see one thing in terms of another that may be entirely unconnected with it.

Humans frequently see weather or natural objects as representing their emotions. This enormously fertile capacity for metaphor seems to develop as a fundamental utility for our symbolizing. If the arbitrary sounds we can make are to be understood as stable meanings, we must, most basically, be able to see the symbols of speech in terms of the things we use them to refer to. Metaphor thus suffuses language. Every sentence is made up from metaphors we have usually forgotten were metaphors. Being able to see these often invisible or forgotten metaphors is one tool of creative language use—it allows us to play with what otherwise we are constrained by. Metaphor enables us to more richly express what we mean and, reciprocally, to understand complex messages from others that enrich what we can mean.

In educating, then, we will want to focus on stimulating and developing students' ability to recognize and use varied rich metaphors. The flexibility and creativity of their thinking is clearly tied up with this skill, so we would be unwise to ignore it or leave it to chance. Preservice teachers can practice recognition of metaphors in their own speech and writing, and can try such activities as are suggested above. They should discover how even some complex tasks can readily engage students' imaginations while also ensuring effective learning.

STORY-SHAPING CURRICULUM CONTENT

Nearly all teacher education programs spend a significant amount of time on how to plan lessons and units of study. This task is, of course, crucial to successful teaching. If the teacher is inefficient in shaping the content into sets of activities that take the right amount of time, then both the conceptual structure of the material and the management of the classroom will likely be inefficient all round. As part of learning to structure curriculum content more effectively, preservice teachers are nearly always introduced to some variant of Ralph Tyler's (1949) procedure for planning. Tyler's general questions designed to help plan effective curricula have been adapted by a number of people over the years into various forms of planning frameworks (e.g., Taba, 1962). These frameworks are important in giving preservice teachers a sense of security and control in making curriculum topics teachable.

These various frameworks all recommend that one should begin one's planning by stating one's objectives for the lesson or unit. They also claim that it is important to state one's objective as clearly and precisely as possible—what should the student know and be able to do at the conclusion of the lesson or unit? The precisely stated objective serves as a criterion that then allows the teacher to select appropriate content, decide on methods of instruction and student learning activities, and devise tests to ensure that the objectives are being attained. Some form of this general model, sometimes simplified in skeletal form as the "objectives–content–methods–evaluation" procedure, is learned by nearly all student teachers in the Western world. In the process of the development of this procedure in education, its industrial source seems to have been forgotten.

"Industrial source?" The procedures taught to preservice teachers for planning their work derive from methods that were found effective early in the twentieth century for building refrigerators and automobiles (Callahan, 1962). The American assembly line was one of the great tools for enriching the country and gearing up its productivity to unprecedented heights of efficiency. To build an efficient machine, like a refrigerator or automobile, one began by planning it in great detail. Once the design was in place, then one could order the components needed to build it. One could also organize the skills required to fit the components together on the assembly line. And, at the end of the manufacturing process, one needed a quality control, to make sure that the components were all adequate and they had been put together properly. That is, one began with a precise objective, gathered the materials one needed, organized the methods and skills for putting those materials together, and then assessed whether one had achieved the objective.

We might appropriately wonder whether the assembly line is the most obvious source we might turn to for ideas about how to educate children. It does not provide a good model for how to make the wonders of the world and human experience meaningful and engaging to children. Indeed, we might consider that our common failure to engage children in schools with the wonders of the world and human achievement owes something to the model that has dominated planning teaching for more than half a century.

Where might one look for an alternative? We are suggesting that it might make sense, if our aim is to engage children with the wonders of the world around them, to consider the tool that has proved most effective at achieving this for millennia—the story. We do not mean simply fictional stories. Our concern is with the real world and all the knowledge about it that we put into the curriculum. So we mean story in the sense that the newspaper editor might use in asking a journalist to get the story on the bridge collapse. The editor is asking the journalist not to invent a fiction about a collapsing bridge but rather to find out what happened and, in describing it clearly, bring out its emotional importance for the paper's readers.

How could the idea of story-shaping become an alternative to the currently universal procedure for planning lessons and units? Even though we are surrounded by stories—both the fictional kind we see on TV, for example, and also the nonfictional kind that fill our newspapers and our casual conversations—most people think they can't make up stories. We do it all day long, of course. We take an event, something that has happened to us or something we have heard, and shape it into a narrative to tell it to others. In some ways, it is much more natural for us to organize content into stories than it is to fit it to the assembly line procedures of objectives–content–methods–evaluation.

How would we do this for a science lesson on the properties of the air or place value in math or any of the usual topics we have to teach? Well, instead of beginning by asking what our objectives are, we will instead ask, "What's the story on the properties of the air," or on place value, or whatever? What is emotionally important about it? We will also want to do what all good storytellers do and evoke a sense of wonder about it, focusing our own attention on bringing into our consciousness what is wonderful about the topic. That is, we will begin with something that might prove—initially at least—a little difficult or at least unfamiliar in teacher education programs: locating within one's self some emotional connection with the topic. If we fail to do this, the likely result will be boredom among the students.

All very well in the abstract, you might reasonable think, but how can we make such an idea work in practice? How can we design planning frameworks from the idea of the story that can help the preservice teacher learn to plan in a different way? The kind of story that engages a typical six- or seven-year-old is different from that which engages the attention and imagination of the typical thirteen- or fourteen-year-old. So just for purposes of demonstrating how this principle can work in practice, let us take the kind of story and topic that is appropriate for the six- or seven-year-old, recognizing that we would need to shift some of the following categories to suit older students. So what is the first step we might take toward story-shaping a topic after trying to attend to what is wonderful about it? Let's take the topic of whales and work it out step by step, even if briefly.

What is wonderful about whales? What is emotionally engaging? The heart of a blue whale is the size of a small car, and it pumps ponds-full amounts of blood with each beat through arteries so big the students could crawl through them. They are the largest animals that have ever lived on earth, and they feed on some of the world's tiniest organisms. They make louder sounds than any other animal and can be heard hundreds of miles away. Our sense of wonder is caught up as we imagine a family of whales struggling through a distant stormy ocean at night and hear those mighty hearts pounding as they swim for thousands of miles in search of food. And what are they doing in the water? They are not fish. They are mammals, like us, with complex family structures; they suckle their young and they communicate in strange and haunting songs, which we cannot decipher. They are strange and mysterious, and these are among the wonders about whales that will form our unit.

How do we go from these images and topics to the story structure? We can begin by observing that nearly all the stories that engage young children are built on underlying binary opposites. Take the Grimm fairy tales, for example. The content level of the story may be about children, forests, animals, and magic, but underlying that surface there are conflicts between good and bad, courage and cowardice, security and fear, and so on.

These underlying binary opposites are crucial to the structure of the stories younger students are most readily engaged by, so we would be sensible to start building our story about whales by looking for a binary structure we can structure it around. Many potential binary opposites may come to mind, but usually one powerful set of opposites can give a clear structure to the lesson and provide depth of understanding and imaginative engagement.

So let us set up a laptop computer with a speaker attached for our first class. The teacher might ask the students to feel their pulse, and, as they locate the pulse, the teacher can play from the computer a normal child's pulse somewhat increased in volume. Then, as the students continue to hold their fingers over the approximately sixty pulses a minute that come from their hearts, the computer can generate at high volume the ten thudding beats per minute of a blue whale's heart.

One could also have a picture of a normal-sized six-year-old superimposed on an average six-year-old blue whale. Such activities can begin to build a sense of the majesty of the whale; they seem invulnerable in their massive strength and size. And yet, these majestic creatures are immensely vulnerable. Though they have existed in the oceans of the world for hundreds of thousands of years, they may not survive this century.

So we have set up a binary opposition for our unit on which we can build the content. In this case, the binary opposites are majesty and vulnerability. We will not detail here the extensive information we would provide in further lessons, about whales and their mysteries, their astonishing journeys through the oceans, and the variety of different whales and their varied wonderful capacities constantly opposed with information about their vulnerability to hunting, to poisoning, to the global warming that might disrupt their krill food source, and so on.

The content of this unit may be only a little different from the content that would be taught using other procedures. But lessons structured this way constantly drive to seek the wonderful, make the content imaginatively engaging to the students, and bring to the forefront the oppositions that give coherence and vividness to how we construct our story. The story of the whales does not only include the use of binary opposites and search for a sense of wonder but also includes the use of imagery, humor, and other features as important element in lesson development, which we'll explore below.

If you are willing to consider this idea worth taking seriously for a few minutes, you may also begin to see teachers not as workers who simply convey information to students but as the storytellers of our extended tribe. They tell the great stories of our mathematics, science, history, and so on. Becoming such storytellers requires teachers to shift a little their perception of their role and also the appropriate skill set that they take into the classroom. That skill set will include knowing how to locate the emotional meaning of these stories and the topics that comprise them and being able to bring out this meaning for students.

So, when we teach preservice teachers how to plan lessons and units, we might consider an important part of this task is for them to learn how to "story-shape" the content. If we wish to go further, thinking these principles are quite important, then we might design an alternative kind of planning framework, such as the framework for imaginative teaching at the elementary level outlined here. Teachers can use this to plan their own lessons and units. (Other related frameworks, some more elaborate, can be found at http://ierg.net/lessonplans/unit_plans.php).

1. Locating importance: *What is emotionally engaging about the topic? How can it evoke wonder? Why should it matter to us?*
2. Thinking about the content in story form:
    2.1. Finding binary opposites: *What binary concepts best capture the wonder and emotion of the topic? If this were a story, what would the opposing forces be?*

2.2. Finding images, metaphors, and drama: *What parts of the topic most dramatically embody the binary concepts? What image best captures that content and its dramatic contrast? What metaphors can be used to help understanding?*

2.3. Structuring the body of the lesson or unit: *How do we teach the content in story form? How can we shape the content so that it will have some emotional meaning? How can we best bring out that emotional meaning in a way that will engage the imagination?*

3. Conclusion: *How does the story end? How do we resolve the conflict set up between the binary opposites? How much do we explain to the students about the binary oppositions?*

4. Evaluation: *How can one know whether the topic has been understood, its importance grasped, and the content learned?*

AFFECTIVE IMAGES IN CURRICULUM CONTENT

Consider the following brief narrative: "I couldn't sleep, so I went for a walk around the neighborhood. It was a warm autumn night, windy, and I could hear leaves falling. A white cat followed me for a block meowing. One house ahead had a large main-floor window lighted up. An old man and woman were inside, dancing. He wore a blue suit and she had on a red dress, both of old-fashioned cut. They were slowly waltzing, and I could just hear the music above the sound of the wind in the trees and the dry rustle of the leaves."

Whether you intended to or not, you have probably formed in your mind some images as a result of reading these black squiggles on the page. The images you have formed will be different in some degree from everyone else's and different from those of the writer of this paragraph. The images will not only have been visual ones; you will likely have also formed images of sounds—the rustle of leaves, the wind in the trees, and the cat's meow. You will have also felt something about the brief narrative—not much, no doubt, but you will have made a small-scale emotional response to the insomniac's nighttime stroll, the nocturnal adventures of the cat, or the old couple dancing in their living room in the middle of the night.

Most teacher education programs spend considerable effort in showing preservice teachers how they can plan to communicate concepts and content efficiently. Usually, instructors teach what concepts are, why they are so important to thinking, and how they can be evoked, clarified, and used in critical thinking. And, of course, this knowledge and skill is important in teaching. What is done much less—indeed, from our own search, we can say is done hardly ever—is instruct preservice teachers on how to evoke the affective images that can give a topic life, energy, vivid meaning, and communicative force.

Consider the introduction to the whales unit already explained. What sticks in your mind? Is it the image of the mighty heart beating in some distant ocean? And doesn't the image of the old couple dancing in the middle of the night remain in your mind more forcefully than our opening paragraph of conceptual material? And why should we ignore such an obvious feature of human intellectual functioning when it comes to teaching? If we want to engage children in learning some topic, then we should enable preservice teachers to become fluent at locating within the topic some affective image. The image that carries an emotional charge will lodge in the mind and lodge in students' minds the knowledge we want them to retain. Every topic in the curriculum is made up, not just of concepts and information, but also of images.

And how are we to do this? In part, by simply exemplifying the use of affective images frequently and then giving preservice teachers random topics and asking them to locate affective images that are a part of the topic. As usual, the more the preservice teacher knows about a topic, the easier such a task will be. If we are to teach about heat to grade 3 students, for example, we might look first for the most vivid images connected with the topic. A good place to start is where our ancestors started when they created those wonderfully vivid stories that give a mythical explanation of phenomena like heat. So, we might start with the story of Prometheus stealing fire from the gods and giving it to humans, bringing out also the image of Prometheus's punishment by Zeus. The myth captures vividly the understanding that control of heat has been crucial to human societies and their development. And, if we want to emphasize the problems of what happens when heat gets out of control, we can tell the story of Phaeton trying and failing to control Apollo's fiery chariot—the sun—around the daytime sky.

But how can we find images for some of the more mundane kinds of information we want students to learn? Take telling the difference between the spelling of words like "to," "two," and "too." How can one find images in such curriculum content such that students will better learn and remember which spelling is appropriate for which meaning? Well, let us introduce you to some of our friends: First there is Mr. Too. He is very big, because he eats *too* much; he is also *too* tall, is clearly hyperactive, and is always going beyond what is sensible. Unlike everyone else in his group, even when he includes the letter *o* in his name, he has to include two *o*'s. (Deriving a personality and physical features for that personality from the spelling of a name may seem a little bizarre, but it is a task that relies on an energetic use of metaphor, and children can usually do this more easily than adults [Gardner & Winner, 1979].) You should also meet our friend Ms. Two. She obviously does everything in pairs when she can—she has *two* cell phones, *two* bikes, and is obviously overcareful; in case she loses one thing, she always has a backup. It is clear from the spelling of her name that she really wishes she were a twin, as she's managed to put a "w" in her name, which is halfway to "twin," even though there is nothing in her name that the "w" sounds like. Then you should also meet Ms. To. She is constantly on her way elsewhere, or pointing to different things and places. She's clearly never satisfied with where she is or what she's got: a bit of a complainer. She's in so much of a hurry that, unlike the other two, she's dropped the third letter from her name and is the slimmest from all her hurrying.

Our point is to indicate that any topic has some images we can locate in it, and these images will often prove the most effective tools in engaging students' interest in the topic, so that they find the topic meaningful and remember it. To teach preservice teachers to be able to find appropriate images in any knowledge topic will be to equip them with an invaluable skill they can use throughout their career. We suspect it will be one that they will find themselves using more and more, and their teaching will become increasingly effective as they do so. Nothing is sacrificed by using affective images; we do not need to reduce the conceptual material or the knowledge content—in fact, evoking images that are a part of any topic can enhance understanding of the concepts and knowledge.

THE ROLE OF HUMOR IN THE CLASSROOM

Humor is often taken to be something that may accompany teaching if an individual teacher has a taste for it, on condition that it doesn't distract from the actual teaching. That is, it is not generally seen as a significant component of a teacher education program. This is perhaps due to its not generally being seen as a constituent of an adequately educated person. Humor, for reasons too complexly intertwined with our cultural history to go into here, is rarely seen as a tool of our understanding—something that adds to our ability to make sense of concepts and the general content of the curriculum. On the contrary, humor can be an excellent tool for understanding. We also think that use of humor in teaching should be seen as a skill that preservice teachers can learn to deploy to improve the effectiveness of lessons about almost any topic.

All babies, unless severely handicapped, begin to smile at caregivers within the first three weeks of life. Even deaf and blind children smile on schedule. We so welcome their smiles and do whatever seems to elicit the smiles most readily. We begin to play simple games, from sticking out tongues to peek-a-boo and making funny sounds in patterns, and then combining the funny sounds and the visual games. Without exploring infant humor in any detail, we can see how it is crucially important, indeed fundamental, to human life in society. Babies use the smile to begin knitting themselves into networks of solidarity with their caregivers. It is one of the great glues of family life and social life. Or, as Merlin Donald puts it, these interactions "interlock the infant's growing mind with those of its caretakers and ultimately the broader society" (1991, p. 255).

Humor, being so fundamental to our nature and culture, merits much more attention in education than it commonly receives. We will mention only one of the ways in which it contributes directly to universally prescribed curriculum aims. Consider the following awful jokes:

Q: What do you get if Batman and Robin get smashed by a steam roller? A: Flatman and Ribbon. Q: When is a car not a car? A: When it turns into a garage. Q: How much do pirates pay for their earrings? A: A Buccaneer. Q. How many ears did Davy Crockett have? A. Three. His left ear, his right ear, and his wild front ear. Q. Were you long in the hospital? A. No, I was the same size that I am now.

All those jokes play with language in a particular way. A shortcut description is to say that they compel the student to see language as an object and not just as a behavior. That is, they contribute to what is called metalinguistic awareness. Being able to see language as an object on which one can reflect is an important step in increasing our grasp of language and enabling greater flexibility in its use. It might seem odd to recommend short periods in the school day for telling jokes, and perhaps also having students in small groups invent jokes of their own. This play with language, and with intricate and complex features of language, contributes directly to sophistication in language use. It would also make school more fun as well as more educationally productive for students.

It may seem even odder to recommend that preservice teachers should be instructed in the use of humor. It is not simply a personality trait, which some teachers might have and others not—though we do need to recognize that some are more readily inclined to use humor. Being able to deploy humor readily in ways that encourage students to increase their flexibility of language use should be recognized as an important skill that each preservice teacher should learn.

While it may seem that nearly all six-year-olds enjoy jokes, it is clear that many are much less sophisticated in the range of jokes they appreciate. Even worse, many are clueless at telling jokes, and even more clueless at thinking about the world in a humorous manner. This is not just a casual failure; it is an educational failure. Sophisticated humor is important for flexibility of language use, which in turn is important for flexibility of thinking. Humor is one of the great lubricants of social and personal life. Consequently, we believe, it needs to be elevated considerably in teacher education programs.

Perhaps it is necessary to indicate that we are not proposing simply telling jokes in class. Rather, we are arguing for more sophisticated and focused uses of humor as a support of teaching and learning. There is a range of research now available showing a number of dimensions of teaching and learning that are aided by humor (for a good summary of this material, and further support, see

Garner, 2005; see also Garner, 2006). What we are suggesting is an additional dimension of learning that is aided by the use of humor. It might be mentioned that this argument is in accord with an educational theory whose concluding achievement is tied up with development of irony (Egan, 1997).

Lewis Carroll, of course, is a classic player with such jokes. His curriculum is made up of things like Reeling and Writhing; , in mathematics, Ambition, Distraction, Uglification, and Derision; with dollops of Mystery, ancient and modern; such artwork as Drawling, Stretching, and Fainting in Coils; and, of course, the classics, Laughing and Grief. His timetable for the different lessons required is as follows:

> "Ten hours the first day," said the mock Turtle: "nine the next, and so on."
> "What a curious plan!" exclaimed Alice.
> "That's the reason they're called lessons," the Gryphon remarked: "because they lessen from day to day."

Such jokes call attention to the way meaning is constructed and may be deconstructed. They enlarge our repertoire of expectations and make more complex and fluid the categories we use in making sense of the world and of experience. Literal, conventional thinking involves forging concepts and categories that reflect reality as far as possible. We commonly—indeed, seem predisposed nearly always to—reify in some degree the concepts and categories we forge. We tend to see them as real like the things they are supposed to reflect, or at least as having a firmness and clarity that is rarely warranted. This confusion is evident in a rigidity of categories that is one of the main hindrances to efficient thinking.

An important constituent of teachers' and students' thinking, then, is the capacity that enables us to constantly keep our concepts and categories fluid and reassess the relationships we establish among them with the reality they are intended to represent. This capacity can in part be evoked, stimulated, and developed by jokes.

Conclusion

Our aim has been to suggest that some commonly neglected activities should be given greater importance in teacher education programs. We have tried to show that these activities are quite practical, even if we have had to restrict ourselves to brief examples. While the topics we have focused on—imagination, metaphor, story-structuring, images, and humor—are far from common topics in teacher education programs, they do each address some central component of all teacher education programs, such as how to plan lessons for effective learning and gain skill in effective methods of instruction.

But how can instructors of teacher education programs find time to add such things into already pressured schedules? While these might sound attractive at one level, they have to jostle with many other concerns, such as legal issues; clinical and field experiences; accommodating multiple intelligences and developmental theories like Piaget's; specialist methods work in particular disciplines; the range of social and psychological disabilities some students will bring to school; and so on and on. We do not have a general answer to this question, understandably. That developing this additional array of skills will take significant time is undeniable. However, some of the items, such as finding images, using humor, and developing metaphoric competence, can become a part of the content of regular classes on methods of teaching and planning. They need not take large blocks of time, and once students have an understanding of them and some practice with them, the skills should become easy to deploy when appropriate.

Learning to use the story-shaping planning framework, however, is going to eat up a significant amount of time. While it should be seen as a supplementary approach to the dominant Tyler-derived models rather than as some kind of competitor, the two approaches make teachers think differently about the content taught, and then make them teach differently. But having alternatives to hand is only to increase the teacher's flexibility and skill set. So, if it is an interesting alternative and worth trying, how can one justify jostling something else aside for such an innovation? Again, there seems no general argument for this, and it must turn on the degree to which any instructor is persuaded that the skills to be gained in learning this approach will later stand a preservice teacher in better stead than some other material that is currently part of the curriculum. This is not an argument we find difficult to make to ourselves. But, we believe, it is one that will become attractive to others only when they see its results in practice.

Note

1. See, for example, www.ed.gov/inits/teachers/exemplarypractices/index.html.

References

Barrow, R. (1988). Some observations on the concept of imagination. In K. Egan & D. Nadaner (Eds.), *Imagination and education.* New York: Teachers College Press.
Callahan, R. (1962). *Education and the cult of efficiency.* Chicago: University of Chicago Press.

Donald, M. (1991). *Origins of the modern mind.* Cambridge, MA: Harvard University Press.

Egan, K. (1992). *Imagination in teaching and learning.* Chicago: University of Chicago Press.

Egan, K. (1997). *The educated mind: How cognitive tools shape our understanding.* Chicago: University of Chicago Press.

Gajdamaschko, N. (2007). Vygotsky on imagination development. *Educational Perspectives, 39*(2), 34–40.

Gardner, H., & Winner, E. (1979). The development of metaphoric competence: Implications for humanistic disciplines. In S. Sacks (Ed.), *On metaphor.* Chicago: University of Chicago Press.

Garner, R. (2005). Humor, analogy and metaphor: H.A.M. it up in teaching. *Radical Pedagogy, 6*(2).

Garner, R. (2006). Humor in pedagogy: How ha-ha can lead to aha! *College Teaching, 54*(1), 177–180.

Judson, G. C. (2006). Appendix. In K. Egan, *Teaching literacy: Engaging the imagination of new readers and writers* (pp. 134–157). Thousand Oaks, CA: Corwin Press.

Lakoff, G., & Johnson, M. (1980). *Metaphors we live by.* Chicago: University of Chicago Press.

Sutton-Smith, B. (1988). In search of the imagination. In K. Egan & D. Nadaner (Eds.), *Imagination and education.* New York: Teachers College Press.

Taba, H. (1962). *Fundamentals of curriculum development: Theory and practice.* New York: Harcourt Brace & World.

Tyler, R. (1949). *Basic principles of curriculum and instruction.* Chicago: University of Chicago Press.

Vygotsky, L. S. (1997). *The collected works of L. S. Vygotsky,* R. W. Rieber & J. Wollock (Eds.), vol. 3. New York: Plenum Press.

Warnock, M. (1976). *Imagination.* London: Faber & Faber.

White, A. R. (1990). *The language of imagination.* Oxford, UK: Blackwell.

CHAPTER 2

Fostering Creativity and Aesthetic Consciousness in Teachers

THEORY AND PRACTICE

Donald S. Blumenfeld-Jones
Arizona State University

Donald Blumenfeld-Jones, Ed.D., is associate professor for Curriculum Studies, Ethics, and Education at Mary Lou Fulton Teachers College, Arizona State University. He specializes in arts-based education research, ethics and classroom discipline, hermeneutics, and critical social theory and curriculum. He has published in such journals as the *Journal of Curriculum Theorizing, Educational Theory, Journal of Thought, Journal of Qualitative Studies in Education*, and *Qualitative Inquiry*. He also has numerous book chapters dealing with dance curriculum, ethics and curriculum, and arts-based education research. Prior to his academic career, he danced professionally for twenty years, studying, performing, and choreographing modern dance in New York City, and he performed, choreographed, and taught throughout the United States and Canada. He presently continues to dance as well as write.

ABSTRACT

In the first section of this chapter, Blumenfeld-Jones critically explores the twin concepts of creativity and aesthetic consciousness by examining their conceptual and classic roots for the purpose of rediscovering their usefulness for all people performing all kinds of acts in the world. This exploration is offered to demonstrate that teachers can "be creative" and already have "aesthetic consciousness." It is also used to set the theoretical grounds for understanding the practice of cultivating creativity and aesthetic consciousness. In the second part of the chapter, which depends upon this theory analysis, Blumenfeld-Jones presents numerous examples from his teaching as to how to cultivate creativity and aesthetic consciousness in teacher preparation and curriculum studies classrooms.

I live around the corner from a neighborhood elementary school. This year, the school has instituted a skills-building program. On a weekly basis, they display on their signboard a "skill of the week" that the whole school is promoting. Most recently, these have been "care," "courage," and, most intriguingly, "curiosity." Aside from the fact that "care" and "courage" aren't skills but actually virtues (although they might be skillfully displayed), the last of these, "curiosity," is perplexing. Is the capacity for "curiosity" a skill or is it a disposition for how to live? It is most dismaying that the school feels the need to focus on developing this disposition in their learners for it seems obvious that children have curiosity in abundance: they are always asking questions about everything upon which their attention alights. Thus, there is a tacit admission by the school people that somehow the children have forgotten this natural proclivity and are no longer employing it. Thus, they need to be taught to be curious.

What can be said of the need to teach people to be curious (again) can be similarly said of "creativity." People are born, I believe, with the capacity to be "creative" but seem to have come to believe that they are not. This is unfortunate for it is my contention that people are already at least nacently creative, and it is my further contention that only through acts of creativity can certain important human capacities be developed for the benefit of the individual and of society.

While I have had this stance during my entire adult career as a dancer, it is the thinking of James B. Macdonald which galvanized it for me. In his later work, he focused on creativity as a prime mode of learning (1995a) in his essay "A Transcendental Developmental Ideology of Education" in which he offered the idea of "centering" as the most future-oriented idea for education. He wrote that centering "calls for the completion of the person or the creation of meaning that utilizes all the potential given to each person" (p. 87). He explored what kinds of activities could provide an opening up of perceptual experience, facilitate sensitizing people to others, develop close-knit community relations, and facilitate the development of patterned meaning structures and enlarge human potential through meaning. I will be discussing, in this chapter, a way toward these developments and facilitations situated in the practice of "creativity" and a focus upon cultivating aesthetic consciousness (Blumenfeld-Jones, 2006).

Please note the inclusion of close-knit community relations and the sensitization of people to others. These two dimensions constitute the basis for building an ethical world. It is not surprising that Macdonald would link aesthetics (patterned meaning-making) and ethics (community building) as this connection is at least as old as the Greek philosophical tradition since the Greeks linked aesthetics and ethics under the term "axiology." They understood them as partner dimensions of one phenomenon: beauty and goodness conjoined.

In more contemporary settings, we have come to understand that a sensitized aesthetic sense aids us in making moral decisions (see Gadamer, 1975; Johnson, 1993). Thus, cultivating aesthetic consciousness contributes to cultivating an ethical consciousness. That creativity, aesthetic consciousness, and ethical cultivation aren't obvious tasks of the educator (aren't simply taken for granted as being of value and as being embodied by every person) has a long history and is a part of our deep cultural milieu. In order to explore issues of cultivation, I will be discussing my own teaching in teacher preparation and curriculum studies programs, but before beginning these descriptions and discussions, first I must situate you vis-à-vis aesthetic consciousness and issues of creativity. Having done this I will present my approach to utilizing art experiences in educating preservice teaching students and classroom teachers in the ways of curriculum.

Aesthetic Consciousness and Creativity: Why Should You Care and What Is It?

The notion of "aesthetic consciousness" is conventionally (these days) connected with the arts. While in my own teaching I do use the arts as the basis for the development of aesthetic consciousness, it should be understood from the outset that the arts are not synonymous with such consciousness. John Dewey (1934) made a great effort to make the case that we can live aesthetically in many situations that have nothing to do with art. However, for purposes of my discussion, I need for you to see that experiences in the arts provide a direct means of developing aesthetic consciousness. At the same time, I caution you to see that, while our cultural reasoning unidirectionally connects "being creative" and having aesthetic consciousness with "talent" in the arts, we in fact do not have to possess artistic talent to benefit from arts experiences. Ironically, however, to benefit from the arts experiences you have to take the experience seriously *as if* you were working toward a life in the arts. This will be elaborated in my description of my work with preservice teachers and masters students who are already certified teachers. By the end of this reading I hope you will see the creative in yourself and that you and all the people you know can live life aesthetically (may already do so) if you so choose and this is of great value for your humanness.

The term *aesthetics* derives from the Greek and means "sense perception or sensation." Immediately, it is clear that we all have sense perception and sensations. Aesthetic consciousness, in it most basic guise, is an awareness of, focus upon, and exercise of judgment about our senses as a human capacity that connects us to the world around us directly and carries information and value for us as a dimension of our humanness. Certainly, if education is about the cultivation of our humanness, it would be about, in part, the cultivation of sensation and our sensitive employment of sensation as part of our humanness. It may be curious to think about cultivating the senses. If we all have them and they are our basic connection to all around us, why would they need cultivation? There are at least two possible answers to this question.

First, our culture has tended to excise the senses from our consciousness as having any value, favoring the mind dominating the body. There are two moments that can make this assertion concrete. In Descartes' now infamous assertion ("Cogito ergo sum"—"I think, therefore I am"), the mind is privileged over all physical reality as Descartes seeks the one fact that he cannot doubt: there is a self who is thinking. This self is apart from all material experience including the body and the senses. The problem with material experience and the senses is that they can deceive us. Only the fact that I am thinking is nondeceptive, and thinking is, therefore, the only venue for finding out the truth. All else is potentially false, unreal, and nontrustworthy.

While Descartes may have expressed this he did not invent the notion—that distinction belongs in the West to the Greeks, especially Plato. For Plato, truth is only that which doesn't change. Since the senses bring this ever-changing material reality to us, the senses are infected by the changing material reality. Therefore, they are untrustworthy for knowing the truth. What is a person to do? It is only this: discover the unchanging essences that underlie all this changeable experience through the use of your mind and reason. Using reason, you will come upon correct *ideas*. These are the only things that are real (because correct ideas are unchanging). As an example, there are all kinds of chairs in the world but what they all share is "chairness" (the idea of chair). Otherwise, we would not know to call all of them chairs. Through our mind we can discover the essence of "chair," the pure form that can't exist in the real world but only in the world of ideas. To bypass the error-filled dispositions of bodily experience, experience must be distilled, purified, and made "true" through correct thought, cleansing it of the contamination of the sensual or emotional. The truth is "true" because I have used the correct mental processes for achieving such knowledge. Truth comes in only one form: correct ideas about "reality." You can see, by this recounting, why the arts, deeply material and sensual, are often marginalized in our society and in our schools.

In the face of this history, to even begin to consider valuing the cultivation of our senses, we must alter our relationship to our senses. For aesthetic consciousness to flourish we must begin to trust our senses as locations of knowledge, not merely conduits of data upon which the mind might work in order to have knowledge. We must see, for instance, that while we usually associate mind with brain and, thus, our mind is in that organ, our bodies are filled with the nervous system. It could be said that we can "think" in our leg or arm or lower back because the mind is there as well. Our bodies are our "minds," not merely our brain as our mind. This requires a reorientation toward what constitutes mind. To credit the value of aesthetic consciousness, the privileging of mind over body must be reversed and body must become a trusted partner in knowing.

How Does "Aesthetics" Fit in This Conversation?

With aesthetics we run into a parallel difficulty with the mind/body split. As asserted earlier, aesthetics is conventionally connected with the arts, and most people see themselves as separate from the arts and from making art. Generally speaking, people do not see that aesthetics, beauty, and sensation fill their lives. For instance, to the degree that people pay attention to personal style in clothing, housing, furnishings, food, and so on, and attend to ways of being with others, to that degree they can be said to be concerned with beauty, sensation, and sensual awareness. They are "living aesthetically." Yet, most people don't see this. Why? This is because the fine arts are thought to be defined by their not having a function (aside from beauty), thus any focus upon function takes those activities out of the art realm. Clothing, furnishings, and food all have function; therefore, they have nothing to do with art.

Further, today, people make their aesthetic choices (about clothing, music, food, etc.) with a consumerist consciousness, connecting beauty and sensation with buying the right food, clothing, makeup, movies, music, books, and so forth, in order to feel as if they are living the beautiful life, leading to improving their chances at success in life. These choices establish public identities that connect them to a particular community and distinguish them from other communities.

All of this and, yet, not art. Why? The art community, generally speaking, sees such consumerism as crass and anti-art. The Museum of Modern Art in New York City does have a design collection that celebrates the beauty of commercial artifacts, but this celebration is always a matter of the objects being separated from their original impetus (making something that would attract and, therefore, sell) in order to be seen as just objects of art. Consumer objects can never be art if seen as consumer objects.

This brings us to the last link in this chain of separation. Real art is not merely "art" but rather high art. Herbert Gans (1974), the sociologist, made a distinction between high art and popular art. High art is part of what Raymond

Williams termed the "selective tradition" (Williams, 1973) that selects some art as icons representing good taste. To appreciate such art is to show oneself to have good taste and to belong in the upper social circles. To appreciate it is to potentially belong in the power centers of society. We notice that those who attend symphonies, theater, museums, and so forth, filling their lives with socially sanctioned beauty, are the people who also have the most material resources who regularly donate to such institutions and sit on their boards. Ironically, these people do not, necessarily, always like "high art," but they participate because being seen with high art provides social leverage and status.

The rest of society lives on the other side of culture in Gans's "popular culture" world. Those who value country-and-western music, television game shows, soap opera, MTV, hip-hop culture, rock-and-roll, and the like, and who purchase paintings of dogs playing cards, bucolic fields, clowns, and doe-eyed children are not involved with art and, therefore, are disconnected from art and, by extension, from aesthetic consciousness and creativity.

As a society, we tend to accept these distinctions as correct. Pierre Bourdieu in *Distinction* (1984) explicitly laid out this terrain as he explored the different social classes' view of what it means to have "good taste." He ably showed the social structures that resulted in the working-class membership viewing itself as having no aesthetic taste but enjoying its lack since the "having of social taste" was onerous.

The selective tradition that performs this labeling is found in school curricula that maintain and nurture the high/low culture distinction and all the privileges that connect with being able to appreciate and participate in high art. Concurrently, popular culture is seen as dangerous and in need of being eliminated from school experience (Blumenfeld-Jones, 2006). In this way, most people are cut off from aesthetic consciousness and creativity in their lives; they are disconnected from *art*. As with the mind/body split, we must recalibrate our thinking to find aesthetics in everything; we can think about our everyday lives in artist's terms without being apologetic.

The above discussion about the aesthetics/art intersection points toward the arts in our lives: the arts and our aesthetic choices are both centered on the making of meaning. Thinking, living aesthetically, and choosing what clothing to wear are all moves made to find, create, and develop a meaningful life as it may be, and, simultaneously, a socially acceptable life that fits with some community. That is, when we encounter art, in any of its forms (even those not considered to be "art"), we are seeking our own meaning of ourselves with the art encounter as the vehicle for coming to self-meaning as well as social meaning.

Hans-Georg Gadamer (1975), in his work on hermeneutics (the study of how we make meaning through our encounters with objects and events in the world), taught us about the arts as he focused his attention, initially, on the act of play (both play in general and being an actor in a play) and experiencing pieces of art as the two venues in which we might understand how we construct self-meaning and a meaningful life.

Gadamer describes the act of play and being in a play as displacing yourself into another state of mind and a role in life, experimenting with being other than who you are at the moment. We all know that play is "just play," not permanent and not real in the usual sense of the word. However, in order for play to succeed (for an audience to believe the actor or for the child to develop a self), the actor, the playing child, must act seriously from within the act of playing a role or simply playing, fully investing her- or himself in the act. At the same time, even the player and the actor must recognize that this is not he or she fully or permanently. Through this paradox of being invested in the play moment and knowing that it is just a play moment, play gets its efficacy for knowing new selves and new possibilities.

Making art is a form of play and is also pursued in a free-wheeling manner that allows for discovery through play with materials. As a self is constructed through the act of play, so a self is constructed through the act of art-making. If this is the case, then making art becomes a valuable location for developing self-understanding, which is, as I have argued, a fundamental goal of all human action. And self-understanding is a key component to ethical life as we must understand ourselves if we are to understand others *and* we can come to see, through arts experiences, the ways each of us constructs a self in the act of making art and the similarities and dissimilarities with our own processes. Thus, we can come into closer contact with another. Ethics is about the ethically good relationships we have with others.

If Play and Making Art Are Playful, Can They Also Help Us Discover Truth?

We are back to the question that concerned Descartes and Plato, how to go about finding truth. Again, Gadamer helps us with this issue. As with Descartes and Plato, Immanuel Kant revered reason and thinking, privileging conceptual knowledge over all other kinds of knowledge. He was concerned with how we find and validate truth. He considered art and aesthetics to be a "subsidiary contribution" to human knowing ("artistic element," "feeling," and "empathy" [Gadamer, 1975, p. 39). However, from an hermeneutic perspective, truth is always temporary (as the moment we find something beyond the truth we presently know, what we already know to be truth must adjust to the new knowing) and discoverable not through the application of reason alone but also through a living experience of sifting experience through our previous experiences. That is, all that we know is based on what we have already experienced, and since new experiences are unpredictable, what we come to know is also unpredictable. Further, since experience is understood through the play of experience, not just pure reason is in use as we come to understand something as well as understanding ourselves.

The arts are a venue where we know what we know through the multiple dimensions of intuition, emotion, body, imagination, as well as reason. Thus, whatever passes for "truth" is only found through access to these multiple dimensions. This makes the arts prime meaning-making sites. From here it is not a far leap to imagine aesthetics and the arts contributing to other domains of knowledge. For instance, we can see the study of mathematics as the study of how to create a meaning mathematically, how to imagine in new ways, and how the feelings of mathematical discovery are part of what is discovered, all of which can be part of our various self-understandings about our place in the world. The same can be said for the sciences, for literature, and so forth. The arts are a pure version of the person using the arts to encounter the world in a meaningful way. This is why Gadamer expends so much energy on the arts in developing hermeneutics and why we must consider the arts not as peripheral to educating people but as central. Art is now not the domain of high art but a mode of living.

Ellen Dissanayake (1995), an anthropologist, understands this idea as she assigns the production of art a biologically evolutionary role in the development of humankind. She writes that the arts have been around a long time "and so have ideas of beauty, sublimity, and transcendence, along with the verities of the human condition: love, death, memory, suffering, power, fear, loss, desire, hope, and so forth." She proposes a "species-centric view of art" that "recognizes and proclaims as valid and intrinsic the association between what humans have always found important and certain ways—called 'the arts'—that they have found to grasp, manifest, and reinforce this importance" (p. 41).

Dissanayake views art as a natural or "core behavioral tendency upon which natural selection could act" (p. 41). She enumerates various instances in which physical adornment in the form of a highly decorated body; in the West, this is often viewed as "superficial . . . nonessential . . . frivolous" (p. 102), but for the Wahgi people of Papua New Guinea, for instance, this adornment is thought to reveal, not conceal. "An adorned person is more important and 'real' than an unadorned 'natural' person" (p. 102). The Wahgi distinguish between an everyday and a special realm. In this way, they use the arts to make sense of their experiences.

> Beautification, such as the use of cosmetics or hair styling, can be regarded as a means to instill culture, to cultivate, to civilize. Some Temne hairstyles require several days to fashion and complete; such plaiting of the hair suggests the order of civilization just as the culti-

vation of the land in fine rows indicates the refinement of the natural earth." (Dissanayake, 1995, p. 105)

Dissanayake names this kind of production "making special." The enhancement of our world contributes to our understanding of that world.

Creating or Recomposing?

"Making special" returns us to the issue of "creativity." I now place "creativity" in quotes, reminding us how this word is charged. When the term is presented, most people respond with, "I'm not creative. I couldn't possibly do this." (I can't "make special" for I haven't the skill or disposition.) However, our daily lives are filled with creative moments, seen whenever we make a decision to do something differently: perhaps we rearrange the items on a shelf for the sheer pleasure of a different configuration, or washing dishes by hand, we contemplate how we will put them differently in the dish rack, not merely for purposes of efficiency but also because the arrangement pleases us visually, sensually. Even these can be moments of "creativity" in that we are making something that wasn't there before and, simultaneously, exercising our ability to expand ourselves, to discover new dimensions of ourselves, to use ourselves in nonlinear, noninstrumentalist ways.

The issue with "creativity" is not, however, exhausted with a discussion of how we could already see ourselves as living creatively in a daily way. It is an open question as to whether "creativity" is the proper term for what we do. George Balanchine, the eminent twentieth-century ballet choreographer who changed ballet irrevocably, is well known to have said, "I am not creative. Only God creates; I compose." This means that Balanchine took the extant ballet vocabulary and melded it with other sorts of movement vocabulary in new ways. He recomposed already existing material. Similarly, my high school sophomore year English teacher, Mr. Cook, told us that there are no new stories in the world; they are all in the Bible; it is in the telling of the story that the difference is made. In Martin Buber's chapter "Education" (2002), he contrasts "creativity" with what he terms "originary instinct." Of creativity he writes that the child is born into the world as pure potential: "Across the whole extent of this planet new human beings are born who are characterized already and yet have still to be characterized . . . ten thousand souls still undeveloped but ready to develop—a creative event if ever there was one, newness rising up, primal potential might" (p. 98–99). He counters this notion with the "originary instinct" (p. 100). "Man [sic], the child of man, wants to make things. He does not merely find pleasure in seeing a form arise from material that presented itself as formless. What the child desires is its own share in this becoming of things; it wants to be the subject of this event of production" (p. 100). The child is building a self through the originary act.

Perhaps creativity is not the direction in which our attention should be directed. As already noted, it holds people away from their own potential. The notion of composition is much less charged. Anyone can practice rearranging what already exists. Anyone can experiment with different arrangements, assessing their impact upon others as well as assessing how they do, do not, or partially express what it is they are thinking, knowing, or wanting to know. Anyone can rearrange for the purposes of discovering new understandings about the world through the process of rearrangement.

Choice-making is the stock in trade of artists. It is what they do, and it really is as little intimidating as that. It is not even necessary to have great physical skill to practice choice-making. When I have my students contribute a movement to a dance experience (to be described in more detail below), they can only contribute movements from the platform of their own bodies and how their bodies work. As we string together movements that are theirs, they can experience how movement fits together. They can begin to think in their bodies as they act in other parts of the daily life. As people think in their bodies, they are practicing what I would term "aesthetic attentiveness." Such attentiveness, when regularly practiced, leads to forming aesthetic consciousness.

With this set of ideas in mind I now move to describe practices I employ in my teaching.

Teaching with, through, and for the Arts

From 1979 to 2002, I was the program coordinator for a cohort teacher preparation program entitled Teaching for a Diverse Future (funded initially by the U.S. Qwest Foundation) that promoted an integrated and anthropological approach to subject matter, classroom community, and concern with justice. One of the "methods" courses I taught was entitled Teaching for the Aesthetic Life. This course was dedicated to students developing their capacity to utilize the arts in teaching academic subject matter but also, and not unimportantly, using the arts as valuable in and of themselves. We made art, we talked about art, we used art to teach subject matter, and we made museum installations of art objects provided by the class. The purpose of this course was to help the students understand the place of the arts in the classroom as well as in various cultures and understand how to integrate the arts into the curriculum, both as a support of other academic endeavors and as an important aspect of human existence, worthy of being part of an educative setting.

As part of this effort, in keeping with the anthropological and justice aims of the overall program, we explored the dilemmas associated with the arts, both in dominant Western culture and in the marginalized cultures that exist within the United States. We had five "strands of experience" threaded simultaneously throughout the course: investigate art as a specific form of human experience; make art; explore themes in which art is one avenue of exploration; research and share alternative multicultural perspectives; and understand art as embedded in daily living rather than considered as a separate entity. All of this was to help them discover the maker of art in themselves, to discover both the beauty/ excitement and kind of work it takes to make art and all focused on purposeful meaning-making both through experience and through studying other cultures and the political dimensions of art-making.

Before beginning to describe how I teach using the arts, I want to share a story from my days with the Phyllis Lamhut Dance Company that will illustrate how the arts can work on behalf of children when those children in no way conceive of themselves as being even interested in the arts. It is a story not about children discovering their inner artist but rather about discovering the life-enhancing experience of simply making art without even, initially, noticing that they are doing so. As this proceeds, the children discover that "making special" (to use Dissanayake's felicitous phrase) is not set apart from daily life but find its truth value in our daily lives and springs forth from that life.

We were on tour for the federal program "Artists in the Schools" and were in residence in Wellesley, Massachusetts. In this program, we would teach dance classes throughout the chosen schools in the district (in this case, the middle school) for two weeks, beginning with a lecture-demonstration and ending with a full-evening concert. One day, Phyllis informed me that I was to teach a class composed of students who had been trouble in their separate classes and had been separated from those classrooms into this one class for the year. I thought, "Great!" But off I went.

Upon entering the room I found the class standing against the walls around the perimeter of the room, all of them with arms folded across their chests, as if to say, "Go ahead. Make me dance." I knew immediately that no standard approach of creative work (which is what we specialized in, bringing movement out of the students and crafting dance experiences based on that movement) was going to work here. So, I needed to change gears immediately.

Realizing I was in New England and it was winter, I asked "Do any of you play ice hockey?" They looked perplexed at the question but warily answered, "Yes." I said, "Great, well let's have a game of ice hockey." Again they looked a bit perplexed but relieved. They wouldn't have to dance. As we weren't in an ice-rink, and there was no puck, hockey sticks, or ice skates, I suggested, "Let's use the eraser as a puck and your legs as hockey sticks." I divided them into teams and we began, with me as the referee. I allowed them to play for about ten minutes. There was tremendous energy for the game. At last I stopped the game and said, "Well, that was great. You know I have an idea to make it more interesting. Let's say this. We'll have another game, but this time you can't use your legs as the hockey stick. You can use anything else you want: arms, head, backs, I don't care, just not your legs. Ok, let's get started."

They were game for this experiment. We kept the same teams and played for perhaps another ten minutes; I then stopped the game again, saying, "That was cool. You know, I have another idea. I'm going to take away the puck. So you'll have to figure out where the puck is even though it's not visible. Same teams, same rules (no legs) and no puck."

We began and these children became engrossed in the challenging task of the invisible puck and the movements flowing from all parts of their bodies. When I at last stopped the game, I said, "That was even better. You know, of course, that what you were just doing was dancing. That's all dancing is: it's moving and paying attention to your movement. It's that simple." They were astonished. They had been afraid, of course, that I was going to make them look like someone they weren't: some ballet type probably. I had done no such thing but had rather allowed them to look and move like themselves, movements that came naturally from them without fitting into preformed molds of what is "dance." This was what was unexpected, that they could dance and also be themselves.

Perhaps, however, the real crux of the story came the next day. A smallish young man wearing a leather biker jacket and engineer boots with gloves pushed through one of the epaulets of the jacket (a young Marlon Brando?) came to find me. He said, "Yesterday you taught my class. I asked my dad if I could stay home because I wasn't going to do any of that dance stuff. I heard it was totally cool and now I'm so bummed. When are you coming back?" We chatted for a few minutes, but unfortunately, I was not scheduled for that class again.

What is the point of this story? It is this I think. I accessed their dance sensibilities, their ability to make improvisational art through what they already knew. As Maxine Greene would have it, I made the familiar strange (hockey) and the strange familiar (dance). I was not afraid to abandon the typical ways in which I worked. I wasn't afraid to look into their lives and find something that was them. I did not manipulate them in order to get them to do what I ultimately wanted (get them to want a "real" dance class). I provided them with their own platform for finding themselves in an activity they would not have freely chosen for themselves because it is filled with social stigma.

They came to see into the heart of this thing called dance, not into the social meanings ascribed to it. They were also able to find themselves, who they really are: movers; hockey might just be an excuse for something more basic to the human experience. That young man who regretted staying away was telling me his friends found something outside of their everyday experience that inexplicably but surely attracted them. This is important, I think. I can't tell you exactly what it is about making art that can attract. But, when presented in a way that draws the art from them rather than imposing art standards on them but is, nonetheless, fully art, people are drawn to their newly discovered potential.

It is in this spirit that I offer the following descriptions and discussions of what I do when I teach people to use the arts educationally. Find yourself from within an activity that is about delving into materials as a way of distancing yourself from yourself through entering into another state. This is partly what Gadamer means by "play," and this play can contribute to the construction of a self, a meaningful life, and community.

Here is how I began the Teaching for the Aesthetic Life course each semester in which it was taught. We began by making art rather than talking about it, focused initially on developing each person's sense of looking for design, thinking about design, and thinking about the "meaning" of relationships (art-making being primarily the act of providing experiences of relationships).

This first activity was dedicated to developing, from the outset, aesthetic sensitivity. As a whole class, we gathered in front of a white board with several markers in different colors. One by one, each student made a mark on the white board. The marks could only be lines and shapes. Any size line or shape was acceptable. The activity was to add to what already existed by previous marks made, paying attention to the emerging set of relationships using one's line or shape contribution to nonverbally comment upon them, provide a counterweight to them, efface them (without erasing them), or any other response to the already existing materials presented by previous learners. This part of the process involved no speaking, and there was to be no talking during the event. There was no preordained order as to who went first. Someone simply made the first mark and others followed as they wished. Everyone had to make a mark and no one could make more than one mark.

Left on the board was a cacophony of colored lines and shapes (both only lined or filled in) clashing, competing, and completing each other. Having completed the design, we would discuss what we thought of what had been done. We talked about what we thought worked and didn't work in terms of the abstract narrative of the design. Was the board too crowded overall? Were there parts that were filled and other parts left more or less empty? What did we think of the distribution of "events"? How did we feel when we looked at the overall design that had emerged (e.g., tense, frenetic, calm, or fluid)? What were people doing to pay attention to what already existed on the board when each person stepped to the board to add to the design? What did we like about it? What did we not like? What kinds of attitudes did we need to take to make it a successful experience?

This last question becomes, am I making my mark in order to leave my mark on the board (let the world know I was there), or am I making my mark in order to add to what I see emerging? During this conversation, I would allow people to voice their sense of inadequacy so that we could, together, show that person that her or his contribution to the whole had a particular and important role to play in the whole. The person didn't have to make a "perfect" mark, whatever that might mean. I wanted people to be able to move past their usual sense of incompetence in the face of the arts without confronting issues of "artistic ability" (thus restriction to lines and shapes).

Having done all this, we erased the design to begin again, this time in response to what we had just done and discussed. We were trying out our abilities to see and to participate in art-making that paid attention to the art, rather than the person doing the art. In this way, the person was set aside and her or his capacities for thinking in this new way became evident. If time allowed, we would do the whole event a third time.

What are the various "learnings" that emerge from such an activity? First, by staying away from representational work (drawing "animals," "people," "structures," "plants," and the like) we stay away from "I'm not an artist because I can't draw" thinking. Second, by focusing on these abstract forms we can focus more on spatial and color relationships and processes of choice-making: "Why did you make the mark you made? What were you trying to do?" We begin to "look" as an artist would look. Third, we are developing a more general sensibility to the world around us as a place of color and emotion (colors carrying hints of emotion). Fourth, by developing such an eye we could each come to understand our abilities as arts thinkers, as people who had an aesthetic consciousness that might not be well explored yet was present.

We were creative and creativity was not restricted to a special few. (In the context of this class, I strategically used the word "creative" because, like it or not, it is always present.) This "creativity" did not demand the making of something wholly new and unique but drew upon common "objects" (geometric forms and various colors) that were arranged in a particular way, composed and recomposed. It is in the act of composition and recomposition that discoveries emerge.

Everyone has a latent aesthetic consciousness that needs, initially, enlivening. This leads to the second dimension of teaching preservice students. The consciousness needs cultivation. That means the learner needs guidance in pursuing its development. As an example of the kinds of guidance I provided, we had one assignment, a fairly typical one for making art with "nonartists": the making of a collage. I asked each student to bring in an array of materials including cloth, colored paper, objects (both natural and humanly made), as well as photographs that, all taken together, pointed toward a theme the person wanted to explore or express through making the collage. (Photographs are not, strictly speaking, collage materials but are, more conventionally, chosen for making photo montages. However, in a concession to people desiring some representational materials, I allowed it.) Whatever theme was chosen and whatever materials secured, the idea was to present not merely a topic (often students would want to do a collage dealing with family or children or nature but without comment upon it) but also an idea about the meaning of "family," "children," or "nature." That is, what exactly does the student artist want to explore about that "topic," and what does the student wish to convey about it that might lead to new understanding of the topic?

The collages were always constructed during a class meeting. I would ask each student to only assemble her or his collage without fixing it to the support (heavy oak tag). I would go around the room, having private consultations with each student. I would inquire into the ideas they were using and what they wanted us to experience as we encountered the collages. I worked to move the ideas beyond what I would call "the sentimental." That is, if a person wanted to have a collage deal with "loving all children," I would ask that person to think of the many ways we actually love children so that there could be a multiplicity of images of "love" that provided the possibility of experiencing various sorts of love, rather than love in general.

I might also investigate their ideas by attempting to guide them toward some of the paradoxes, conflicts, and confusions that might be explored through art and perhaps even temporarily resolved through the art-making. (This is important: something can be learned about the "topic" through the art-making that wouldn't be available through other forms of exploration.) Then we could talk about how to arrange those images on the collage, remembering that I asked that there be quite a few abstract areas not using photographs or words. How would the person "translate" the ideas into abstract images of color and form that might move the experiencer toward "love"?

The difficulty in this kind of teaching pertains to people's sense of ownership of their art. It is conventional that learners will not want to have their ideas about making the collage questioned: their thinking is off limits to critique. They feel quite possessive of it. Thus, when I ask the kinds of questions described above, the learners have sometimes felt that I am interfering with their creative process. I have to remind students that just as we teach people to write more effectively and sometimes ask people to alter their present voice or to find a new voice that is still theirs, in this case I am providing guidance for them to understand the artistic process. It is not about interfering with their creative process but about giving that process more gravity, more clarity, and more sureness.

Making art is not haphazard or unsystematic. It is also not done by following rules. Being a matter of cultivating improved choice-making about the selection of a focus, the selection of materials, and studying ways to organize and manipulate those materials, it makes sense to have a teacher facilitate that choice-making.

It's important to notice that I never tell students what they want to do is not acceptable. I only give guidance for effective ways to bring about what is desired. As an example of guidance, in this particular activity, learners often intended to use all the materials they had brought to class. I would urge upon the learners the general principle that "less is more." One line in a drawing carefully situated speaks volumes in the tensions and energy it creates vis-à-vis the whole.

I remind everyone of the opening activity of the semester. I asked them to accept my critiques not as interfering with their creative process but as helping them hone that process through my experienced guidance. This is a central tenet of the work: by manipulating materials (in this case, collage materials), by focusing on the purely sensory aspect of the work, by keeping in mind the idea being explored, by grappling with the ways in which the materials aren't always cooperative in finding resolutions to either aesthetic or conceptual problems (or both), or by providing what artists have in their minds about the final product, something might be learned about the idea at hand that was not available without performing the artistic process.

Discovery through art was a central theme of concern for our curriculum and, consequently, for preparing teachers to teach. Our culture is fixated upon the scientific method. Douglas Sloan (1983) labeled our age one of "scientism": science is useful for coming to understand some things, but we have come to over apply it, as if it is the only avenue for understanding. Our curriculum is laden with academics that appeal only to the mind and logic. Even when there are pedagogical efforts that may bring in some form of artlike-making (creating poster-board presentations on writers or creating shoebox dioramas of a book), the art-making is entirely secondary to the mind material that is supposedly enhanced by this activity. The quality of the resulting product is rarely evaluated or valued.

The notion that we might know something through art-making that is not knowable through any other means is not part of our daily thinking about education. The development of aesthetic consciousness is, therefore, more than merely a nice addition to the quality of life. Aesthetic consciousness and aesthetic attentiveness is part of our knowing and, more importantly, a profound component of our connection with the world around us. As already pointed out, we are not disembodied brains; the brain is throughout our bodies, and paying attention to our bodies is another way of understanding. We are not born being able to use our bodies adeptly for knowing beyond our cognitive capacities. We must learn to know in our bodies just as much as we learn to know from our minds. Thus, teaching toward aesthetic consciousness is important and crucial.

As a corollary activity to the above, the students were asked to choose an art medium of any sort and make several "objects" during the semester. We would, at the end of the semester, have a "gallery opening" in which everyone would display their objects and tell us about the experience of choosing the medium, working through the medium, and conceptualizing and executing the specific project. The project could be quilt-making, T-shirt dying, drawing, making music, cooking, photography, and the like.

When I did this task as a graduate student, I took on drawing with oil pastels that I owned. I drew two portraits of my wife. They weren't skilled productions, but the process of really looking (in some ways for the first time), trying to move through my hand, and choosing colors to render something on paper that might be construed to be faithful to what I saw brought home to me both the joy and frustration of making art. Of course, I had known this during my long career as a dancer, but here I was reconfronting the daunting task of developing some skill for a purpose while privileging the reason for making the art over worrying about my ability to make it. During that experience, I found some things were very satisfying (drawing her hair, for instance, seemed to go well the second time), and even if the whole struck me as not what I really saw and wanted, I could still look to elements and feel the goodness of those elements.

I asked them not to make the project writing. I was trying to move them away from words to other modalities of imagination in order for them to open up to their own unrealized potential as artists. At the same time, I desired them to take on a project of personal meaning as an experience of what it would be like to place such work in their own classrooms and feel confident that, having done this for themselves, they could offer guidance to their learners as their learners embarked on their own activity of self-discovery. It was also important for them to see that they could do such work and leverage it for personal value. To the degree that they allowed themselves to engage in this activity, they would have something to offer their own learners.

I teach that a curriculum is worthy of our attention only when it addresses three areas of concern: the acquiring of knowledge and skill, the construction of a self through activities that focus upon knowledge and skill, and the dedication to building an ethical society through learning in an environment of self-development. This curriculum was dedicated to a demonstration and experience of this three-part proposition. The class participants were to come to know something about making art and its processes. They were to come to construct a self that could make art and value the experience of so doing. And they were to come to think about how this art affected their community (contributing to building an ethical society because they were paying attention to their responsibilities toward that community).

I have focused, so far, on the act of art-making as art-making. It is clear, however, that work with the arts also affords an avenue into understanding cognitive things in new ways that give new access to knowing. Again, an example is important here. Returning to my experience with artist in the schools, while on a two-week school residency in Camden, New Jersey, my teaching partner, Natasha Simon, and I were asked to do a dance class dealing with fractions as the fourth graders were having difficulty with the idea of "fraction." We chose the following.

We gathered all the children to one side of the room, in three lines. Three students at a time, we asked them to draw a large arc through the space, beginning at the floor where they were and ending at the other side of the room. They did this back and forth several times (to drum accompaniment). Then we asked them to draw two smaller arcs, the first arc ending in the middle of the room and the second arc ending at the other side of the room. Again, we had them all do this several times. Then we asked for thirds. We moved to drawing without their hands. And we strung spatial divisions of various amounts together, creating a dance that could work as a dance, not just as a support of academic knowledge. Eventually, we had the students improvise dances of dividing the space in smaller and larger parcels, employing fractions language in doing so.

In this way, the students embodied fractions rather than simply trying to cognize them. Perhaps Piaget would have been disparaging: by their age, they were to be beyond the "concrete" phase of learning. However, as we saw it, we created the basis for a dance, not an illustration. We insisted on the dance aspect: "Pay attention to your bodies, how they feel when you draw these arcs, what it's like drawing with your leg or your head." We provided a movement vocabulary out of which to create improvised dances. It was crucial the dance aspect of this event be genuine and not simply illustrative. The students had to be invested in their bodies, not in the cognitive information. In this way, they saw space differently. It became substance to them whereas before it was merely something unseen through which they passed. We had put them into contact with a basic substrate of all existence in a way that made it real. The teacher later reported to us that they understood in a way she hadn't thought possible.

This narrative presents various dimensions of the use of the arts in teaching subject matter. First, and foremost, the art aspect of the teaching must never be short-changed, otherwise the teaching is weak. Neither thinking aesthetically nor thinking academically becomes robust. Second, there need be no complex art activity for the art to be present. Please note that, so far, all the examples I have presented work with simple materials and simple ideas. Despite this, I would argue that they are sophisticated as they demand the highest level of aesthetic considerations: design, relationships, formation of vocabulary, and wise choices made, all dedicated to finding something out about the "topic" at hand, whether that topic is design and emotion (the group drawing activity), the discovery of meaning about an idea (the collage activity), or cognitive knowledge (the fractions activity). Third, this "finding out" is based in the art, and while some of the "learning" might be accomplished by other means (e.g., the fractions example), the location of the learning (the body and the senses) allows other learning to be simultaneously accessed (body and senses learning), and orientations toward what is learned are changed.

What is learned is unique to the mode of learning and is found in no other way than through the art activity. I am emphasizing "activity" as opposed to "talking about" what is learned and accessed. This is not to say that "talking about" is not, itself, a sort of activity but rather that the kind of activity it is (one which is favored by conventional education) is removed from that which is under examination. What is learned is a "cognitive disposition toward" and "adeptness at thinking about" separate from the thing under examination. One is not preferable to the other, but they are distinctive, one from the other.

The issue of forming a vocabulary of aesthetics brings me to another activity I utilized with my teacher preparation students. When artists work, they always work with vocabulary of one sort or another. Even Jackson Pollack, in his famous action paintings, worked with vocabulary of splashing; he flung, wiped, dashed paint with his body as a vehicle for that splashing, flinging, wiping, and dashing. Wassily Kandinsky asserted that color had meaning and that through assembling colors in certain ways he could stimulate particular responses on the part of viewers of his paintings. He didn't mean this behavioristically but only that people respond to color with meanings.

These are both examples of abstract artists who didn't present recognizable representations. This is important because while vocabulary might be construed as what is being represented (Georgia O'Keefe's paintings of flowers, for example) it is actually not that at all. Vocabulary, for her, would be how she manipulated colored paint in the space of the canvas in order to re-present nature to us. Many people could paint the flowers she painted, so the real genius lies in how she saw the flowers and how she manipulated materials to bring that vision to us. The resulting paintings are an amalgam of seeing and materials interacting and modifying each other in the process of making the painting. Her need was to discover a vocabulary of color and form that would do for her what she desired.

In that spirit, I worked with my preservice teachers to create nonverbal vocabulary through their responses to poetry. Prior to this, we had already had several dance experiences in which we created movement vocabulary. As an example, in one class, standing in a circle facing each other, I asked each person, one at a time, to provide a movement for a body part. We then learned that person's movement, imitating it as best we could. When we had gathered perhaps four or five of these we linked them together and danced the short dance we had just created several times, honing our ability to get the movement correct and our ability to perform the transitions between movements so that the whole dance felt complete.

It is significant that this dance was generated from the students, not from official dance movement vocabulary. I emphasized that this was "legitimate" dance and "legitimate" art, not anything less. This was not a manipulation to encourage them to continue. In my estimation, it qualifies as art. They were not going to be practicing artists and did not see themselves as such and weren't going to live their lives seeing events and simultaneously seeing possible dances (something endemic to all artists). Nevertheless, this was art.

In later classes, we worked on dance improvisations. I would provide a simple idea (walking forward backward or walking on tiptoes walking low to the ground), and they would then begin to perform that idea. In this case, they would only be able to walk forward, backward, on tiptoes, or low to the ground. That was the vocabulary. They could vary the speed, they could pause, they could imitate another person, or they could have momentary duets, trios, or quartets of walking (walking alike or walking differently), or anything else that occurred to them. They were learning to be aware of others in the space, aware of how their movement would change when joining another; they were learning new ways to be in their bodies as they imitated someone else and learning how to craft art in an immediate way that did not give time for self-editing.

Another idea I often employed was to have the teachers' arms be their brains—they must go where the arm wants to go, do what it wants to do—not thinking about it, just doing it. They experienced themselves as thinking in movement rather than thinking about movement, being directly with their body rather than studying their body. These kinds of activities enabled them to see that all movement is potentially dance movement if you approach it correctly.

This experiencing of movement, then, became the basis for working with the poetry. For working with poetry, I selected some poems to which I asked them to respond in small groups. First, each group read their poem together. There was to be little discussion of the "meaning" of the poem. Rather, the preservice teachers were to focus on the feel of the poem, on the actions suggested by the poem or the mood of the poem. However, the purpose was not to "act out" the poem. If a poem was gloomy, one wouldn't do movements that represented being glum. Rather, one would take inside oneself the mood of the poem (gloom) and make a dance in which no matter what you did, it would feel gloomy. There weren't specific movements that translated into "gloomy" but rather a way of dancing that attempted to experience the essence of gloom. As a concrete example, I will recount the following. Phyllis Lamhut, my choreographer, told us of making a dance having to do with the "evil eye."

She did not merely make glaring actions. Rather, she took inside herself "evil eye," experienced through what "evil eye" might be and then generated movements that were at the "essence" of "evil eye." Her solution to this "problem": she sat in a corner, knees drawn up, shivering and huddled. This movement was her sense of the essence of "evil eye." This is what I mean by "experience the essence of gloom." How you would, finally, choreograph and dance "gloom" wouldn't be easily or conventionally predictable.

The process described above is available to anyone, both as a student and as a pedagogue. Most of the above are not complicated activities and do not require a great physical skill. This does not mean that those wishing to work in this way shouldn't study dance, drawing, music, photography, and so forth, but people can begin to conceive of themselves as people capable of sharing such work with students. Thus, certainly teachers might want to cultivate the experiences for themselves prior to using it in the classroom. I wanted my own students to understand their own potential to use the arts to illuminate subject matter without feeling intimidated and wanted them to experience drawing upon the resources of the students.

My lessons were always accompanied with meta-lessons where we would stop in the midst of our work and I would ask the class what we had just done and what the principles behind teaching in that way are. We would analyze the teaching itself so that they could see how they could use it because they now better understood it. Experiencing it is not sufficient: talking about the practice itself is necessary in order for it to be useful in their later practice.

It is important to note that none of the above described activities are drawn from popular culture. That is, none of them draw from break dancing, hip-hop, jazz, modern dance, or ballet. They do not draw from any official form, all of which would impede the success of the experience. The success is based on a, relatively speaking, unedited response to poetry, to fractions, to an idea rather than an illustration of poetry, fractions, or ideas. These were not "representations of" but were a "response to."

It is not only preservice teachers who benefit from art experiences. I also use art experiences when working with certified teachers who study curriculum development. There are two experiences I will describe here, neither of which has to do with dance but both of which have to do with the senses (aesthesis).

The first of the experiences used with master's curriculum development students was developed out of a passage in Buber's chapter "Education" (2002). At one point, Buber is exploring the responsibility of a teacher who wishes to lead his students out, to enable them to discover themselves. He describes the following scene:

The teacher of the "free" school places on the table a twig of broom, say, in an earthenware jug, and makes the pupils draw it. Or he places it on the table, tells the pupils to look at it, removes it, and then makes them draw it. If the pupils are quite unsophisticated soon not a single drawing will look like another. Now the delicate, almost imperceptible and yet important influence begins—that of criticism and instruction. The children encounter a scale of values that, however unacademic it may be, is quite constant, a knowledge of good and evil that, however individualistic it may be, is quite unambiguous. The more unacademic this scale of values, and the more individualistic this knowledge, the more deeply do the children experience the encounter. . . . The pupil gains the realization only after he has ventured far out on the way to his achievement, his heart is drawn to reverence for the form, and educated. (p. 105)

In response to this passage, I present my students with an object such as the twig described by Buber, a wooden block, a candle, a pen, or any other small object. Everyone is given a good sized piece of paper and an array of drawing materials (markers, crayons, and pencils, both colored and black) from which to choose. The assignment is "Respond to the object thinking about curriculum. What is your immediate relationship to this object before you? Don't think too long on the relationship. Simply look and respond." I make it clear that this is not an art exercise but another way of contacting their thinking. The quality of the "art" isn't important. The response in another form (nonverbal and bodily) is important. That is why I ask them to not overthink the relationship. We take approximately twenty minutes to create our images and, then, one by one, we share with the class the image and we speak to what it means to us, how the image provides an expression of the response. I ask everyone not to apologize for the "art" work but to see this as experiencing a different way of thinking about something, in this case, curriculum, but it could be any topic or any area and the object could be any object. The object itself is not important. It is merely a prompt for aesthetic responsiveness.

Both these injunctions and the subsequent activity adhere to Buber's notion of presenting an unacademic scale of values (not emphasizing a "correct" way to draw or think) that is individualistic (personal), thus leading to the students experiencing more deeply their own achievements in thinking in this new way. Simultaneously, we do not succumb to the falseness of pure individuality as we come to see the commonalities in our thinking about the themes at hand, the commonalities of our responses to the request to draw in the first place, and something of the origins of our own thought as we probe the "why did you respond in this way" question. All of this allows each of us, as we encounter another's response to the task, to look to ourselves and our responses to the task,

thus forming ourselves as thinkers of certain kinds, thinkers that can be "successful" at thinking in this way because there are no barriers to thinking; we need not
prevent ourselves from thinking because our approach doesn't fit official molds.

The second activity I use with my masters curriculum development students
is more conventional: we watch a film. The film, however, is not an education
film and is not a conventional story form. It is *My Dinner with André* (1981), a
Louis Malle film with Andre Gregory and Wallace Shawn. Gregory and Shawn
had been having a series of interesting dinner conversations at a restaurant in
New York City. Later, relating these events to Malle, he suggested they re-create
these conversations for a film, condensing them into one evening. Shawn and
Gregory played out their conversations for several months, recording them.
Subsequently, Shawn consolidated, edited, and reorganized those conversations
into a screenplay that was then filmed. This is, ostensibly, a "talking heads" film.
However, as the two "characters" traverse, defend, and question the very different trajectories of their own lives (Gregory on a world-crossing, in more than
one sense, seeking of self through mythic activities, emotional, desperate, and
beautiful, and Shawn playing the stable, stay-at-home, occupy-his-small-nook-
of-his-world, in this case the theater world, character), we find a film filled with
emotion, contrasts, conflict, and all the other underpinnings of our everyday
lives.

As my students watch this film, I ask them to consider the stories of these
two men and what each of the stories might mean for the curriculum that they
teach and that they consider to be of worth (which, of course, might be different from each other). I am purposefully attempting to disrupt their taken-for-
granted living of their education lives. Andre is also trying to do this. His tale is
one of great emotion as well as confusion and paradox. I want my students to
feel the emotion as Andre tries to connect himself with the world around him
through other than conventional means. I want them to judge neither Andre nor
Wally but rather consider what their very different views of meaning might have
to do with teaching and curriculum.

The film is important as a vehicle, and without it there could be no such
consideration of difference. At the same time, it is more than an intellectual
vehicle. Often "talking heads" films are just about ideas. *My Dinner with André*
is not just about ideas but also about a life lived, replete with fear, love, paradox,
effort, and all the rhythms of poetry and music.

It is important to see art and art encounters as not representations of X
but rather a direct experience of X. It is only in the direct experience of X that
learning occurs. As with the drawing activity, the purpose here isn't to become
a distanced film critic or responder to ideas but to engage with the people in
the film, with their lives as lived and feel the connections to their own lives,

especially their own curricular lives. I want teachers and students to feel, not just think in a disembodied manner.

Conclusion

In all of the above, I have attempted to respond to the call for this yearbook. The editors wrote, "The importance of developing curious and creative minds has existed in the field of education for close to a century. Yet, the idea has never been fully embraced or enacted in ways that would fuel large-scale educational and societal change." Further, they requested writing that would address "what practices and strategies spur the development of curious and creative minds." In the aforementioned writing, I have tried to lay out the conceptual terrain that enables me to conceptualize an education for curiosity and creativity. The practices I have employed are dedicated to my learners finding either a new or renewed relationship with their own capacities to be creative and curious. If I have a hope for you, the reader, it is not just that I have convinced you of the salience of the arguments but also that you may begin to shift your relationship to yourself and who you might become. I ask myself, and you, How else might we improve this world in which we live if not through discovering ourselves as multifaceted human beings living fully engaged lives? Enjoy. Compose. Create. Imagine.

References

Blumenfeld-Jones, D. (2006). Aesthetic consciousness and dance curriculum: Liberation possibilities for inner city schools. In J. Kinchloe, K. Rose, K. Hayes, P. M. Anderson, & G. Press (Eds.), *The Praeger handbook of urban education* (pp. 508–517). Westport, CT: Praeger.

Bourdieu, P. (1984). *Distinction: A social critique of the judgment of taste* (N. Richard, Trans.). London: Routledge & Kegan Paul.

Buber, M. (2002). Education. In *Between Man and Man* (R. G. Smith, Trans.). New York: Routledge.

Dewey, J. (1934). *Art as experience.* New York: Minton, Balch and Company.

Dissanayake, E. (1995). *Homo aestheticus: Where art comes from and why.* Seattle: University of Washington Press.

Gadamer, H.-G. (1975). *Truth and method* (2nd ed.). New York: Crossroads.

Gans, H. J. (1974). *Popular culture and high culture: An analysis and evaluation of taste.* New York: Basic Books.

Johnson, M. (1993). *Moral imagination: Implications of cognitive science for ethics.* Chicago: University of Chicago Press.

Macdonald, J. B. (1995a). A transcendental developmental ideology of education. In B. J. Macdonald (Ed.), *Theory as a prayerful act: The collected essays of James B. Macdonald* (pp. 69–98). New York: Peter Lang.

Macdonald, J. B. (1995b). A vision of a humane school. In B. J. Macdonald (Ed.), *Theory as a prayerful act: The collected essays of James B. Macdonald* (pp. 49–68). New York: Peter Lang.

Malle, L., Shawn, W., & Gregory, A. (1981). *My dinner with André*. New York: Wellspring.

Sloan, Douglas. (1983). *Insight-imagination: The emancipation of thought and the modern world*. Westport, CT: Greenwood Press.

Williams, R. (1973). Base and superstructure in Marxist cultural theory. *New Left Review, 82*, 3–16.

CHAPTER 3

Sunshine and Shadows
OPENING SPACES FOR CREATIVITY, METAPHOR, AND PARADOX IN TEACHING AND TEACHER EDUCATION

Dixie K. Keyes
Arkansas State University

Dixie Keyes, Ed.D., is an associate professor of middle-level education in the Department of Teacher Education at Arkansas State University in Jonesboro, Arkansas. Her research interests cohere around
teacher knowledge and the narratives of teachers as curriculum
makers, with a specific focus in adolescent and critical literacy issues.

ABSTRACT

This chapter follows the traditions of narrative inquiry in its use of
restorying and makes use of a conceptualization called "tracing" to
collect images and stories from various plotlines and multiple contexts of people's narratives. These "traced stories" from both teachers
and a teacher educator reveal particularities of creativity, empathy,
and paradox that guide the individuals in their decision making and
narrative authority. By collecting these varied images and stories,
practices and strategies that stir the development of curious and
creative minds can be found and readers can see what curious and
creative teaching and learning look like. I hope this display answers
Cheryl Craig's and Louise Deretchin's call (2008) to "offer possible
pathways for a resurgence of intellectual energy and action in the
field of teaching and teacher education" (p. 1998). In this chapter,
the capacity for creativity and the pathways toward understanding
paradox are described and found critical in both educational and
social realms.

In a turning point of the dark comedy *Little Miss Sunshine* (2006), Dwayne
wishes he could skip all the "high school crap" and everything associated with
it. As he and his genius uncle, Frank—a Marcel Proust scholar—reflect together

on a dock by the water, Frank immediately makes a literary reference describing Proust's background. Proust was a French writer, gay, considered a loser who never had a real job, and unsuccessful in love, and he spent a large chunk of his life writing a book almost no one reads. Frank goes on to share how Proust looked back on those years of suffering as his best years, ones that made him who he was, as opposed to the happy years where nothing was significant. Then Frank looks Dwayne square in the eyes and offers this advice: "High school—those are your prime suffering years. You don't get better suffering than that."

Introduction

The paradox of high school days—instrumental suffering—is an oxymoron that aptly describes what fifteen-year-old Dwayne wishes he could forego. As I watched *Little Miss Sunshine* for the second time a few weeks ago, I enjoyed the authenticities of a below-middle-class family and the family members' fierce, dysfunctional love for one another. Toward the end of the movie, Uncle Frank tells the teenage boy, Dwayne, whose dreams of a career in the air force have just been crushed (he's color blind) about Proust's writings—that Proust was declared an atrocious writer and belittled by the people of his era, although he is arguably the greatest writer since Shakespeare. Frank was feeling the depths of pain himself; a Proust scholar and professor, he had just lost his job for having an affair with a graduate student. Then he tried to kill himself and was ordered to live with his sister's family for a period of healing. By sharing the story of Proust—how the author did not value the hard times and struggles of his life until the end of it—Frank is also reconciling his own situation.

Upon my second viewing of this story, I saw the clarity of an embedded metaphor in the movie. The old Volkswagen van that had to be pushed by the entire family to start in second gear is the receptacle of their elusive dreams, their problems, and ironically their support of one another. Each person in the family (Mom, Dad, Uncle Frank, Dwayne, and Olive [Grandpa died on the way]) carry their own personal dilemmas in life, but each one pushed the van to get it started when it was time to move on, even little Olive. They collectively placed their problems within the family van, pushed it together, and embarked on another part of their journey. Even if they sometimes temporarily forgot one another—like when they left Olive at a gas station—they rolled back around and remembered, acknowledging their mistakes. They even partook in risky behavior. As they swung around a gas station parking lot to gather the forgotten Olive, they did not completely stop. They reached out several arms shouting, "Run, Olive, run!" and she managed to jump into the side door of the van as it swerved past the gas tanks.

The Volkswagen van, to me, forms an image of dysfunctional resilience. Those who learn are constantly in the midst of risk, reflection, change, renewal and reacceptance of themselves and others. But how often do we revision or restory this theme? How often do we value metaphor, oxymoronic views, and paradox? Does the lack of space for creativity limit our space for confronting or even seeing contradictions, both helpful and problematic? Is this space necessary for young people to make sense of their world and to embrace critical thought and change?

In and Out of the Swampy Lowlands

I begin with my own narrative from the past few years. It may be especially helpful for teacher educators who are early in their careers and who wrestle with different states of mind during their transition into higher education. After re-visiting my early realizations of paradox during my doctoral dissertation defense almost three years ago, I bumped into a decision I had made before I attained a position in higher education —a decision to remain in the swampy lowlands as a practitioner and a researcher. "There are those who choose the swampy lowlands. They deliberately involve themselves in messy but crucially important problems and, when asked to describe their methods of inquiry, they speak of experience, trial and error, intuition, and muddling through" (Schön, 1983, p. 43). I had decided to embrace the peripeteia, the trouble, the mire, while think-ing through, while inquiring, while studying every muddy footstep, and while tracing every storyline—mine and those beside me. Often when we choose to embrace, we may be letting go.

Things were rolling along well, I began my "dream job," and I was com-placent and not learning anything beyond the mundane. I made the easy jump *out* of the swampy lowlands onto the more solid ground of being a professor, of knowing more than others, of sharing knowledge I thought would benefit others despite the knowledge they held or wanted to share. In the dimensions of present time, I return to my past searching and see an acknowledgment, a "finality" of sorts in the last paragraph of my dissertation:

> I feel as if I have emerged from the jungle in which most beginning researchers find themselves, and that I can now lay my machete down. . . . Now I venture forth, not only with a stronger meta-phorical voice, but with the newly acquired respect for others and for myself that comes with any honest, hard-earned achievement. I am ready to travel down the river of narrative research with my own stories, following and sharing in the storied lives of others.

I never noticed the error of my unconscious decision to leave the swampy low-lands until the very moment of writing this line for this book chapter. "Knowledge is a paradox dancing as the truth" (Dell'Aversana, 2002).

I purposefully fill this introductory space with story and metaphor in an attempt to share the power of resonating stories, of finding that "two sets [of stories] correspond metaphorically to one another" (Conle in Phillion, He, & Connelly, 2005, p. 220). At the point in the movie where Uncle Frank points out the paradox of strife (beneficial strife, if you will), I realized that the doldrums, frustrations, and doubting experiences after my first six months in higher education made up the timely, instrumental suffering that would impel me away from complacency. The "narrative moment of encounter" provided by Uncle Frank and Dwayne as they made sense of their peripatetic experiences instigated a "partial reshaping" of the lessons I needed to learn from my return to the swamplands over the past two years, and I began to return to my stories and notice patterns (Conle, 2003, p. 11). I journaled about reembracing paradox and having faith in myself and in other people, which I identified as the center, the nugget, of my perceived deficiencies. I was able to return to the abovementioned Paolo Dell'Aversana quote, one that I had focused on previously, remembering that throughout my first narrative inquiry research experience, I had looked for one thing and found another (from Cervantes' *Don Quixote*).

Knowledge does dance in front of us, teasing us with verisimilitudes moment by moment in our lives. The more knowledge I seemed to encounter, the more I was taunted with layers of questions. When I thought I had control over a narrative of mine, it simply led to the beginning of another. As soon as I felt the beginnings of comfort in the role of a narrative researcher, I knew it was time to revision myself as a participant. To step away from a conflict or confusion, I understood I had to step back into it. Metaphors arrived in my thinking, guided me, and broadened my understanding. But soon after, I would find them restrictive and they would leave me, having served their value. I tracked this history of paradox back to the theme of my dissertation defense, realizing the word paradox had not come to mind over the past two and half years—not until I chose to "go back and fetch it," this message retrieved from the Sankofa symbol (see figure 3.1) written of by Mary Bateson (2000, pp. 167, 171).

The long-necked bird reaching back reflects an active approach to looking forward, an action I needed to take as I continued my third year as a teacher educator. Bateson noted that the ways to wisdom include a continued child-like curiosity, a sense of cherishing the experiences of others, and an attitude of continuous learning.

By restorying our stories (Clandinin & Connelly, 2000), we "reaffirm them, modify them, and create new ones," which leads to new knowledge, new understandings (p. xxvi). I follow in the footsteps of Carola Conle (in Phillion, He,

Figure 3.1. The Sankofa symbol

& Connelly, 2005), Margaret Olson (in Craig & Deretchin, 2008), and Cheryl Craig (2008), all narrative inquirers who have engaged in experiential self-study, a historical overview of teacher education program development, and an exploration of self-study to advance development as a teacher educator, respectively. The readings above have encouraged me to move forward as I am currently involved in restorying. Although I am humbled in knocking on the door of Conle's explorations for themes in her ten years of writing, I attempt to follow her method of presenting research stories and of noting narrative resonance as I make sense of my early years as a narrative researcher and teacher educator.

In the tradition of Olson's concept of narrative authority (1995), I will share a narrative of a teacher candidate who opened spaces for creativity and empathy during a teacher education course and conference presentation, and note how she recognized her developing narrative authority. Craig's indelible scholarship, which draws on Joseph Schwab, Michael Connelly, and Jean Clandinin, has as its aim to inform her "teaching and research practices and, at the same time . . . to offer possible pathways for a resurgence of intellectual energy and action in the field of teaching and teacher education" (2008, p. 1998). I am not yet well versed in self-study research, but the expectations I hold for myself include similar goals as those mentioned by Craig, and I follow behind her in my journey.

Over the past two years, I have sought to increasingly include narrative practices in my teacher education courses. Narrative curricula practices "have become established in graduate and preservice teacher education and professional development" (Conle, 2000, p. 49). As I continue to plumb Schwab, Clandinin, Connelly, Craig, Conle, and Olson and envision their modeling and ideas onto my professional knowledge landscape (Clandinin & Connelly, 2000), it is my hope that my adventures in the swampy lowlands may contribute to the "intellectual energy and action" to which Craig refers.

My self-derived peripatetic experience (the upset of expected sequence) as a beginning teacher educator is a gift, and I am offered a "hoist up" toward understanding by Jerome Bruner (2002) as he advocated that Aristotle's concept of peripeteia should be as "widely taught to school kids as the geometer's less magical notion of hypotenuse of a right triangle."

The notion of paradox enters again, as well as that "murky" narrative that also often "bestows . . . a title of reality" upon the things of the real world (pp. 5, 8). Stories always have a particular message, or one stance of verisimilitude, upon which others can reflect and ponder. The rest of this chapter lies in the murkiness of the lowlands as I share narratives of irrational but inventive thought, of the strain of metaphor, of the recognition of paradox, and of the whirlwind of expectations in education. I offer my own particularities, in narrative fashion, as a researcher and teacher educator, and as a human who questions and inquires and who tries to avoid complacency.

Methodological notes: "The incorporation of theory into narrative inquiry can over-power an experiential narrative unless the theory in turn becomes a part of the story. After all, our encounters with ideas, reading, and theories are experiences as well and the meaning we make of them can become part of our narrative" (Conle, 2000, p. 58).

I have already acknowledged the educational researchers and theorists whom I follow, some of whom offered narratives beside which I can lay mine. Beyond that, I would like to make use of several conceptualizations and incorporate them into my narrative.

Craig and other narrative inquirers make use of multiple modes or tools of analysis within the process of their research (burrowing, broadening, and restorying). I shall use restorying mostly at the end of this writing as a tool for an effective coda, or "retrospective evaluation of what it all might mean" (Bruner, 2002, p. 20). Additionally, I will make use of a conceptualization, or tool, which I call "tracing." Generally defined as "the discovery and description of the course of development of something" (www.thefreedictionary.com/tracing), we may also think of tracing that involves the reproduction of an image made by copying it through translucent paper.

Although the processes of Craig, Conle, and Olson inspired me, the tool of tracing allows me to more specifically describe my process of reproducing various storied images together from separate contexts and histories, effectively bringing them together to one central location—just as a child might trace three or four images of interest onto one piece of paper (see end of chapter). I use this tool metaphorically as it attends to the temporal dimension that a "sensitive inquirer will spontaneously, almost without forethought, live these shifts in place and time and along the personal and the social" effectively dealing with the ambiguity involved in field texts (Clandinin & Connelly, 2000, p. 91). The tracings

I share are derived from my past writings, both personal and professional, and from field notes and transcriptions from two studies conducted in the tradition of narrative inquiry research with a focus on critical literacy in middle-level teaching and teacher preparation.

After dealing with the murkiness of ambiguity, I rely on tracing to bring three additional images of creativity together in this present piece. Returning to the purpose of this chapter, these images of creativity depict possible strategies that stir curious and creative minds toward empathy and art. As readers see through my lens and the lenses of my participants what curious and creative teaching and learning could look like, they will note the relational aspects of teacher and teacher educator created spaces for learning opportunities (rising forth from the swamplands). And like Dwayne, the resulting realization of paradox and contradiction presents us with a constant puzzle to solve.

I now share portions of three narratives: that of William Gordon and Synectics, of sixth-grade teacher John James who opens spaces for creativity, and of Glenda Rockton, a teacher candidate who values and implements analogical thought with a teacher's narrative authority.

Revisioning Creativity

> There is something antic about creating, although the enterprise be serious. And there is a matching antic spirit that goes with writing about it, for if ever there were a silent process it is the creative one. Antic and serious and silent. Yet there is good reason to inquire about creativity, a reason beyond practicality, for practicality is not a reason but a justification after the fact. The reason is the ancient search of the humanist for the excellence of man: the next creative act may bring man to a new dignity. (Bruner, 1971, p. 17)

Bruner—a connoisseur of folk knowledge and perhaps the greatest thinker of issues of epistemology—historically writes about his processes and his methods of arriving at conclusions or further questionings. He tells of the persons who influenced his thoughts, his personal observations that provoked relevant connections, and content of what he read and his responses to various texts. He continually brought his new knowledge into the realm of education. The quote above and the one following are from my favorite book of his, *On Knowing: Essays for the Left Hand* (1971). He wrote of the personal convictions educators should consider in the chapter "After John Dewey What?": "The structure of knowledge—its connectedness and the derivations" that make one idea follow from another—is the proper emphasis in education" (p. 120).

I chose to spotlight Bruner in this discussion of creativity, metaphor, and paradox for two reasons. First, he fervently addressed each of these topics—interconnected though they are—throughout his lifetime. His writings maintained an open, progressive stance and acknowledged his own changes in thought over the years. Secondly, he knew and respected Gordon as they spent time together at Harvard and in other contexts.

A Creator of Creativity: William Gordon and Synectics

"Synectically is the way people think, not just a way," Gordon stated in his first book, which Bruner, by the way, encouraged him to write (Gordon, 1961, p. 108). Synectics derives from a similarly spelled Greek word, *synektikos*, which means the joining together of different and apparently irrelevant elements. Gordon explained it as "an operational theory for the conscious use of the preconscious psychological mechanisms present in man's creative activity" (1961, p. 3). His second and last major book, *The Metaphorical Way of Learning and Knowing: Applying Synectics to Sensitivity and Learning Situations* (1973), was published four times in two editions and describes his research using Synectics in varied schools and in multiple content areas, mostly with disadvantaged learners. He outlined the Synectics hypothesis in the foreword, acknowledging the foundation of metaphorical thought:

> Creative perception depends on making metaphors that are necessary and sufficient connective conditions between known and unknown, and between known and known. Learning in art and science is simply an extension of creative perception. Invention in art and science is an extension of learning. The process of invention and discovery is one of testing daydreams. Observations of people learning (from sophisticated scientists to under privileged students) strongly suggest that learning (or discovery) is closely related to creativity. The Synectics hypothesis about creative thought applies directly to learning.
>
> 1. Learning efficiency in people can be increased markedly if they understand the psychological processes by which they operate.
> 2. In the learning process the emotional component is as important as the intellectual, the non-rational as important as the rational.
> 3. These emotional and non-rational elements can and must be engaged in order to increase the probability of successful learning. (1973, pp. ix–x)

(Remember Dwayne and Frank as the above hypothesis is considered. Dwayne tested his daydreams, found the emotional component of learning important, and brought together the irrationality of his experiences into meaning.) Here are the two avenues of Synectics:

MAKING THE FAMILIAR STRANGE

1. Describe the topic: *teacher has students describe the topic as they see it now.*
2. Create direct analogies: *students suggest direct analogies, select one, and explore (describe) it further.*
3. Describe personal analogies: *students "become" the analogy they selected in phase 2.*
4. Identify compressed conflicts: *students take their descriptions from phases 2 and 3, suggest several compressed conflicts, and choose one.*
5. Create a new direct analogy: *students generate and select another direct analogy, based on the compressed conflict.*
6. Reexamine the original topic: *teacher has students move back to original task or problem and use the last analogy and/or the entire Synectics experience.*

MAKING THE STRANGE FAMILIAR

1. Substantive input: *teacher provides information on new topic.*
2. Direct analogy: *teacher suggests direct analogy and asks students to describe the analogy.*
3. Personal analogy: *teacher has students "become" the direct analogy.*
4. Comparing analogies: *students identify and explain the points of similarity between the new material and the direct analogy.*
5. Explaining differences: *students explain where the analogy does not fit.*
6. Exploration: *students reexplore the original topic on its own terms.*
7. Generating analogy: *students provide their own direct analogy and explore the similarities and differences.*

Note: Compiled from multiple sources (Gunter, Estes, & Schwab, 2003, pp. 150–153; Joyce & Weil, 2008, pp. 223, 227).

Returning to Gordon's story, I must refer back to Bruner's involvement in the late 1950s with a "curious group" of industrial scientists who had gathered to create protective clothing for missile loading teams who handled highly corrosive propellants. Bruner also mentioned critical "long discussion" with Gordon, who was then in his early years of studying the creative process. The roots of Synectics were embedded in Gordon's way of knowing from early in his life. During the context of World War I when he was a combat salvage diver, he found his first observation of a wondrous problem solver, General Bernard Montgomery. Sunken boats needed to be cleaned from Tripoli Harbor, and this general responded creatively. He thought of his mother and how she used to rake piles of dirt down from mounds into her garden. Hence, Montgomery used this analogy in his decision to blow the boats to pieces and rake them out of the harbor. Energized by this observation and by his own inventive interests, Gordon created an unstoppable system for retrieving experimental torpedoes (an inflatable balloon that floated torpedoes to the surface).

These two events began a lifetime of study focused on "beside-the-point imagery" and "constructive irrelevancies" (Fincher, 1978, p. 27). Gordon knew the importance of temporal observations to continue validation of his development of Synectics, so he looked back at history for examples of invention based in "necessary irrelevancies," writing about August Kekule's discovery of the benzene molecule (by thinking of a snake eating its own tail), Alexander Graham Bell's comparison of the inner ear to the workings of a telephone, and William Harvey's discovery of the pumping heart as noticed in a fish that was cut open. He continued to be convinced of the power of analogical and metaphorical thought, eventually moving his work into educational writings and school settings.

I refer to Gordon as the "creator of creativity" because he believed in each person's creative capacity and, after many years of ongoing research, defined the Synectics hypothesis about creative thought and how it applies to learning and invention. In his 1961 book, he wrote, "Training the individual to understand and celebrate metaphor (in poetry and in literature as well as in science) and training the individual to make metaphors (even though they are generally descriptive) is training him in habits of mind consonant with the functional principles of the underlevels of brain and nervous system" (p. 117).

Tracing leads me to place a recent episode of Synectics brainstorming next to Gordon's story. Table 3.1 depicts a Synectics brainstorming session I led in Liverpool at an international conference for educators. There was an ongoing teachers' strike in Liverpool that was all over the news upon my arrival there. Holding the "Familiar to Strange" avenue of Synectics in my mind, I opened the session by inviting descriptions or words evoked when "teacher empowerment" is thought of.

After choosing "roads/paths" as the metaphorical route to think of empowerment, the group brainstormed a variety of interesting ones. We collectively chose "side road," contributed by a Dutch colleague as *sluipweg*, and we *became* side roads, noting our emotions and attitudes *as* side roads. This led to the development of a number of oxymorons, or compressed conflicts: empowered misuse, overlooked recognition, happy abuse, chipped whole, lonely love, and battered appreciation.

Although we attempted a further analogy with music, the group returned to the compressed conflict column to reach reflective conclusions about teacher empowerment, which are listed in the last column of table 3.1. The paradoxical descriptions of "lonely love" and "happy abuse" could be the root of the labor issues currently ongoing in the country. Are teachers misunderstood and overworked? Are they damaged in the profession? Do they need protection from honest mistakes? Could they benefit from an acknowledgment of their risk-taking? The purpose of this particular session was to generate reflection on an important topic for teacher educators, and due to metaphorical thought, which led to paradoxical phrasings, the group left a bit more enlightened about what teacher empowerment means.

The group appreciated the sparks of creativity as they considered teachers through the metaphor of "chipped teapots." Bruner noted that "combinatorial acts that produce effective surprise . . . almost always succeed through the exercise of technique" (1971, p. 22). From metaphor to paradox to creative surprise, all are interconnected through the Synectics process. I am still trying to figure out why such processes like those Synectics provides are largely absent in classrooms today, and I submit to educational audiences today the tracings of Gordon's legacy and one example of the use of Synectics.

The Hot Seat with John James

Freak the Mighty (2001) is a coming of age novel for young adolescents, which portrays an intense friendship between Freak (a highly intelligent small person) and "Max the Mighty," a giant of sorts, known to be brawny with a torrid family history. As their friendship evolves, Max eventually carries Freak upon his shoulders, symbolic of their symbiotic relationship. My next tracing involves this novel and sixth-grade reading teacher, John James, who has included it in his curriculum for more than ten years. His own social, emotional, and intellectual past as an adolescent included a learning disability and victimization from bullying, hence his selection of a story that converges with his own, and he believes, with those of his students.

With popcorn in Styrofoam bowls on group tables and each child with a soda, the atmosphere of John's room was student centered and friendly. He held a plastic bucket with each student name on a 3 × 5 card and shared that he would model the Hot Seat activity by portraying Max's grandfather, Grim. Then he drew student names and provided them with the chance to role-play a

Table 3.1. Results of Synectics Brainstorming at ETEN Conference, 2008

Familiar concept or topic	Direct analogy I	Personal analogy	Compressed conflicts	Direct analogy II	Revisiting the original topic for reflection
Teacher empowerment	Roads/paths	Be a "sluipweg" or side road . . . how do you feel?	Music		
					A) How can any of the metaphors or paradoxes we created inform our views of teachers?
Appreciative inquiry	Potholes	Lonely	Relaxed energy	Jazz	Teachers are seen as living lives of "lonely love"— they love what they do but don't feel respected for it or understood by society at large. They also live with "happy abuse," in that they are overworked and generally put up with it.
Power to teachers	Long & winding road	Peaceful	Safe crash	Folk	
Ways of reflecting	Missed road	Overlooked	Empowered misuse	Rock	
Feedback	Road not taken	Happy	Overlooked recognition	House	
Guts/courage	Boulevard of broken dreams	Relaxed	Crashed safety	Heavy metal	
Parent contact	My way, or the highway	Lost	Happy Abuse	Opera	
Image of the ideal	Mud path in the grass	Appreciated	Peacefully broken	Blues	
		Needed	Chipped Whole	Pop	
		Tired		Punk	
		Overloaded		Retro	
		Battered		Easy listening	

Organizational flattitude	Water buffaloes in Romania	Invigorated	Tired	Reggae
Equal level of input	Route 66	Taken advantage of	invigoration	Trash
Community of learners	Moose in Alaska	Loved	Lonely love	Mariachi
Decision making	Waterways	Empowered	Loved	Hip-hop
Leaders as teachers	Highways	Helpful	loneliness	Doom
We've lost the power!	Auto Bahn	Broken	Overloaded	Rap
Choices	Skyway	Proud	relief	Folk
Respect	Dead end	Recognized	Battered	Country
Resilience	Ventweg	Abused	appreciation	Gothic
Dedication	Sluipweg	Misused		
Most don't know what empowerment is	(Dutch for "side road")	Burned out		
Pay raise	Moose in Alaska	Chipped		
Attitude		Relieved		
Prestige		Crashed		
Proud				

B) How can the emerged ideas impact how we prepare teachers?

Respect should allow for imperfections. It's okay to take risks because we learn from challenges and mistakes. Teachers aren't perfect teapots sitting on shelves—they're actually "chipped." If they are chipped too often or damaged greatly in the profession, their purpose could dissolve, just as a teapot with a huge crack can no longer be functional.

character. As he modeled the Hot Seat task, I appreciated the critical nature of this learning activity as the students created their questions for Grim and began depicting understanding of different perspectives. Hot Seat invites particular students to fully empathize with a character from literature by pretending to *be* that character. Students are encouraged to walk, talk, and act like the character in every way. Interestingly, this parallels the personal analogy step of Synectics—the "becoming" of something else.

After John's modeling, one young man agreed to role-play Max. A student in the audience asked, "Why are you friends with Freak?"

"I never had a brain until Freak came along." He chose to cite this line from the book, although his ability to immediately ensconce himself as Max amazed me. Another student was asked to role-play Max. "Why are you so big?" another student questioned.

"Because my dad birthmarked me." He had entered the room sauntering, with his hands over his face, saying several times aloud, "I don't like myself."

As another student played the role of Tony D, the antagonistic gang leader who brought the most conflict to Freak and Max, a student asked him why he is violent.

"Because I like to see blood."

"Would you be willing to change if given the chance?"

"If I had the chance, but I can't find one."

The first student, as Max, recognized himself as "brainless," which is at the opposite pole of the paradox Freak represents, Freak being a total brain in Max's estimation. He was able to imagine himself brainless without Freak but powerfully intellectual *with* him. Paradoxical thought from a preteen.

The second student turned the noun "birthmark" into a verb, giving a new metaphor to us for genetic commonalities. Remarkable to me, and notable of metaphoric thought, is the surprise effect of the connotation of "birthmark." Birthmarks are permanent, often unattractive and obvious, and "mark" someone as similar to another in their genetic lineage. Max's father had supposedly killed his mother, so his father was an obvious cause of Max's low self-esteem and far from possible emulation. Further, Max was "birthmarked" because of the similarity in size to his father—another symbol of the power of one's history and past, the burdens that are carried. Again, how can a preteen create such a metaphoric concept, representative of Gordon's knowledge of the generative power of metaphor through Synectical thought?

The third student could not *find* a chance to change; he was lost in violence. The young man portraying Tony D chose to personify "chances," as if chances were hiding from him, as if they had all run away. This personification of lost chances provided empathy for Tony D, just as the irrational thoughts of the two other student Hot Seat characters promoted empathy. If teachers and students are aware of the birth of metaphors involved during this time of role-play, they can further analyze, dispel, and create additional metaphors to enhance understanding and empathy, which will instigate additional critical thought possibly leading to social action.

John values the educative function of learning activities such as Hot Seat, although he questions the time involved in including them within his curriculum. I asked him why he still did it if time is a constant issue.

"It fosters creative thought, helps them draw inferences and make conclusions." He mentioned the constructivist model of literacy—"building on what they bring" and "digging down to find out what they already know." He also noted the value of providing them with the opportunity to "go back to something else later and get something different from it the second time around."

Throughout all of my interviews with John, a constant is the battle he feels between teaching them to ask deep questions and modeling reading skills necessary for accountability test success. When we spoke of the three students who participated as characters in Hot Seat, I noted the compelling metaphorical thoughts that had erupted. John noted that all three were African American students and shared that, in his opinion, their literary knowledge is not reflected through their writing. "Their culture values strong oral traditions versus written fluency." Although they may not always produce the written competency required in testing, their verbal and dramatic interpretations of the characters from this novel were unique, critical, and strong. "Minority interpretations aren't valued enough," declared John. I thought of the hegemonic systems in place in regard to accountability practices and how activities like Hot Seat are even more valuable for students who need their voices heard in a different way—the students who can create metaphor, something Aristotle thought was a mark of genius.

Mind-Melding with Glenda Rockton

As I trace Glenda, emotions well up in me. Glenda found me as I was stuck in some quicksand within my jungle, offered a hand, and pulled me out; her energy as a curriculum maker and her response to critical literacy reenergized me when I did not yet appreciate my quicksand. Nevertheless, as she decided to join me as a co-presenter at a state curriculum conference for teachers, we met on weekends and after school to discuss critical literacy strategies we wanted to share at the conference. During this time, she was also a student in one of my teacher education courses, Literacy through Literature in the Middle Grades, where critical literacy is a dominant theme.

I began the course by inviting students to select a novel of their choice from a wide variety of historical, realistic, or fantasy fiction. Glenda quickly snapped

up *Where the Great Hawk Flies* by Liza Ketchum (2005). Upon our first preparation meeting for the conference, I came to know why. At age 24, Glenda discovered that half of her heritage was Native American Cherokee. Below is an excerpt
from a transcription where she shared her reaction after a telephone conversation
with her biological father.

> He told me a little about himself. He was working construction and
> that he had always tried to keep tabs with me and anytime I was in
> the paper he cut it up for a scrapbook his mother had made of me
> throughout the years and the last thing he had heard was that I had
> gotten married which had been four or five years before that. He was
> just as ecstatic as he could be; I on the other hand was still completely
> stunned. Come to find out again, that his family was Native American
> Cherokee and I found out that I was half. And at first I thought that
> most people who've grown up in this area have some percentage of Na-
> tive American in them whether it's Mohawk or Cherokee . . . whatever.
> That didn't really hit me until I began thinking about it . . . y'know
> I was HALF of a minority group, and that hit me like a ton of bricks
> because I had always been a little white girl. And so finding out that I
> was half of a minority group—one of the smallest minority groups . . .
> one of the minority groups that's disappearing. And that in five to six
> generations, there will be no more pure Native Americans. And that re-
> ally hit me, so I doing a bunch of research on the heritage . . . I thought
> "I can't let this pass. I need to find out more of my makeup." Since
> then I've had a soft spot in my heart for Native American literature and
> Native American books and I was striving to catch up with what I felt
> any child growing up in a normal setting would have—these stories
> would've been just passed down . . . on the random Sunday afternoon.
> Like here's your family's heritage. Or like on Christmas, Uncle's secret
> gets blurted out. So I guess I was really trying to capture 24–25 years
> of knowledge about a specific culture.

Glenda pondered the paradox of being a "white" Native American but simultaneously explored the different points of view involved in this discovery as
she read *Where the Great Hawk Flies.*

> It is written in alternating chapters and it's one continuous story
> throughout and the first chapter and the intro are written by Daniel
> who is half Pequot and half an English child so he was half and half
> like me. So the story progresses through alternate points of view, and
> I love how it's written because you not only have one main character
> you had two or three, and you allowed yourself to submerse yourself
> in the story because you got to see both points of view.

Consider Olson's concept of narrative authority at this point in Glenda's story. As noted in the particulars of our conversation below, her personal narrative played an important role in the development of mind-melding. The creation of empathy was central on the plotline of her narrative and became central to her plans for teaching.

> GLENDA: The mind-melding strategy really hit home for me because in whatever I do I try to see opposing viewpoints and that's just how I look at the world. Here I am, but there they are, but what's their thought process? What are they thinking? Mind-melding really illustrated to me *how* to teach others how to do that. The first rule to getting along with anybody is to appreciate their opinion and appreciate their points of view. What helps me appreciate others' opinions is being empathetic . . . really identifying with them and their struggles and their point of view. Because I feel like by identifying with it I can respect it more and that really relates and makes everything cohesive in my head.
>
> ME: Do you think that drive toward empathy was fueled by a possible desire for you to find respect for your father that you didn't know?
>
> GLENDA: I feel it was definitely fueled by finding respect for what I felt was my lost heritage. And definitely a part of that was reconciling in my head who he was, what he had gone through since I had been born and coming out on the better side of things.
>
> ME: Do you think through literature that we find redemption? That we find people who go through things like what we go through and we relate it to our lives?
>
> GLENDA: Absolutely. Even if it's a fictional character you feel like you're not alone. If I see a student who's going through a certain situation, he may not speak to me about it. However, if I find a book with a character who's going through a situation, then that opens up an avenue for that student to talk about the character and really put himself in the situation of the character. It gives them more of an outlet to possibly educate others about their struggles or their place. So I definitely think books are crucial in that they provide a voice for people or students or whomever when they might not otherwise have a voice.

As I listened to Glenda that day, I turned back (Sankofa symbol) and thought of the many ways literature had saved me or allowed me to find my redemption, especially in my younger years. I lived vicariously through characters who had heroic powers; I recognized myself and my hopes in Madeleine L'Engle novels. On a coincidentally powerful note, I restoried two narratives of my own as I wrote my dissertation, both about my father. Observing Glenda as she made sense of her curriculum-making experiences allowed me to revalue my own like experiences, those that, as she put it, "gives them more of an outlet to possibly educate others about their struggles or their place."

Coda: The Tracings Together on One Page

I now bring the images of creativity and paradox together in this chapter, with captions that will show the temporality—the moving backward and forward in time—involved in the narrative that has been pieced together (see figure 3.2).

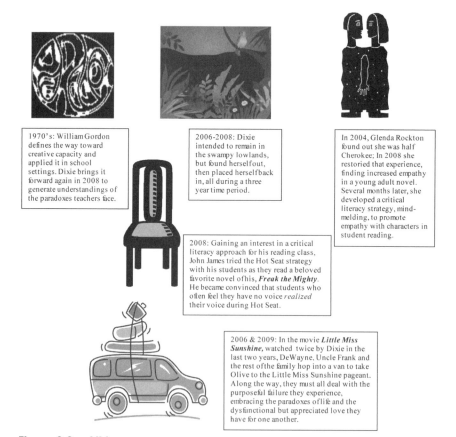

1970's: William Gordon defines the way toward creative capacity and applied it in school settings. Dixie brings it forward again in 2008 to generate understandings of the paradoxes teachers face.

2006-2008: Dixie intended to remain in the swampy lowlands, but found herself out, then placed herself back in, all during a three year time period.

In 2004, Glenda Rockton found out she was half Cherokee; In 2008 she restoried that experience, finding increased empathy in a young adult novel. Several months later, she developed a critical literacy strategy, mind-melding, to promote empathy with characters in student reading.

2008: Gaining an interest in a critical literacy approach for his reading class, John James tried the Hot Seat strategy with his students as they read a beloved favorite novel of his, *Freak the Mighty*. He became convinced that students who often feel they have no voice *realized* their voice during Hot Seat.

2006 & 2009: In the movie *Little Miss Sunshine*, watched twice by Dixie in the last two years, DeWayne, Uncle Frank and the rest of the family hop into a van to take Olive to the Little Miss Sunshine pageant. Along the way, they must all deal with the purposeful failure they experience, embracing the paradoxes of life and the dysfunctional but appreciated love they have for one another.

Figure 3.2. All images

I display this collection of tracings hoping other teachers and teacher educators may do the same. Particularities of creativity or stories relived and shared again can convince us to open those important spaces to embrace irrational connections and explore impossible truths.

How else shall our young people, in their struggles and disappointments, grow into an understanding of antimony—how can something so brittle contribute to great strength? How shall future teachers better embrace both the sunshine and shadows of education—the challenges and the fulfillments? How can our future scientists revel in relaxed alertness as they embrace an intuitive knowing that at any moment a disjointed connection may lead them forward in the invention process? Gordon (1973) advised encouraging students to rouse their own metaphors and analogies:

> It is critically important that students be encouraged to conceive of their own metaphors rather than passively depending on the comparison of a teacher. Otherwise, students will not learn the habit of metaphorical learning and knowing; and they will not have the skill for developing intellectual leverage when presented with new situations. (pp. 85–86)

Both teachers and teacher educators, along with preservice teachers, can use the processes involved in Synectics to create metaphor and oxymorons and to generate new ideas. Although all of Gordon's books are out of print and incredibly difficult to find, longtime educational researcher and author Bruce Joyce identified Synectics as a "model of teaching," beginning with the first edition of his seminal textbook in the 1970s. Eight editions later, Joyce recently updated his chapter on Synectics with a research scenario I wrote about a high school writing student. The two avenues of Synectics, reviewed earlier in this chapter, were compiled largely from the Joyce text. This information provides educators with a practical way to "make the familiar strange" and "make the strange familiar." This can be used as a guide for group brainstorming using the Synectics process, or it can effectively guide a lone user through the steps. I hope readers will experiment, play, and communicate with these tools, and revive Gordon's belief in the power of "synectical thought" when possible. Our students deserve the opportunity.

Joyce and Marsha Weil (2008) described the instructional and nurturant effects of Synectics: group cohesion and productivity, tools for metaphoric thinking, problem-solving capability, self-esteem, adventurousness, and achieving curricular content (p. 239).

The use of metaphors in writing (as delivered by Synectics brainstorming sessions in my language arts classroom) has assisted my students in structuring their thoughts, as well as in making sense of their experiences. Synectics has helped many of my students find their voices in writing and has raised their self-esteem (as they recognize their creativity being honored) by pushing them toward an often first successful writing experience.

Gordon (1961) noted that the communal experience of creative responsibility and emotional acceptance promoted successful inventive ideas (pp. 75–77). I find elements of culturally responsive pedagogy and teacher efficacy in Gordon's Synectics. Indeed, he developed Synectics workbooks (and teacher guides) that were used with black, inner-city students who desperately needed to catch up to white counterparts in reading and writing achievement. He found that his materials using the metaphorical approach provided sensitivity along with "sensible innovation."

Gordon mentioned a concern in metaphorical research that seemingly less intelligent students may fail "embarrassingly" with a metaphorical approach to learning but hoped that was due to the existent unjust labeling that still occurs in education today. He determined that "their potential had gone underground, but it might be recovered by the metaphorical approach" and that "perhaps children who were always searching for the 'whys' of the universe would inevitably get lower grades than children who accepted the world on face value."

This thought parallels John's empowered decision to make the time for creativity connections. If students were offered a better grasp of science through metaphorical thought, underachievers may be drawn out. Data gathered from schools in Spanish Harlem, Sacramento, Philadelphia, New York City, and other cities supported Gordon's hypothesis, with underachievers showing radical improvement. After interviewing the students involved, Gordon determined that the reasons for large shifts in learning appeared to be "the caring tone of the materials" and student acceptance of the honesty of educators who really listened and helped students find the process of arriving at connections (pp. 66–67).

Norvella Carter (2003) edited what I consider a foundational book for me as an early teacher educator caught with others in an age of accountability. The book entitled *Convergence or Divergence* challenges us to first "understand the political dimensions of school reform" and then, secondly, and as demonstrated in the tracings of Gordon (during his research), Glenda (preservice teacher), and John (inservice teacher), to "prepare teachers as change agents with moral purpose . . . and incorporating pedagogically informed disciplinary and multicultural competencies into the curriculum" (p. 29). Making use of sensitive, respectful learning events such as the process of Synectics and the validating, meaning-filled Hot Seat matches Geneva Gay's call for culturally responsive teaching (in Carter, 2003, p. 62). Facilitating the narrative authority of preservice teachers as they develop efficacy and build high expectations for all learners is critical. Glenda's empathy-building, mind-melding strategy moved her "from words to action" and guided her to address challenges in the form of practices "for educational environments that encourage all students to learn to the best of their ability" (p. 65).

Through restorying my experiences with creativity, metaphor, and paradox, along with others—the Synectical voice of Gordon, the concerned teacher John in whose room I spend much time, and Glenda the teacher candidate entering her career in education with an uncanny awareness of cultural relevance and analogical thought—I have picked up my machete again and remain in the jungle with them. John and I continue a longitudinal journey. Glenda and I are writing together. Gordon's voice reminds me each day to finish the book I started about Synectics. Most important is that for the moment I no longer feel negativity toward the paradoxical elements in my personal and professional life as a beginning teacher educator—it has shoved me forward into an even more dense area of the jungle. But what lies ahead? Confusion or illumination? Critique or adventure? Sunshine or shadows? Possibly. Probably. What do I know for sure? I will expect the peripeteia and the paradox, and I hope to find stories from others, particularly teacher educators, who are doing the same.

References

Arndt, M. (2006). *Little miss sunshine.* Los Angeles: Fox Searchlight Pictures/Twentieth Century Fox.

Bateson, M. C. (2000). *Full circles, overlapping lives.* New York: Ballantine Books.

Bruner, J. (1971). *On knowing: Essays for the left hand.* New York: Atheneum.

Bruner, J. (2002). *Making stories: Law, literature and life.* New York: Farrar, Straus and Giroux.

Carter, N. (Ed.). (2003). *Convergence or divergence: Alignment of standards, assessment, and issues of diversity.* Washington, DC: AACTE Publications.

Clandinin, D. J., & Connelly, F. M. (2000). *Narrative inquiry: Experience and story in qualitative research.* San Francisco: Jossey-Bass.

Conle, C. (2000). Narrative inquiry: Research tool and medium for professional development. *European Journal of Teacher Education, 23*(1), 49–63.

Conle, C. (2003). An anatomy of narrative curricula. *Educational Researcher, 32*(3), 3–15.

Craig, C. J. (2008). Joseph Schwab, self-study of teaching and teacher education practices proponent? A personal perspective. *Teaching and Teacher Education, 24*(8), 1993–2001.

Craig, C. J., & Deretchin, L. F. (2008). *Imagining a renaissance in teacher education.* Teacher education yearbook XVI. Lanham, MD: Rowman & Littlefield Education.

Dell'Aversana, P. (2002). Agreeing and disagreeing on the creative process. *First Break, 20*(2), 88–89.

Fincher, J. (1978). The new idea man. *Human Behavior, 7,* 27–32.

Gordon, W. J. J. (1961). *Synectics: The development of creative capacity.* Cambridge, MA: Porpoise Books.

Gordon, W. J. J. (1973). *The metaphorical way of learning and knowing: Applying Synectics to sensitivity and learning situations.* Cambridge, MA: Porpoise Books.

Gunter, M. A., Estes, T. H., & Schwab, J. (2003). *Instruction: A models approach* (4th ed.). Boston: Allyn and Bacon.

Ketchum, L. (2005). *Where the great hawk flies.* New York: Scholastic.

Joyce, B., & Weil, M. (2008). *Models of teaching* (8th ed.). Boston: Pearson.

Olson, M. (1995). Conceptualizing narrative authority: Implications for teacher education. *Teaching and Teacher Education, 11*(2), 119–125.

Philbrick, R. (2001). *Freak the mighty.* New York: Scholastic.

Phillion, J., He, M. F., & Connelly, F. M. (Eds.). (2005). *Narrative and experience in multicultural education.* Thousand Oaks, CA: Sage.

Schön, D. A. (1983). *The reflective practitioner: How professionals think in action.* New York: Basic Books.

CHAPTER 4

No Less "Real" in My Mind

USING FICTION AS CREATIVE CURRICULUM IN AN UNDERGRADUATE TEACHER EDUCATION COURSE

Chris Lasher-Zwerling
Alianza Charter School, Watsonville

Kip Téllez
University of California, Santa Cruz

Chris Lasher-Zwerling, M.A., is a bilingual teacher at Alianza Charter School in the Pajaro Valley Unified School District. She has an M.A. in Education from the University of California at Santa Cruz and an M.A. in English from CSU Chico.

Kip Téllez, Ph.D., is associate professor and chair of the Education Department at University of California at Santa Cruz. His research interests are teacher education and second-language instruction. He earned his Ph.D. from Claremont Graduate University.

ABSTRACT

Management, medical educators, and researchers have long identified reading fiction as a particularly useful tool in promoting self-reflection and creating a broadened professional outlook among their preservice teachers. In contrast, the research in teacher education has rarely examined the role fiction can play in developing new teachers. The research reported here invited fifty-one undergraduates enrolled in an Introduction to Teaching course to read five varied fictional works of literature on teachers or teaching. The qualitative results suggest that this innovative curriculum of fictional works helps preservice teachers understand the conflict between a teacher's personal and professional lives, the complexity of teaching, and the importance of teacher-student relationships, among other compelling themes.

Creativity and imagination go hand in hand with teaching. Differentiating instruction to effectively educate the very unique students one might find in any K–12 or teacher education classroom requires constant and inspired changes in strategies, materials, and delivery of course content. This type of teaching requires thorough self-reflection and a dedication to student learning. This approach to instruction does not come from textbooks and is not static. Why is it then that introductory teacher education courses often introduce prospective teachers to the teacher profession using unimaginative, dry curriculum?

Sharon Feiman-Nemser and Helen Featherstone (1992) argue that introductory teacher education courses are too commonly textbook driven, introducing students to a so-called practitioners' perspective on education along with a myriad of unrelated facts about teachers and schools. A field experience is also typical in such courses, encouraging potential teachers to gain direct experience in the classroom as a way to gauge whether teaching might be an appropriate career choice. However, as the aforementioned authors further suggest, this curriculum often fails to promote self-reflection and leaves students' assumptions and beliefs about teaching and teachers unaddressed.

After much personal and shared reflection, we decided that our own Introduction to Teaching course was fraught with similar shortcomings. As we considered whether our introductory course could be creatively modified to promote a deeper consideration of teaching and learning, we sought a medium that would allow preservice teachers to understand better the emotional and moral aspects of teaching.

Our search led us to read a wide variety of approaches to introductory "professional" fields courses, which focused on broadening student perspective and deepening an understanding of the profession. In our research of management and medical education, in particular, we found several instances of instructors who had identified reading fiction as a particularly useful tool in promoting self-reflection. In medical education, for example, the use of literature as an effective means of widening students' perspectives was well documented (Montgomery Hunter, Charon, & Coulehan, 1995).

Given the common use of reading fiction in other professional fields, it was surprising for us to find that few studies in education have examined the effects of reading fiction on the self-reflection and professional understanding (e.g., moral and psychological) of preservice teachers. Once we had decided to use fiction, we set out to find appropriate works, decided upon a diverse set of texts (see appendix A), and developed two primary research questions: How does the fiction used in this class illuminate a preservice teacher's beliefs about teaching in a different or more meaningful way than expository text or field experiences alone? What concerns of teaching and preservice teachers might these fictional accounts address?

The use of literature as a tool for learning and reflection has many advocates—Dorothy Walsh (1969) is foremost among them. In her classic work, *Literature and Knowledge*, Walsh (1969) notes that literature brings with it a specific kind of knowledge, "an experience to be experienced" (p. 130), while noting the novel's capacity to teach as a relic of a specific culture within a specific historical context, what Walsh has called realization. "Literary education," she writes, "can enormously expand the range of humanistic understanding" (p. 133). By way of clarification, Walsh does not equate this understanding with a search for clear answers but instead suggests that "the realm of literary art is a realm too diverse, too various, too rich in multiple perspectives, to provide anything in the way of simple directives" (p. 134). Tzachi Zamir (2002) makes a similar point, suggesting that using literature for the sake of learning must never be equated with pure didacticism or functionalism.

Our interest in the role of fiction as a tool for reflection on teaching grew out of a more foundational concern that asks how readers interpret texts. As teachers with an abiding belief in reader response theory, we approached our work with preservice teachers from a poststructuralist stance, relying on the work of Roland Barthes (1974) in particular. Such a view demands that we recognize how the experiences of our readers influence their reading of fictional works; indeed, like many teachers of literature, we take a distinctly phenomenological approach to reading, sharing David Bleich's (1978) view that readers must be encouraged to create an inner dialogue between their own experiences and the texts they read. Further, sharing this dialogue with other readers serves to refine the negotiation of meaning between the text and the reader.

We have also been greatly influenced by the work of Judith Langer (1989), whose concept of envisionment offers a particularly engaging view on how readers create their own conceptions of the text. As we hope will become clear, our pedagogical aims are all oriented toward the creation of a negotiated dialogue between the reader's experience and the text. The pedagogy that we share builds directly on the foundation laid down by this research.

While we consider the work of poststructuralist theory important in our work, we also rely on an earlier tradition by building on the arguments John Dewey (1934/2005) made in *Art as Experience*, as well as drawing a theoretical frame from neopragmatic philosophers such as Richard Rorty (1989), who speaks openly on the "uses" of fiction. Rorty (1989) suggests that literature, unlike writing in the social sciences, gives the reader "the ability to think of people wildly different from ourselves as included in the range of 'us'" (p. 196). Edmund Gordon (1990) also recognizes that fictional and imaginative works help us to understand different cultural, social, and epistemological points of view and, like Rorty (1989), points out that the underlying explanations for human phenomena are often better explored in artistic and fictional work than in typical social science research. Rorty's (1989) claim, in particular, encouraged us to wonder whether fiction could promote a better understanding of teaching than either research on teaching or anecdotal, autobiographical accounts of teaching.

Another source we found useful was Robert Coles's (1989) book, *The Call of Stories: Teaching and the Moral Imagination*. This book examines how literature, from Leo Tolstoy to William Carlos Williams, has affected the author's own understandings of his patients and his medical students. Coles emphasizes the moral analysis and reflection that stories can ignite in their readers and mentions many examples of students', doctors', and teachers' experiences in using literature to make connections to real human experience. He concludes that the power of imaginative stories lies in their ability to promote self-reflection, and in how readers, whether they be medical students, English teachers, or college students, can make connections between their own "moral conduct" and the "moral imagination of writers and the moral imperative of fellow humans" (p. 205).

Studies regarding the research literature on fiction in the medical professions demonstrated that fictional works can encourage cultural competence among nursing students (e.g., Anderson, 2004) and self-awareness among preservice physicians and nurses (Charon et al., 1995). In public administration classes, researchers have used fiction as a means to capture students' imaginations and lead to richer conversations (Marion, 1988). In management education, researchers have reported that using fiction can give a sense of the "plurality," or multiple perspectives of the various participants in organizations to preservice management students (Cohen, 1998).

A few writers within teacher education have argued in favor of using fiction in preservice education courses as a way of creating a deeper understanding of and useful reflections on children and youth (Marlowe & Maycock, 2001; Morrison & Rude, 2002; Tama & Peterson, 1991; Wear, 1989). In particular, William Morrison and Harvey Rude (2002) suggest several benefits of using literary fiction over common textbooks in special education teacher programs. They argue that fiction serves as a tool for helping preservice teachers sympathize with students who have learning challenges. We relied on their paper for our own theoretical framework, hoping to add to the research regarding the use of fiction with preservice teachers. Mike Marlowe and George Maycock (2001) studied preservice teachers' reactions to fictional works on special learners. Their aim is to help emerging teachers understand students, while ours is to help emerging teachers understand teachers and teaching through using a creative curriculum of fiction.

Carrol Tama and Kenneth Peterson's (1991) work comes closest to our interests. They developed a set of alternative readings (both fiction and nonfiction) and later asked their teacher education students for their reactions. Their cursory data analysis suggested that the works (e.g., Mike Rose's *Lives on the*

Boundary) resulted in a "grounding effect" on the students, that is, reading works of literature provides students with a more realistic understanding of what they might expect to experience as teachers. The mixing of fiction and nonfiction works in this study was compelling to us, but we wanted to focus on the use of fiction alone. Finally, Delese Wear (1989) recommends using fiction but does not engage in work with students and thus reported no data. There appears to be a need to fill in gaps in the research relating to the use of a creative curriculum that includes works of fiction in teaching preservice teachers.

Because the promotion of reflection of some kind is one of the goals of this study, we want to provide a provisional definition of the term. We do not think that an operational definition is warranted in this case, and others who have used the term have also used more general definitions. For instance, Donald Schon (1983) whose landmark work, *The Reflective Practitioner: How Professionals Think in Action*, defined reflection as a professional habit of the mind. Schon's work tends to emphasize reflection on the technical aspects of teaching, which is not our intention. Our "reflective" goal in this study is based largely on another landmark work on teacher reflection, Kenneth Zeichner and Daniel Liston's (1987) study on teaching student teachers to reflect. Their goal was to encourage preservice teachers to see the wider consequences of a teacher's action and reappraise the daily moral dilemmas of teachers. One might say that their goal was to "problematize" teaching so that teachers-to-be would not be so easily convinced that teaching was the delivery of content alone. Since this watershed work, many other teacher educators have further defined the term. For instance, Peter Hoffman-Kipp, Alfredo Artiles, and Laura López-Torres (2003) have cast reflection as a form of cultural-historical activity theory, in which

> reflection is understood as a process that is embedded in everyday activities situated in school cultures that are social in nature, where interactions with others are an important medium in which reflection occurs. Teachers interact with colleagues in goal-directed activities that require communication and the exchange of ideas where reflection itself is not contained wholly in the mind of the individual but is "distributed" through sign systems and artifacts that are embedded in the social activity. (p. 250)

The result of this type of reflection is a widening of the individual's conception of teaching. This is the kind of reflection we were hoping to elicit in our own students through the use of an innovative and creative curriculum of varied literary accounts of teachers and teaching as we engaged in our research study.

Specifically, we are suggesting that reading fictional accounts of teaching encourages deep reflection, potentially offering an exploration of teaching worlds that *could* be. In fiction, authors are free to explore relationships and predicaments that one might never encounter in practice but that, if believable, cause us to re-consider the conditions of teaching.

Of course, the selection of the fictional works we invite students to read is critically important in any such endeavor, and it surprised us to find so few compelling works on this topic. Learning from teachers is a nearly universal experience, and yet few fiction writers find the classroom a suitable context for a novel. After two classes in which we experimented with various works, we settled on the following books: *The Water Is Wide* by Pat Conroy, *One Child* by Torey Hayden, *The Education of Hyman Kaplan* by Leonard Ross, *A Jest of God* by Margaret Laurence, and *The Prime of Miss Jean Brodie* by Muriel Spark (see appendix A for a synopsis of each book). Some "classic" novels were tried and failed. For instance, *To Sir with Love* by Edward Ricardo Braithwaite was not selected; students had found it too "dated."

The Study

The university course used as the site for this study was an Introduction to Teaching course of 120 students. (A syllabus of the course in one of its more recent iterations can be viewed at http://people.ucsc.edu/~ktellez/e180w07.htm.) The class requirements included a variety of assignments (e.g., a letter to a former teacher; a scholarly education article summary and review; a lesson plan/presentation/reflection; a response journal; thirty hours field experience in an elementary or secondary teacher's classroom; an interview with their observation teacher; and a group literature circle presentation). The required texts of this course were two books of essays about becoming a teacher and one of six different literature circle books. The literature circle books were all narratives written by or about teachers, or works of fiction about teachers. While some of the students in the course read nonfictional accounts of teachers or teaching (e.g., Tracy Kidder's *Among Schoolchildren*), this study examined the effects of the fictional works only. Of the 120 students enrolled in the course, 51 read works of fiction.

Our chief question was how effective were these works of fiction at introducing students to a practitioner's perspective in teaching, as well as inspiring a level of reflection deepened by fictional works. In order to understand what students learned about teachers from fiction and how fiction allows another perspective than other curricula used in the course, three types of data were examined: (a) open-ended "quick-writes"; (b) student literature circle presentations; and (c) semistructured interviews (see appendix B).

The "quick-writes," averaging one handwritten page each, were completed by all students who had attended the lecture the last week of the course and completed after students had presented their literature circle books in section class.

Students answered the prompt, "What did you learn about a teacher's perspective from reading, planning, and presenting the book you read for your literature circle?" The inclusion of planning and presenting the book of fiction as well as the actual reading of the book in the "quick-writes" prompt is an acknowledgment that the discussion of the book between group members also contributed to student learning. The quick-writes data and literature circle presentations were audio-recorded, transcribed, and organized by themes and categories.

The Participants

One student representing each work of fiction was interviewed using a semistructured protocol based on the design suggested by Tom Wengraf (2001). The resulting five interviews, four female and one male undergraduate, were also recorded, transcribed, and analyzed for themes (Bogdan & Biklen, 1992). Each interview lasted from twenty to forty minutes and was conducted in an informal setting after the academic quarter had ended. Participants for the interviews were chosen based on quick-write data, willingness, and fictional work read. Because students self-selected books to read, only those students who selected a fictional work were part of the interview participant pool.

Initially, we attempted to use quick-writes data to determine which participant to interview for each work of fiction. Quick-writes comments that were particularly interesting or unique and needed elaboration in order to be better understood identified the first group of students who were asked to participate in the semistructured interviews. The subsequent interview data (five students), the open-ended response quick-writes data (fifty-one students), and the project presentations (twelve audio-recorded presentations) were analyzed to determine what students had learned about the perspective of a teacher from the fictional accounts and what students reported as being different or unique about their experience of reading and learning from a work of fiction in contrast to other curricula employed in this course.

The Results

Our overall data revealed that 94 percent of the participants reported reading fiction as a positive learning experience and that the assignment to read a book about a teacher and present a creative book report with other students was a worthwhile and valuable exercise. Various themes that emerged from the data included (a) the difficulties of reconciling teachers' personal lives with teachers' professional lives (the thoughts and feelings of a teacher, how the personal and professional lives of a teacher are intertwined, and how teacher beliefs affect what and how a teacher teaches); (b) the importance of student-teacher relationships (the influence of a teacher over students and the influence of students over a teacher); and (c) the complexity of teaching (the complexity and difficulty of being a teacher, the importance of differentiating instruction according to student needs, cultural differences between teachers and students, and the power administration has over a teacher).

Students also indicated that reading fiction allowed them to gain a unique perspective due to their emotional involvement in the story. The presentation of a teaching situation from multiple viewpoints and the knowledge that the story is not "real" gave the preservice teachers more time and a safer place for reflection than a field experience. Additionally, the stories allowed readers to experience a teacher's thoughts, motivations, and experiences beyond the classroom and see how such thoughts and experiences affected their teaching. The comments of the undergraduate participants indicate that the innovative and creative curriculum of reading fiction in preservice education courses supports the growth of reflective teachers.

Data Sources

The three forms of data gathered for this research—presentations, "quick-writes," and interviews—offered varied answers to the research questions presented:

PRESENTATIONS

The audio-recorded student presentations were as varied as the books students read and offered insight into what particular themes students felt were important enough to present to other students and the instructors. Because these presentations were graded, they cannot be taken strictly as direct evidence of what students really thought of the book (i.e., what students chose to present may have been influenced by knowing that their presentations would affect their overall grade in the course)—nor can it be presumed that these presentations are the opinion of one or all students in the presenting group. However, the presentations are evidence of a group effort to present the themes that they found to be most important or pertinent to the course. Presentations included haiku poetry summaries, skits from the different stories, a "big book" of the story, letters written from different characters perspectives, a modern day parody, an interview panel with story characters and historical figures, and a skit with characters talking to a psychologist. Themes emerging from students' creative presentations included (a) how teachers' beliefs affect practice; (b) how outside school factors affect classrooms; (c) teachers' personal and professional lives; (d) the difficulty and complexity of teaching; (e) student-teacher relationships; and (f) critiques of pedagogy.

Though each presentation focused on some aspect of teaching from the novels read, the presentations that focused on a teacher's perspective were those that addressed the themes of a teacher's personal lives in contrast to their professional lives, and how teacher's beliefs affect practice. Presentations that focused on these particular themes gave the most evidence that participants were considering teaching from a teacher's point of view. Presentations that focused on how outside school factors affect teaching, the difficulty and complexity of teaching, and student-teacher relationships to some extent also addressed issues of education from a teacher's perspective. However, such themes took into account a more general understanding of how schools work. True evidence of student "realization" of a different perspective came from presentations whose themes focused on teachers as individuals, as human beings whose own personal beliefs and emotions were affected by and in turn affected their professional life.

Though each presentation offered a slightly different interpretation of the book read, some books seemed to be more or less effective in eliciting student responses that focused on a teacher's perspective. For example, the presentations of *The Education of Hyman Kaplan* focused on the complexity of teaching and pedagogy critiques. Students tended to present this book from the perspective of the student, Hyman Kaplan, and gave very little evidence of an attempt to understand the teacher's perspective. None of the Hyman Kaplan presentations fully addressed the perspective of a teacher or indicated a better understanding of the teacher's perspective, but each did attempt to understand the book from the perspective of a student and did address the complexity of teaching in some way. In contrast, the presentations of *A Jest of God* offered substantial evidence that the novel had encouraged the type of reflection we had hoped for.

The *Jest of God* presentations included a news interview skit and artistic posters of the themes of the novel. Both of the presentations focused on the character Rachel, the teacher who narrates the story. Students interpreted Rachel's actions in her classroom as linked to the other occurrences in Rachel's life. Their focus on the teacher's perspective included judgments on Rachel's choices and connections to the time and situation in which Rachel found herself. One participant in the second presentation reported that she liked the book because it was a "feminist novel." She shared in the presentation, "It shows the expectations and frustrations that women have to go through because of society's standards, and how not being a mother has taken a toll on her . . . how everyone else sees her . . . the fact that she's not a mother." These presentations suggest that *A Jest of God* is an effective and creative tool for leading students to examine moral dilemmas and "realize" what teaching might be like.

QUICK-WRITES

The themes we uncovered in the "quick-writes," though similar to the themes of the presentations and most certainly influenced by the activity of creating group presentations, offered a much more specific and detailed explanation of what students felt they had learned from the novels they read. As previously mentioned, a total of fifty-one responses to the fictional works were collected and analyzed.

Based on a textual analysis of the quick-writes, three primary themes emerged: (a) connecting teachers' personal and professional lives; (b) student-teacher relationships; and (c) the complexity of teaching. Though some of these themes overlap (any of them could be categorized as the "difficulty and complexity" of teaching), they are organized to the specific focus of the quick-write. A particularly thoughtful example of a student comment that fits the theme of "connecting teachers' personal and professional lives: how teachers' beliefs affect what and how a teacher teaches" came from a student who read *The Prime of Miss Jean Brodie*. The student reflects,

> Through Miss Brodie, however, I learned that there is a definite distinction between a creative approach and a self-righteous creative approach. . . . Teaching is not about creating clones of yourself (i.e., the Brodie set). Teaching is about helping an individual gain the tools necessary to become whoever and do whatever they desire. (personal communication, November 29, 2004)

Here is another student example that addresses this same general theme of a "teacher's personal and professional life" but from a participant who read a different work of fiction, *A Jest of God*: "I learned that what a teacher does in the classroom affects all of their lives and that what happens at home to a teacher can't necessarily be left out of the class either. In the book, Rachel's emotional and social problems came into the classroom far too often" (personal communication, November 29, 2004). This student noticed that teachers' personal and professional lives are intertwined and that teachers should be aware of how their personal and professional lives affect one another. Another participant writes of similar realizations: "It is interesting to think that teachers are regular people who deal with their personal lives outside the classroom as well. She (the teacher) had conflicts between the relationships in her life with her mother, her friend, and her colleagues at school" (personal communication, November 29, 2004).

This student began to understand how teachers, like all people, have multiple worlds in which they exist and that those worlds are all part of a teacher's life.

A quick-writes explanation was categorized under "student-teacher relationships" if the student mainly discussed the teacher's interaction with students as opposed to a specific focus on the teacher's thoughts or beliefs alone. Students who read *One Child* and *The Prime of Miss Jean Brodie* mentioned the importance of the teacher-student bond in being an effective teaching practitioner. One student wrote,

> In our group we had some great discussions about the power and control teachers have in their classrooms and over their students. Miss Brodie from the novel really took advantage of her position of power and became over-involved with her students' lives and choices. This book taught me that there is a limit to how involved a teacher should get with their students. (personal communication, November 29, 2004)

Another student, who read *One Child*, also discussed the boundaries of student-teacher relationships in terms of limiting involvement with students as a necessity of the teaching profession: "I feel one of the biggest things I learned was how to foster a teacher/student relationship. . . . There comes a point in each school year where as much as you would want to keep your students for many years, you have to let go so they can grow and become self-sufficient" (personal communication, November 29, 2004). These two novels seemed to encourage students to look at teaching from this perspective, to consider the teachers and their responsibilities while also considering the necessity and limits of developing relationships with students.

"The complexity of teaching" was the most prominent theme. Students who read *The Water Is Wide* overwhelmingly discussed the complexity and difficulty of teaching in terms of cultural conflict between teachers and students, the control that administration has over teachers, and differentiation of instruction. A few of the students who read *One Child* also discussed the difficulty of teaching but more in terms of the difficult choices a teacher might have to make. One noted, "It is hard to explain what I learned from *One Child*, but I really did. It kind of made me realize how grossly unprepared I am both to be an adult and a teacher. I'd like to tell myself that I would do the brave things Torey did, but would I?" (personal communication, November 29, 2004). Also of interest in the quick-write responses were data that referred to why students felt that fiction was a different or useful curriculum to use in this course. One student felt that

> reading a fictional account of a teaching situation was no less "real" in my mind than reading a piece of non-fiction because after a while

characters are people and people are characters. The fictional aspect of this book allowed me, the reader, to see the various viewpoints of teachers, administrators, and students with the same relative objectivity. In non-fiction someone is usually telling the story—it's the teacher or the students. While both perspectives may be presented, only in fiction is one able to flow through all of the perspectives with ease. (personal communication, November 29, 2004)

Another comment addressed the emotional perspective of the fictional teacher:

By reading *One Child* it gave me the emotional state of the teacher as well as hopes, aspirations, and downfalls, and disappointments. Rather than a non-fiction book where the teacher might feel the need to write in a more scholarly approach and might not even express her own feelings too deeply, this book allowed the reader to be touched by the children in the same or perhaps similar way a teacher would be touched. She also covered some problems that the non-fiction writers and educators discussed in detail in our readings. Yet, I will probably remember more from the fictional reading of *One Child*, than the other books. (personal communication, November 29, 2004)

This quote is of particular interest within the context of the research questions of this study. That the student found reading fiction more memorable, or somehow a stronger lesson than reading expository text, supports Wear's (1989) hypothesis that fiction "can portray" problems in teaching that expository text cannot (p. 54). The participant suggests that the emotional experience of reading the book adds to the power of fiction over nonfiction as a way to understand a teacher's perspective.

INTERVIEWS

The five semistructured interviews focused on the participants' perceptions of the teacher in their works of fiction and the differences between fiction and other curricula used in the course such as classroom observations, reading essays about teaching, course lectures, and other writing assignments. (See appendix B for examples of interview questions). Each participant read a different work of fiction, and thus each had a different insight as to why fiction was a useful curricular medium to use in an introductory education course.

The interview participant who read *A Jest of God* was a female junior undergraduate. She reported that the experience of reading fiction was different from her classroom observations in that "the teacher is put on a pedestal [in a classroom]," that they are not really a "person," whereas "the book really gave you background on what's really going on in a teacher's life" (personal communication, April 2, 2005). The book allowed this participant insight into the reality of being a teacher that gets past the façade that one might observe from the outside, from sitting and watching a teacher at work. That *A Jest of God* is written in first person most likely influenced this student's observations, for the entire novel is written as the uncensored thoughts of a teacher as she encounters an odd but not unbelievable life. The student also became aware through her experience of reading this book that "school is like a spider web that affects every part of her [the teacher's] life" and that this realization will give her a new "perspective" with which to consider the profession of teaching (personal communication, April 2, 2005).

The interview participant, a senior male undergraduate, who read *The Prime of Miss Jean Brodie* also indicated a better understanding of the motivations of a teacher. He found the book more helpful in understanding the perspective of a teacher than his classroom observations because he "had a longer time to get the perspective of Brodie." Even though *The Prime of Miss Jean Brodie* is written in a very different style than *A Jest of God,* both of these participants found value in these works of fiction, which allowed them to really understand a teacher's perspective over a classroom observation.

The interview participant, a female freshman undergraduate, who read *One Child* also found the experience of reading fiction to be beneficial in getting to understand a teacher's perspective, but her assessment directly related to the medium of fiction: "The book is beneficial because it is a relief to know it is just a book. You can take time off. There is an emotional attachment though it is not real [really happening]" (personal communication, February 16, 2005). This particular participant was very effusive in her enjoyment of reading the book and, during the presentation and in her quick-writes, repeatedly stated how much she loved reading *One Child.* She assessed the benefits of reading and of having an imaginative experience over a real experience as being the unlimited time she was allowed to reflect on what was happening in the story, as well as the safety of knowing that the situation in the book was fictional.

The interview participant, a female junior undergraduate, who read *The Education of Hyman Kaplan* found the literature circle assignment useful in that it allowed her "to see another perspective." She also felt that reading fiction about teachers was a beneficial assignment in this class in that, unlike in her observation classroom, she was able to see "the result" of an assignment and was better able to see different "aspects and effects" of teaching. This participant felt that the lens fiction afforded her was more holistic than what she was able to understand as an outsider who observed snippets of real classroom experience. Like the other interviewees, this participant appreciated what the book she read allowed her to "experience," while at the same time stating that being in a real

classroom and observing was meaningful and helpful in developing her understanding of what it means to teach and be a teacher (personal communication,
March 20, 2005).

Like the other interviewees, the junior female undergraduate who was assigned *The Water Is Wide* found the experience of reading fiction a unique way
to understand teachers. When comparing her observation teacher to Conroy
(the main character) from the novel, this participant was quick to point out that
she felt Conroy was an inferior teacher. Yet, she appreciated that she could see
"into Conroy's head" more than her observation teacher's, and that the book
allowed more understanding of Conroy's "background and history." "The book
was more in depth about the person," she explained, observing, "Mr. B [her
observation teacher] was more in depth about the teaching" (personal communication, April 2005).

Conclusions

We began our study with the somewhat inchoate belief that fictional works on
teaching would promote preservice teacher reflection in a way that other curricula and experiences could not. We strongly felt that an innovative and inter-
actional curriculum that included creative literature group presentations would
encourage both creative and unique teaching and learning experiences for our
undergraduates. As we reflected back on our original motivation for the study,
we realized that we were also willing to require our students to read these works
because fiction about teaching had meant so much to us.

It now appears that our generalization was a qualified success, qualified
partly because not all the works appeared to be of equal value. Though the
themes that students described in the data of this study are varied across the five
works of fiction, a careful analysis of the data shows that some of the works of
fiction seem to have been more helpful in introducing students to the perspective
of a teacher and encouraged the kind of reflection we sought. Though all books
were reported as useful and all students described learning more about the topics
of teachers and teaching from the literature circle assignment, participants who
read *A Jest of God, The Prime of Miss Jean Brodie,* and *One Child* seemed to be
more moved to deep reflection about teaching and teacher's lives.

These three books seemed to be those that matched our students' conception of teaching as they had experienced it. As Langer (1989) notes, readers
undergo a process of interacting with the text and are influenced at each point
by their own life circumstances. The book that seemed least likely to promote
reflection, *The Education of Hyman Kaplan,* lacked sufficient "envisionments"

(Langer, 1989) for our students. As we considered this fact, it became clear to us that *Kaplan*, although written from the teacher's point of view, is set in an adult English as a second language (ESL) classroom and in an earlier era (1930s). We should point out that the book resonated deeply with both of us, but we had both taught adult English learners and could appreciate the tender classroom moments in the novel that may not have been so obvious to our students.

While our intent in the research was not necessarily to determine which of the books we selected was the best for our students, we are suggesting that *The Prime of Miss Jean Brodie* seemed to promote the deepest reflection—owing to the manner in which Muriel Sparks's engaging work explores most deeply the relationship between a teacher and her students. Because Miss Brodie's methods are questionable at times, students could consider carefully the moral implications of a teacher's work without the concern that this was a real teacher teaching real youth. Most importantly, perhaps, the book helped them to reflect on the larger goals of education and the transparency of the teacher. Teaching, they grew to realize, is not about the teacher but rather about student learning.

If we are to trust the developmental literature on teachers, this insight seems to come only after years in the classroom. We are not suggesting that the students in our course who read *Brodie* will enter the classroom focused entirely on student learning, unconcerned with their own glory (or shortcomings) as teachers, but it was indeed exciting to see preservice teachers reflecting on this idea so early in their development.

Finally, as we read over the transcripts and quick-writes and considered the students' shifting "selves" and identities as they negotiated the course, we were struck by how much they altered their views from beginning to end. Although finding change over time was not part of our research, we could not help but notice it. Clearly, their direct experience observing and assisting in classrooms had altered their views on teaching and, of course, inspired much reflection about the kind of teacher they wanted to be. We also came to notice their references to the fictional works as sources of reflection. There was an almost daily reconstruction of their identities as emerging teachers (St. Pierre, 2000).

Implications for Future Study

Future research regarding the use of fiction in preservice education courses might focus on which teaching strategies are most effective for fictional texts; how to fruitfully integrate students' field experiences and other course curricula into fictional studies; and a description of the criteria that mark fictional works that are particularly successful in allowing preservice teachers to critically assess and broaden their understanding of teachers and the teaching profession. As prospective teachers move from student to teacher, introductory education courses are critical in the development of a comprehensive and accurate understanding of the teaching profession. We believe our study has shown that fiction can offer a unique view of teachers and teaching, a view that assists preservice teachers to reflect deeply on important themes.

Appendix A

The following is a list of titles and plot summaries.

THE WATER IS WIDE BY PAT CONROY

This story accounts the experiences of a teacher and his students as they struggle to learn amidst great poverty, racism, and limited resources on an island off the coast of North Carolina during the late 1960s.

ONE CHILD BY TOREY HAYDEN

This story describes the year in the life of a special education teacher and an extraordinary student who is placed in her classroom. This book has previously been used in special education and literature research (Marlowe & Maycock, 2001; Morrison & Rude, 2002).

THE EDUCATION OF HYMEN KAPLAN BY LEONARD Q. ROSS

The chapters in this humorous work of fiction each account a different class period in an adult ESL school and relate the misinterpretations and difficulties experienced by the adult immigrant students and their teacher as they attempt to learn and teach English.

A JEST OF GOD BY MARGARET LAWRENCE

This first-person story of a teacher's life in 1960s Canada weaves classroom and personal experiences together. The novel is about the personal growth of a spinster teacher and how social norms affect her perception of herself and her job. Tama and Peterson (1991) and Wear (1989) recommend this text.

THE PRIME OF MISS JEAN BRODIE BY MURIEL SPARK

This classic work of fiction, set in Scotland during the 1920s, follows a group of students and their avant-garde teacher as they challenge social norms and redefine their roles as student, teacher, friend, and confidante.

Appendix B

The following are interview questions (semistructured interview).

1. Describe _____ (a character) from the book you read. What kind of teacher was he/she?
2. Did you think that the character was realistic? Why or why not?
3. Did they do anything that you wouldn't have done? Why or why not?
4. What do you think their philosophy of teaching was? Did you agree with their philosophy of teaching? Why or why not?
5. Did you feel differently about the character when you finished the book than when you first started reading? If yes, what happened that made you feel differently about the character?
6. What were the character's strengths and weaknesses as a teacher?
7. Could she or he have been a better teacher? How?
8. Did the character's personal life interfere with her or his professional life? How?
9. Do you feel that you understood _____ better than the teacher in your observation classroom? Why or why not?
10. How was the experience of reading the story about _____ different and/or more or less beneficial than your classroom observation experiences in understanding the mindset of a teacher?
11. Did he/she remind you of any teachers you have had? How?
12. Do you think you would be like _____ if you become a teacher? In what ways or why not?
13. Do you plan to become a teacher? (If yes) Have you always wanted to be a teacher? What kind of teacher do you imagine yourself being?
14. Do you think that reading this book has influenced your ideas of what it is like to be a teacher? How?

15. How was the experience of reading the book different or more or less meaningful than the other assignments of the class?

References

Anderson, K. L. (2004). Teaching cultural competence using an exemplar from literary journalism. *Journal of Nursing Education, 43*(6), 253–259.

Barthes, R. (1974). *S/Z: An essay* (R. Miller, Trans.). New York: Hill and Wang.

Bleich, D. (1978). *Subjective criticism.* Baltimore: Johns Hopkins University Press.

Bogdan, R. C., & Biklen, S. K. (1992). *Qualitative research for education.* Needham Heights, MA: Allyn and Bacon.

Charon, R., Trautmann Banks, J., Connelly, J. E., Hunsaker Hawkins, A., Montgomery Hunter, K., Hudson Jones, A., Montello, M., & Poirer, S. (1995). Literature and medicine. *Annals of Internal Medicine, 122*(8), 599–606.

Cohen, C. (1998). Using narrative fiction within management education. *Management Learning, 29*(2), 165–181.

Coles, R. (1989). *The call of stories: Teaching and the moral imagination.* Boston: Houghton Mifflin.

Conroy, P. (1972). *The water is wide.* Boston: Houghton Mifflin.

Dewey, J. (1934/2005). *Art as experience.* New York: Perigee.

Feiman-Nemser, S., & Featherstone, H. (1992). *Exploring teaching: Reinventing an introductory course.* New York: Teachers College Press.

Gordon, E. (1990). Coping with communicentric bias in knowledge production in the social sciences. *Educational Researcher, 19*(3), 14–19.

Hayden, T. (2002). *One child.* New York: Avon.

Hoffman-Kipp, P., Artiles, A. J., & López-Torres, L. (2003). Beyond reflection: Teacher learning as praxis. *Theory into Practice, 42*(3), 248–254.

Kidder, T. (1989). *Among schoolchildren.* Boston: Houghton Mifflin.

Langer, J. (1989). *The process of understanding literature.* Albany, NY: Center the Learning and Teaching of Literature.

Laurence, M. (1983). *A jest of God.* Chicago: University of Chicago Press.

Marion, D. (1988). Using fiction to expose a fundamental theme in American public administration. *Teaching Political Science, 15*(2), 44–49.

Marlowe, M., & Maycock, G. (2001). Using literary texts in teacher education to promote positive attitudes toward children with disabilities. *Teacher Education and Special Education, 24*(2), 75–83.

Montgomery Hunter, K., Charon, R., & Coulehan, J. (1995). The study of literature in medical education. *Academic Medicine, 70*(9), 787–794.

Morrison, W. F., & Rude, H. A. (2002). Beyond textbooks: A rationale for a more inclusive use of literature in preservice special education teacher programs. *Teacher Education and Special Education, 25*(2), 114–123.

Rorty, R. (1989). *Contingency, irony, and solidarity.* New York: Cambridge University Press.

Ross, L. Q. (1937). *The education of Hyman Kaplan.* New York: Harcourt Brace.

Schon, D. A. (1983). *The reflective practitioner: How professionals think in action.* New York: Basic Books.

Spark, M. (1961). *The prime of Miss Jean Brodie.* Philadelphia: Lippencott.

St. Pierre, E. A. (2000). Post-structural feminism in education: An overview. *Qualitative Studies in Education, 13*(5), 477–515.

Tama, M. C., & Peterson, K. (1991). Achieving reflectivity through literature. *Educational Leadership, 48*(6), 22–24.

Walsh, D. (1969). *Literature and knowledge.* Middletown, CT: Wesleyan University Press.

Wear, D. (1989). What literature says to preservice teachers and teacher educators. *Journal of Teacher Education, 40*(1), 51–55.

Wengraf, T. (2001). *Qualitative research interviewing.* London: Sage.

Zamir, T. (2002). An epistemological basis for linking philosophy and literature. *Metaphilosophy, 33*(3), 321–336.

Zeichner, K., & Liston, D. (1987). Teaching student teachers to reflect. *Harvard Educational Review, 57*(1), 23–48.

CHAPTER 5

The Power of Art in Observation

Kathryn L. Jenkins
University of Houston–Downtown

Joyce M. Dutcher
University of Houston–Downtown

Kathryn L. Jenkins, Ed.D., is assistant professor of early childhood education in the Department of Urban Education at the University of Houston–Downtown. In addition to co-investigating the observation skills of preservice teachers, Dr. Jenkins's research explores the developmental levels of play and oral language of at-risk preschoolers and professional development models.

Joyce M. Dutcher, Ed.D., is adjunct professor in the Department of Urban Education at the University of Houston–Downtown and past director for the Center of Professional Development of Teachers. In addition to co-investigating the observation skills of preservice teachers, Dr. Dutcher's research explores the longitudinal effects of the art observation model on teacher preparation.

ABSTRACT

High-quality observations of young children involve awareness and critical thinking and require creative teaching and planned assessment. There are fundamental observation skills that must be introduced prior to entering the classroom to ensure teachers develop curiosity while collecting key information. It was conceived by university-level faculty that preservice teachers would benefit from an opportunity to develop their observation skills in small group sessions. With prior research of medical students as a model, and in partnership with the Museum of Fine Arts, Houston, a visit that exposed education students to specific art pieces and helped to stimulate curiosity was the centerpiece for this session. Using an abridged version of Visual Thinking Strategies, participants worked in small groups, shared their observations, and provided evidence to justify their analysis of each piece. It was found that participants gained confidence, increased competency, and developed creative and critical thinking skills useful to observing and assessing their own students in future classrooms when they engaged in abundantly creative, collaborative experiences of their own.

When a researcher investigates the use of the arts in the curriculum of schools, the majority of the information found leads to the results of introducing children of many ages to musical scores of historical notice and to famous art masterpieces. For some reason, art educators and professionals in the field of education and in art have rarely continued to provide the benefits of art to older students on the collegiate level. If we believe that the arts should indeed "serve as a model for the rest of education" as artist and educator Elliot Eisner (2002b) asserts, then it is reasonable to believe that his statement includes all levels of education, not merely elementary and high school students.

Rather than simply investigate the effects of introducing the arts at a collegial level, this chapter addresses how the arts provide university students in urban education studies an opportunity to develop curious minds in creative ways and to construct new knowledge about teaching and learning. This chapter specifically centers on the effects of observation skills and the elements of discovery that emerge in urban education (UE) students at the University of Houston–Downtown (UHD) when they are exposed to teaching strategies and experiences that support inquiry and curiosity.

The faculty in the Department of Urban Education (DUE) at UHD knows that what makes a suitable teacher of young children is the ability to observe and understand what is going on with each and every child. Quality observations of children necessarily include awareness and critical thinking (Beaty, 2006). Many times, teachers begin to rely on other avenues to complete assessments of young children. In some instances, teachers make quick judgments, infer too much about a situation, or rely too heavily on previous experiences with assessment.

Honing observation, analysis, and critical thinking skills through creative experiences enhances not just their assessment skills but also their overall abilities as educators. Positive relationships between students and their teachers are the key to children's play, exploration, and learning (Howes & Ritchie, 2002). Developing an attitude of curiosity and accepting varied responses during their teacher preparation experiences impacts teacher candidates' lesson planning, instructional strategies, and assessment.

There are fundamental basics of observation that must be introduced to future teachers prior to their classroom-based experiences. It was conceived that preservice teachers, referred to in this chapter as DUE students, would benefit from an opportunity—once a semester—to analyze their observation skills and develop creative thinking through the use of art. Therefore, DUE faculty scheduled focused visits to the Museum of Fine Arts, Houston (MFAH), to reinforce the importance of using real-world experiences to develop observation skills. DUE faculty felt that experiences using real art for purposes of observation would be authentic and key to the advancement of the DUE students' critical analysis abilities and would motivate their use of aesthetic experiences to enhance their teaching.

Although authentic assessment is a theory that is strongly believed in and taught at UHD, the faculty sensed that the skills of conducting observations and analysis could not be overemphasized. Observation is an art that requires practice. Observation is the first important step before any further analysis, judgment, or diagnosis of a child or curriculum because first reactions and first impressions are lasting and not always accurate. When one is responsible—as teachers are—for communicating students' strengths, abilities, needs, and issues, accuracy is nonnegotiable. Therefore, the DUE faculty believes it is imperative that all future classroom teachers learn strong observational skills before leaving the program. Strong observation skills and understanding of individual differences lead to more creative teaching.

The art educators at the MFAH know that what makes an effective art experience is the time to observe, peers to collaborate with, and an opportunity to share thoughts. In coordination of these major premises, an organized experience (one of four) was made available during a long semester for DUE students enrolled in a prerequisite course of the early childhood education program, whose focus is on aesthetic awareness and creativity integrated into teaching. The museum's role in this partnership was to provide the platform of integration between education, art, and observation. The art museum educators recognize the importance of sharpening observation skills for many professions but especially for educators of young children where observation is valued as an important data-gathering tool for assessing young children.

During the prerequisite course at the university and prior to the museum visit, DUE students learned about the basics of art, the purpose of art in the classroom, the developmental stages of art, and the effects of using art in appropriate ways with young children all through creative teaching and curiosity-driven emergent curriculum. Students also engaged in discussions of the long-term effects of art for children. These discussions resulted in understanding that the arts develop the creative mind, enhance children's problem solving, encourage perspective taking, teach the recognition of subtleties, encourage collaboration, and promote the discovery of meaning and true expression, without words (Eisner, 2002a).

Prior to visiting the museum, DUE students were given an outline of what to expect from their museum field experience: viewing art, discussing impressions and observations, and a whole group reflection and share-a-thon. The students in this prerequisite course were selected for the first of four experiences (phase I) for two reasons: (1) the course is required and data collected would contribute to the collection of longitudinal data, and (2) the course is a natural fit because of its content base and course objectives in art based on creative instruction and assessment.

In organizing the experiences for the university students, the MFAH and UHD-DUE faculty collaborated to determine the model that would serve as the frame for the phase I experience. The purpose of the experience was to build and enhance urban education students' visual perceptions; support their curiosity concerning the use of aesthetic experiences in teaching, specifically through observations, creative thinking, and critical analyses; and hone their communication skills to better prepare prospective teachers for working with students and families in creative ways.

It was determined that the course model needed to include opportunities for students to observe, infer, classify, predict, and follow their curiosity, as well as share their thoughts with colleagues. Previous research had been conducted using art to teach basic observation skills to medical students (Braverman, 2001; Elder et al., 2006; Reilly, Ring, & Duke, 2005). These research studies provided a solid basis to design the study that would further enhance the observation skills of educational professionals (Yenawine, 1997). With observation at the forefront of interest in education, studies that provide further skills and techniques have an impact on the field.

A Review of the Literature

Observation has been defined as "watching to learn" (Jablon, Dombro, & Dictelmiller, 2007). Teachers are most effective when they are confident and capable observers—watching their students to learn their abilities and needs in order to make informed decisions that drive instruction. Skills in purposeful observations, assessment and application of resulting knowledge are important in building relationships between children and teachers. Effective educators use their past observations to plan how to carefully listen to their students, guide their behaviors, and interact with them (Howes & Ritchie, 2002; Shonkoff & Phillips, 2000; Stipek, 2006).

Although most educators agree that observing is key to success as a teacher, not all are aware of how to develop observation as a skill. Very few collegiate-level courses in education use a set of standards or steps to specifically teach preservice teachers how to observe. Even within most assessment courses, the focus is most likely on recording and analyzing authentic tools and not on observing. Skilled observation is not an ability that is maturational. It includes a process of outlining, reflecting, and making decisions (Jablon, Dombro, & Dictelmiller, 2007). Observing young children involves asking questions to consider while documenting behaviors and skills.

The challenge to preservice or novice teachers is that experiences in the classroom with young children move rather quickly. It is intimidating and difficult to hone beginner observation skills while children are present and trying to engage in creative learning experiences. With this in mind, situations that would allow preservice teachers to ask themselves questions, to reflect, and to analyze without children present must be uniquely designed in order to be effective. One such idea is to use art as an impetus to teaching and advancing observation skills. Viewing a piece of art allows preservice teachers, in a less threatening way, to ask questions before making judgments or analyzing intentions. Because art is displayed and not constantly changing (as are active elementary school children), preservice teachers can more deeply and methodically, as well as slowly, practice observing and reflecting on their observations and follow their own curiosity.

Observation, like art, captures a moment or event in time. Observers of art bring in past experiences, prior knowledge, and their own creative insight. Teachers also utilize these aspects when observing children. Therefore, the key is to utilize these components and to match them with additional skills that can ensure observations are done in a detailed and methodical way that will help educators tune into specific qualities of settings.

The model for this study developed as a result of much medical education research that has been successfully completed using art to enhance observation by medical students (Braverman, 2001; Elder et al., 2006; Malone, 2003). Many medical studies have created partnerships with museums and galleries to use their facilities and techniques to provide a unique learning situation for their students. These studies have produced results that support the need for systematic teaching of description and interpretation to hone observation skills (Elder et al., 2006). Noticing and interpreting visual cues is valued in the medical field and can be enhanced using art and small group settings (Berger, 2001).

With heightened observational skills, doctors who have undergone small group art sessions can often use questioning strategies to correctly diagnose patients, eliminating the reliance on formal tests (Braverman, 2001). Programs involving medical students using art have varied from using busts, photographs, and portraits (Malone, 2003). These studies have also produced results that indicate students who have participated in small group art sessions have a higher retention of detail and impressions (Malone, 2003). The design of small groups and discussion opportunities coupled with the use of a specific art analysis model was found to be key to positive results in the medical studies (Elder et al., 2006; Reilly, Ring, & Duke, 2005). A deliberate focus on perception was one area that appeared to enhance these experiences for the medical students. According to Shari Tishman (2005), art museums naturally couple active learning and personal agency. The evocative trait of museums and the standard use of visual thinking assisted greatly in the design of these prior studies.

The Program

VISUAL THINKING STRATEGIES

Part of the design for these medical students' experiences was based on elementary art education. Visual Thinking Strategies (VTS) is a method that has been shown to be effective in increasing elementary students' observational awareness, communication, and analytical- and creative-thinking skills (Visual Understanding in Education, 2001). A five-year longitudinal study, conducted by Abigail Housen, Philip Yenawine, and Karin deSantis (Housen, 2002) revealed that elementary students' creativity and critical-thinking abilities increased in a relatively short period of time through the repetition of observing increasingly complex art, responding to open-ended questions, and by participating in group discussions. Furthermore, the results showed a transfer of acquired skills and knowledge in other contexts and content areas (Housen, 2002; Yenawine, 1997).

Using VTS to develop and enhance preservice teachers' observations and communication evokes creative and critical thinking, and it promotes effective strategies for classroom use, thus creating a win-win situation for preservice teachers and their future students. VTS is a group discovery approach to learning that is designed to stimulate aesthetic awareness and creative and critical thinking (Housen, 2002). In the longitudinal study conducted by Housen, Yenawine, and deSantis (2002), students traveled to an art museum for specified sessions with their teacher and an art educator. They were asked to examine visual art pieces of varied mediums and periods and to focus on three questions:

1. What's going on in the picture?
2. What do you see that makes you say that?
3. What more can we find?

There were two roles involved in VTS sessions: the facilitator's and participant's. During each session, the facilitator listened, paraphrased responses, validated different opinions, and encouraged building of interpretations and connections through observations. The participants, pre- and postobservations, shared basic evidence and developed their observations to include ideas, constructive meaning, and collaboration of opinions through group sharing of ideas. While VTS may appear relatively simple, it has grown in popularity beyond the elementary classroom. It has been an effective method to use with medical students to stimulate focused observations. The medical field found that it increases listening skills, analytical thinking, and finding multiple solutions in the medical training process (Reilly, Ring, & Duke, 2005). These findings hold promise for the field of education at the collegial level because these are skills that would also benefit aspiring teachers.

The DUE faculty believes that modeling is the most effective way of growing knowledge of developmentally appropriate practices in the classroom. As the model of VTS worked well for previous studies in the medical field using observation of art, the university and the MFAH agreed to use VTS for the preservice teachers' small group discussions.

VTS is used to examine and find meaning in visual art and is learner centered. Its usefulness is not isolated to art, as it also supports curiosity in instructional strategies and enhances communication, observation, reasoning, thinking, and problem solving. In addition to understanding the experience as a learner, the practice and refinement of democratic collaboration, problem solving, and making connections to art are key professional development traits. Although the participants in our study were adults, the honing of the skills listed above was still a necessity and priority.

RESEARCH STUDY PARTICIPANTS

Located in the central business district of Houston, UHD serves a diverse student population. Upon graduation, many alumni stay in the area to serve UHD's inner-city communities. This is especially true of the graduates of DUE. Approximately 240 DUE elementary and secondary generalist and bilingual teacher education students begin to teach in Houston's inner-city schools annually.

Participants in the study were sixty teacher education students enrolled in two sections of the early childhood course, Aesthetics and Physical Development. The DUE faculty is committed to preparing future teachers for working in an urban environment. It is also committed to partnering with the MFAH to increase student preparedness.

The MFAH is committed to serving the city's vast educational communities. The MFAH Education Department is staffed with museum educators and volunteers (docents) experienced in working with PreK–16 students. The MFAH education coordinator, along with one other art educator, coordinates the partnership efforts at the museum and host the sessions with preparation of materials and leading the discussions. Museum docents assist as needed during each session, guiding students through the museum exhibits and prodding them to think deeply and follow their curiosity during small group activities.

UHD-MFAH PARTNERSHIP

The partnership between the MFAH and the UHD-DUE was formed with the intent of a long-term commitment that was a minimum of two years. It initially involved two DUE course sections consisting of sixty students.

At the end of the two years, it is expected to host fourteen to sixteen class sessions per semester with student participants from multiple sections of four courses. This would involve approximately 250 participants. The MFAH is committed to programs for teachers and their students that integrate art creatively in context and content across the curriculum. The MFAH is receptive to growing an innovative educational program that is similar to the medical center program they are facilitating with the University of Texas Medical School.

The UHD-DUE students selected for the program were scheduled to attend a Power of Art in Observation experience at the MFAH once a semester for a two-year period. The first experience (phase I) was scheduled during a prerequisite course. Experiences associated with phases II, III, and IV were scheduled during core courses, occurring once each semester for the remaining three semesters of the students' degree plan. The purpose of each set of experiences stayed constant, but the focus for each phase changed. Phase I focused on awareness and critical thinking through observation. Phase II incorporated observation as a means of understanding the learner. Phase III used the observation process skill to promote curriculum integration, contextual language, and common denominators. Phase IV addressed current trends, social justice, and assessment of an urban environment.

The first phase I experience was initiated in fall 2006. Students who attended at this time participated in phases II, III, and IV experiences in subsequent semesters. The phase II experience, on understanding the learner, occurred during a required education psychology course. The phase III experience, on curriculum integration, occurred during a required content methods course, and the phase IV experience, on current trends and social justice, occurred during the students' final semester when they took a required course on issues in urban teaching. This process was designed so that, as each group of students moved to a new phase, a new group of students began. By spring 2008, experiences in all four phases were offered each semester equating to approximately three hundred students moving through the program at any one time.

With each set of experiences, the structure of the experiences stayed the same, but the questioning and art forms varied. For example, each set of experiences was planned for students to: (a) complete a presession questionnaire; (b) respond to visuals of art and probing questions by the museum educator; and (c) regroup into small groups and study a specific work of art in a gallery with a trained docent (docents were trained not to provide information at this time but instead guided students' observations through questioning). The remaining time was spent on students returning to the large group. There they shared their particular observations; the docents shared a more detailed analysis of each work of art; the museum educator gave summary statements; and the UHD-DUE faculty tied it to course content. The initial questionnaire was then repeated as a postsession questionnaire, and a set of short answer questions were added for the students to complete. All pre- and postwritten information was submitted anonymously.

The questioning and art forms visited varied with each session. For example, in phase I the students were exposed to VTS, and they viewed cultural three-dimensional art, while in phase II they concentrated on deliberate-looking methods of inquiry and looked for visual cues as they experienced the two-dimensional art of portraits. These variations provided rich discussions and exposure to different perspectives and art forms without repetitious experiences. Each set

Figure 5.1.   Observing art at the Museum of Fine Arts, Houston

of experiences was designed to challenge students to think about possible classroom implications. As an added incentive, the MFAH provided students with free passes good for future visits to the museum to encourage them to use the museum on a more regular basis and to independently begin to see the power of art in observation (see figure 5.1).

DATA COLLECTION

Data were collected from a variety of sources. First, the students were given a questionnaire to determine their presession beliefs about the use of art, observation of art, and cultural issues. The questionnaire included ten statements focusing on art observation, assessment, cultural sensitivity, and the purpose of using art. Participants completed the questionnaire by marking whether they thought the statements were true, thought they were false, or were not sure. Once this information was gathered, students participated in a whole group discussion. As the participants were reflecting, sharing, and observing, their thoughts and opinions were recorded with audio equipment. As they visited the museum and made observations about their art work in small groups, the docents anecdotally recorded their opinions and statements of observation. Finally, once students shared-out to the whole group their reflections of the art pieces, they completed the postsession questionnaire. This was the same questionnaire with the ten statements that they categorized as true, false, or not sure. In addition to the original statements, students were asked to complete six open-ended questions:

1. What is your overall impression of what the artist was feeling, thinking, and/ or expressing in the work of art?
2. Why do you think that?
3. What part of the art work was most important and/or informative from the artist's point of view and, then, from your own perspective, and why?
4. Did this session change your perception about art observation, and if so, how? Did this session cause you to think critically about any piece or section of an art work, and if so, how?
5. How do you see this session increasing an observer's communication skills?
6. What application or impact do you see art observation having on a classroom teacher?

RESULTS

The results reported are a collection of data compiled from the sixty participants who were enrolled in a UHD prerequisite course that focused on aesthetic development and growth of children. Beginning with the presession questionnaire, participants' responses indicated that they saw art and its use in a traditional manner. The data from the questions revealed that participants believed the primary purpose for observing works of art was for pleasure. The participants were not sure or did not agree that observing art made them more aware of their surroundings. A large number of the participants did not initially see connections to making inferences and art observations, nor did they connect art experiences to enhancement of communication skills. A larger majority did determine that art may bring a common language to second-language learners and that it may develop critical-thinking skills, although another group of participants was not sure of either of these statements. One-fourth of the participants recorded on the presession survey that they did not believe or were not sure that observing art could create cultural sensitivity, enhance understanding of others, or develop skills for effective assessment.

Moving forward to the data collected from the middle of the session, students were led through open discussion and asked first to share what they knew about observation. The majority of participants gave answers that related specifically to observation of art or art itself. When asked what was going on in certain works of art or pictures, participants mostly gave responses that were inferences, not straight observations. They suggested that "taking your time is key, more time allows for more detailed observations" and that "with observation comes meaning and with meaning comes understanding." When probed as to what inspired their thinking, participants were quickly able to point to a specific piece or detail of the art that influenced their statements. They shared that "creative and critical thinking forces the learner to make connections, to look beyond the art" and their thought that "careful observation and following your curiosity" inspired them to want to know the "why of the art and characteristics of the artists themselves." The majority of responses came when asked these first two questions. However, when the third question, "What more can we find?", was posed, there was a dramatic decrease in the number of responses or repeats of previously shared observations or opinions.

Finally, data were collected and analyzed from the postsession questionnaire and the six open-ended questions. The postsession questionnaire revealed that participants were more decisive about what they believed. Substantially fewer "not sure" responses were marked for all ten statements. The largest variation between pre- and postresponses were with the following: (a) *My ability to make inferences is enhanced through art observations,* and (b) *Art observation develops skills to assess objectively.* Two statements that showed little variation in belief were as follows: (a) *Observing works of art creates cultural sensitivity,* and (b) *Art observation enhances my ability to understand others.*

Participants tended to believe from the start of the session that these two statements were true. Part A results can be viewed in table 5.1, in which the presession responses are in the top row and the postsession responses are in the bottom row. Section A was administered at the beginning and end of each session.

In analyzing the six open-ended questions, it was found that participants began to attach new meaning to art observation. A representative sample included statements such as "critical thinking plays an important role" and "there are always reasons for creating and doing things, and analyzing art or people correctly can lead to higher understanding of many parts of the art or person." Participants responded that "this helped make connections to [their] own culture and background and those of others." As far as increasing an observer's communication skills, the participants said it "enhanced their ability to articulate what is being observed." Finally, it inspired the participants to appreciate student curiosity and creative thinking in a more in-depth way, forcing them to

Table 5.1. Pre- and Post-session Questionnaire Results
(Presession responses given in top row; postsession given in bottom row)

	True	False	Not Sure
1. The primary purpose for observing works of art is for pleasure.	32 26	18 31	9 2
2. Observing art makes me more aware of my surroundings.	42 56	10 2	8 1
3. My ability to make inferences is enhanced through art observation.	33 57	8 0	18 2
4. Visual arts help me to build contextual language.	39 53	3 2	18 4
5. Art observation enhances one's communication skills.	37 53	9 3	13 3
6. Art brings a common language to second-language learners.	41 51	4 3	15 5
7. Art observation develops/enhances my critical-thinking skills.	50 55	3 3	7 1
8. Observing works of art creates cultural sensitivity.	51 57	3 1	6 1
9. Art observation enhances my ability to understand others.	47 53	3 3	10 3
10. Art observation develops skills to assess objectively.	38 56	5 1	17 2

open their minds "to normal views and consider individuality and its importance."

Overall, participants made many connections between what they learned from this Power of Art in Observation session with their role as a future classroom teacher. They felt they would appreciate students and student diversity in a more in-depth manner. They concluded they could use creative teaching and assessment more comfortably. In addition, they would pay attention to detail when writing lesson plans and incorporate a variety of tools to elicit critical thinking, support curiosity, and integrative creativity in all content areas. Furthermore, participants saw that observing art enhanced their communication skills. Ultimately, they felt these experiences opened their own creative minds and enhanced their overall curiosity for teaching using aesthetic experiences.

Conclusions

Through the use of teaching strategies that are developmentally appropriate for young children and the VTS system, the DUE faculty created a learning model to encourage DUE students to work together, to spark motivation to express opinions, and to enhance vocabulary, problem solving, and observation skills. The results of this observation session and opportunity to visit the MFAH indicate that this model has indeed had positive influences on several areas of growth for preservice teachers. This first-time experience produced results that show that the DUE students benefited from the model, from the opportunity to use the VTS strategy in a museum setting, and from being pushed to share and provide evidence to support their observations.

The session and the research conducted imply that the DUE students gained confidence, increased competency, and developed a philosophy based on the importance of using engaging, intriguing, and collaborative experiences to observe and assess their own early childhood education students in their future classrooms. The qualitative data also indicated that DUE students wished to have more time in the museum to look at their own selected art pieces and analyze them independently. As a result, this was added and changed for the following semesters' course experiences.

Because the results are from the first time and only one sample group of participants, additional experiences and data are needed to extend the implications for future research. In building on the positive results of this first semester's experience, DUE faculty have created a long-range timeline for future experiences and data collection. They have added a required course of study for each semester, which includes making use of VTS. Students in each of the courses will visit the MFAH during a regularly scheduled class time to experience an observation session utilizing developmentally appropriate practice and theory of aesthetic development in support of creative teaching and assessing.

Each class will view a different selection of art from those presented in other phases of the program. The selections are meant to challenge and motivate growth in DUE student participants. Art pieces for each phase will be selected by the MFAH in consideration of the focus established by the DUE faculty. With the long-range implementation, students will visit the museum for the first time during a prerequisite course taken before their organized field experiences and student teaching. As students move through their field-based courses, they will build their experiences at the MFAH to enhance observation skills, which will help them to understand the learner and the teacher's role in effectively providing learning experiences for all children.

References

Beaty, J. (2006). *Observing development of the young child* (6th ed.). Upper Saddle River, NJ: Pearson Education.

Berger, L. (2001, January 2). By observing art, med students learn art of observation. *New York Times.* Retrieved July 25, 2007, from www.nytimes.com/2001/01/02/health/by-observing-art-med-students-learn-art-of-observation.html.

Braverman, I. (2001, October 15). Artwork can sharpen medical diagnostic skills, Yale researchers report. Message posted to AAAS: www.eurekalert.org/.

Eisner, E. W. (2002a). *The arts and the creation of mind.* New Haven, CT: Yale University Press.

Eisner, E. W. (2002b). What can education learn from the arts about the practice of education? Paper presented as the John Dewey Lecture for 2002, Stanford University. Abstract retrieved November 20, 2007, from www.infed.org/biblio/eisner_arts_and_the_practice_of_education.htm.

Elder, N., Tobias, B., Lucero-Criswell, A., & Goldenhar, L. (2006, June). The art of observation: Impact of a family medicine and art museum partnership on student education. *Family Medicine, 38*(6), 393–398.

Housen, A. (2002). Aesthetic thought, critical thinking and transfer. *Arts and Learning Journal, 18*(1), 99–131.

Howes, C., & Ritchie, S. (2002). *A matter of trust: Connecting teachers and learners in the early childhood classroom.* New York: Teachers College Press.

Jablon, J. R., Dombro, A. L., & Dictelmiller, M. L. (2007). *The power of observation for birth through eight* (2nd ed.). Washington, DC: Teaching Strategies.

Malone, M. A. (2003, February 19). Lines blur between art and medicine in new course. *Stanford Report.* Message posted to http://news-service.stanford.edu/news.

Reilly, J. M., Ring, J., & Duke, L. (2005, April). Visual thinking strategies: A new role for art in medical education. *Family Medicine, 37*(4), 250–252.

Shonkoff, J. P., & Phillips, D. A. (Eds.). (2000). *From neurons to neighborhoods: The science of early childhood development.* Washington, DC: National Academy Press.

Stipek, D. (2006). Relationships matter. *Educational Leadership, 64*(1), 46–49.

Tishman, S. (2005, September). From edification to engagement: Learning designs in museums. *CAA News, 30*(5), 12–13, 41.

VUE: Visual understanding in education. (2001). Retrieved from www.vue.org/.

Yenawine, P. (1997). Thoughts on visual literacy. In J. E. Flood, B. S. Heath, & D. Lapp (Eds.), *Handbook of research on teaching literacy through the communicative and visual arts* (pp. 810–812). Mahwah, NJ: Lawrence Erlbaum.

Summary and Implications

Cheryl J. Craig

Louise F. Deretchin

The chapters in division 1 stirred minds and offered a multitude of creative possibilities. Centered on teacher education, this group of essays surveyed what was missing or not appropriately attended to in the teacher education enterprise. Moreover, ways that identified oversights that could be productively addressed were generated.

Division 1 began with what was needed: a sizing up of the teacher education field and an elucidation of "Some Neglected Components of Teacher Education Programs." Authored by Anne Chodakowski, Kieran Egan, Gillian Judson, and Kym Stewart, chapter 1 dealt with the paucity of opportunities afforded approaches that unavoidably involve the emotions and imagination and stand to greatly enrich students' learning. The authors asserted that this set of emotional and imaginative dispositions is not peripheral—on the contrary, they are of critical importance to the teacher education enterprise.

Donald Blumenfeld-Jones continued this argument in chapter 2, "Fostering Creative and Aesthetic Consciousness in Teachers: Theory and Practice." However, he avoided referring to curiosity and creative thinking as a particular skill set or even a group of virtues. Instead, he declared curiosity and creative thinking natural proclivities that have strangely become lost in the formal education process of educating teachers and students. An especially interesting aspect of this chapter was how the author drew on his own rich background in dance and aesthetic ways of knowing to cultivate preservice teachers' nonverbal responses to poetry, for example.

In chapter 3, Dixie Keyes used the plotline of the movie *Little Miss Sunshine* to open up a discussion of paradox and how it presents itself in preservice education, which, in turn (it can be argued), mirrors life itself. Most specifically, she used the "traced stories" conceptualization to uncover and blend the narratives of William Gordon and Synectics, of sixth-grade teacher John James who opens spaces for creativity, and of Glenda Rockton, a teacher candidate who appreciates and enacts analogical thought with a teacher's narrative authority. Amid a whirl of complexity, metaphor, and paradox, the perspective and practices of a literacy teacher educator, Keyes herself, shines through.

Following Keyes's chapter 3 came Chris Lasher-Zwerling and Kip Téllez's chapter 4, "No Less 'Real' in My Mind: Using Fiction as Creative Curriculum in an Undergraduate Teacher Education Course." In that work, the authors held to the position that creativity and imagination go hand in hand with the practice of teaching—and learning to teach. Hence, they probed how the reading of fiction could broaden and deepen preservice teachers' capacities to engage in reflection in and on their developing understanding of teaching and the teaching profession. Such an approach, claimed Lasher-Zwerling and Téllez, contributed to the daily construction and reconstruction of teacher candidate's identities as future teachers.

Chapter 5 rounded off the division 1, "Teacher Education," offerings. Contributed by Kathryn Jenkins and Joyce Dutcher, "The Power of Art in Observation" captured how preservice teachers' observational skills of young children were refined through observing works of art made possible through a partnership between their College of Education and a local museum. As a result of the process, prospective teachers' confidence, competency, and creative and critical-thinking skills were developed in ways that readied them to more ably observe and assess students in their future classrooms.

Division 1's chapters were filled with narrative exemplars showing how teacher education strategies, curriculum, and programs have been lived in ways that promote the cultivation of curious and creative minds—and that ready both teacher educators and prospective teachers for the vital roles they play in the formation of young people's minds and worldviews in an increasingly diverse world.

STUDENTS, PROGRAMS, AND SCHOOLS

Overview and Framework

Cheryl J. Craig

Louise F. Deretchin

Unlike division 1, division 2 addresses a potpourri of topics relating to students, programs, and schools. Such foci necessarily carry with them implications for teaching and teacher education and thus are of vital importance in the cultivation of curious and creative minds.

Ginny Esch's chapter 6, "Young Children: Creativity in the Classroom," defines creativity and maps the characteristics of creative children. In addition, Esch explores how children's creativity can be nurtured in the classroom in her chapter contribution.

Chapter 7, authored by Julia Cote, focuses on "Arts-Based Education and Creativity." Cote offers the theoretical and human rationale for arts-integrated curriculum. She then shows, through real-world examples, how a faculty at an elementary school breathed life into its individually and collectively held vision of teaching and learning.

"Labyrinths for Creativity and Peace in Schools," the focus of chapter 8, offers another interesting way to cultivate curious and creative minds in schools. Contributed by Sandra Wasko-Flood, the work explores the labyrinth as a sacred space. It shows how children's interactive experiences in labyrinths forge connections between art, science, technology, and nature and position students in ways that could foster both inner peace and world peace.

Beverly Klug and Patricia Whitfield are the authors of chapter 9, "A Mind with a View: Education through the Kaleidoscopic Lenses of the Arts." In their chapter, they assert the primacy of the visual and performing arts in children's education. They feature the Reggio Emilia approach and curriculum adaptations for American Indian children as ways that "the whole child" can be formed.

In chapter 10, Sharon Friesen, David Jardine, and Brenda Gladstone discuss "The First Thunder Clap of Spring: An Invitation into Aboriginal Ways of Knowing and the Creative Possibilities of Digital Technologies." In their chapter, the authors focus on how to use new digital technologies to preserve and communicate aboriginal ways of knowing without subverting historically underserved people into dominant culture—while simultaneously including aboriginal communities in the knowledge society.

Jacqueline Sack, in chapter 11, focuses on "Fostering Creative Minds through Problem Solving in a 3-D Visualization Design Research Program" and her work with grade 3 dual-language (Spanish/English) students in the fourth largest urban center in the United States. In the program, children's creativity was nurtured through teacher-student and student-teacher relationships, the classroom environment, and the 2- and 3-D activities in which the students engaged.

"A Report on the Introduction and Resulting Effects of Novel Teaching Strategies in Increasing Creativity and Independent Thought" is the title of chapter 12, which was contributed by Teresa Leavitt and Madalina Tanase. In this essay, Leavitt and Tanase capture their international work aimed at promoting creativity (creative thinking) in English language learners in China through the use of readers' and writers' workshop strategies.

Chapter 13, "Poetry from Report Cards: Children's Understanding of Themselves in Relationship Their Teachers," is authored by Shaun Murphy. The chapter tells of how students wrote "Found Poetry" poems that conveyed their stories of their reactions to the narrative texts on their report cards written by their teachers. The work illuminates how student identity is nested in relationships and context.

Together, the chapters in division 2 tell of students, programs, and schools and of how curious and creative minds are actively being cultivated in a multiplicity of ways.

CHAPTER 6

Young Children
CREATIVITY IN THE CLASSROOM

Ginny Esch
University of Tennessee at Martin

Ginny Esch, Ph.D., is professor in the Department of Educational Studies at the University of Tennessee at Martin where she teaches early childhood math and science, creativity and play, and children's literature. Some of her recent publications are on diversity, bullying, and an introduction to China for early childhood.

ABSTRACT

Young children have a preponderance of curiosity and innovation. Creativity is prevalent in many forms yet appears to be elusive in definition. This chapter is a position paper that espouses the support and promotion of creativity as a positive attribute; the creative component can nurture the cognitive, social, and emotional development of students who might be overlooked in other endeavors. Many opportunities for stimulating creativity in young children can be encouraged in the classroom; however, educators must be aware of some of the misconceptions that arise with creative abilities. Some recommendations serve as guiding factors in dealing with the possible reluctance that teachers of young children may have in promoting creativity as a positive attribute.

Did you hear the one about the small boy who drew a colorful garden on his paper? He used bright red and yellow for his flowers, and the stems and grass were a vibrant green. Then he proceeded to color over his entire picture with black crayon. Upon seeing his completed work, his teacher considered many appalling and sinister options regarding his behavior. Instead of immediately reporting this disconcerting observation to the school psychologist, she asked the youngster about his picture and why his beautiful garden was covered with black crayon. The explanation was simple: the picture was of a garden at night. There was no deep-rooted malevolence or angst; the child was merely making a depiction of the image in his imagination.

This is creativity at work. The thought processes, imagery, fantasies, inventions, innovations, and problem resolutions are all a part of children's vivid imaginations. Converting all of these characteristics into usable resources is a major cognitive feat for the children themselves and for those who deal with children on an everyday basis. The element of creativity can be a challenging one to define because the meaning indicates several facets of significance. There is artistic creativity, scientific creativity, and creativity in movement or in sound. Creativity contains no limit on the fluency of ideas or facility of problem solving. The Encarta World English Dictionary characterizes creativity as the means to utilize the mental capabilities in extended novel and unique thoughts, while Webster's New World College Dictionary portrays creative aptitude as imaginative or inspired ingenuity. Linda Naiman (2006) stated that "creativity is the act of turning new and imaginative ideas into reality. Creativity involves two processes: thinking, and then producing. Innovation is the production or implementation of an idea. If you have ideas, but don't act on them, you are imaginative but not creative." According to Mary Mayesky (2009), "Young children tend to be highly open, curious, and creative" (p. 4). Jane Piirto (2004) stated that origin of the word *create* is derived from the Latin *creâtus* and *creâre*, which denote the meaning of "to make or produce" or "literally, to grow" (p. 6). Regardless of which definition one selects for usage, the characteristics of creative individuals are as varied as the designations are for the term of creativity. Young children acquire perceptions that adults take for granted and turn them upside down. They can explain the unexpected, draw the unpredictable, and imagine the impossible.

Characteristics of Creative Individuals

Creative people are fascinated with invention. They are autonomous in decision making and intrinsically motivated in making these decisions. They are spontaneous and impulsive as well as tolerant of ambiguity. They are persistent in their beliefs but can be motivated to change perspectives when necessary.

A key element in the portrayal of creativity is that of diversity. Children come to the classroom with myriad experiences and attributes. Diversity in the broad sense usually connotes cultural disparities and plays a central role in curriculum planning, instructional methodology, and classroom management strategies. Often, diversity is restricted to race and ethnicity, but these are only a segment of a larger picture. Other aspects of diversity that must be addressed within the classroom include traditions, religious diversity, alternative lifestyle and family life, and the diversity of special needs.

In order to analyze and evaluate the huge range of diversity topics, researchers have concentrated on what has occurred in the past and how past influences have manipulated current educational practices. Gaile Canella (1997) indicated that many programs have deliberately directed students toward normalcy. This means that educational practices have been geared toward overcoming any type of diversity that is not meeting contemporary societal standards. It also means that the creative child is often overlooked or criticized because of variant behavior. According to Linda Darling-Hammond (1997), schools have traditionally subjugated the personal differences of students to accommodate narrowly defined standardized curricula.

The scope of a pluralistic society encompasses several facets that are not ordinarily contemplated in classroom settings. Jeffrey Trawick-Smith (2000) discussed the variance of characteristics and behaviors that include temperament, socioeconomic status, and gender. Kelvin Seifert (1999) concentrated on the issues of culture and gender in his treatment of diversity awareness.

What sparks the creative element in children comes from all of these diversity factors with which each child arrives in the classroom. Creativity can be genetically inherited and fostered in the home. It can be a delightful new experience for children who have never before encountered the materials or freedom to experiment. It can be an escape factor for abused or neglected children. Regardless of the basis for creativity, classroom professionals must be prepared to motivate as well as stimulate the creative process.

Creative people have several mutual traits that indicate a propensity for originality. Ann Gordon and Kathryn Browne (2008) indicated that fluency is a vital component of creative proficiency in young children and define fluency as the capability of formulating myriad ideas. Combined with flexibility, fluency allows the individual to generate a variety of alternative concepts in different situations. Rebecca Isbell and Shirley Raines (2003) included being adventurous and uninhibited as characteristics in young children. Robert Schirrmacher (2006) incorporated elaboration as a creative trait because of the complexities of expression. Frank Smith (1990) indicated that two additional components are necessary for involved creative concentration, which consists of the establishment of options and a choice among those options.

Another defining attribute of creativity is the willingness to take risks. Exploring various possibilities from a safe environment permits the child to undertake a challenge without fear of recrimination or reproach. Taking a chance allows a child to encounter an assortment of opportunities and discern multiple options. Because children are not fearful of making mistakes, they are amenable to trying novel tactics in problem resolution and discovering new ways of performing complex tasks. Being creative involves taking chances. Being permitted to make mistakes in secure surroundings allows children to learn from their errors as well as feel safe in trying an endeavor again. Wendy Libby (2002) stated that success needs to be an essential expectation of children in order to gain self-assurance and confidence in their communication skills. Our educational system rewards those who have a dread of failure and do not make errors. This backward thinking is unfortunate because producing flaws is a genuine factor in learning.

An additional indicator of creativity, according to Deborah Tegano, James Moran, and Janet Sawyers (1991), is a remarkable sense of humor. The sense of humor for young children is far different from that of adults. Because children are learning to function in their individual worlds, they employ concepts of integrating concrete impressions with cognitive function. They do not care for abstractions or double meanings because they do not understand them, but they do find silliness in incongruous situations that appeal to the implication of the absurd such as an elephant wearing a tutu and ballet slippers.

Children develop at varying rates and learn in diverse ways. The Center for Arts and Culture (n.d.) stated that, while competence in reading and using numbers are necessary life skills, the modes in which students learn are extensive and complex. Howard Gardner (1983/1993) epitomized this methodology through his theory of multiple intelligences. This theory states that passageway for student success lies in alternative approaches instead of only literacy and mathematics, and currently has established ten different types of intelligence (M. K. Smith, 2002/ 2008). Gardner himself acknowledged intelligence as "the capacity to solve problems or to fashion products that are valued in one or more cultural setting" (Gardner & Hatch, 1989).

Another important perspective that needs to be taken into consideration is Urie Bronfenbrenner's Ecological Systems Theory (1979). His developmental theory revolves around the child as a universal center with increasingly complex systems emanating from the child. This approach has been instrumental in the study of the effect of surrounding environmental factors on the growth of an individual child. How ecological features impact development can influence the child's propensity toward being creative as well as the attitude regarding inventiveness. Barbara Clark (2002) used a novel approach to the topic of sustaining a productive environment by listing a series of stipulations that hinder creativity. Among these are the following:

- Everything must be useful.
- Everything must be successful.
- Everything must be perfect.
- Everyone must like you.
- You shall not prefer solitude to togetherness.
- You must not diverge from culturally imposed sex norms.
- Do not rock the cultural boat. (p. 93)

These inventive aspects of revising instructive teaching have allowed a substantial number of educators to reexamine their conventional methodologies and perspectives in pedagogy. This means that several facets of the educational process can be revised to modify the conventional mechanisms used for mastering valuable skills, adhering to prescribed curricula, and the evaluation of progress.

Opportunities for Creativity of Young Children in the Classroom

According to Gera Jacobs and Kathy Crowley (2007), young children express their emotions through art media prior to communication with verbal interaction. Because of vocabulary limitations, children are restricted in articulating their thoughts and ideas to others. However, they are able to connect their opinions and feelings through their choices in art supplies such as paint or clay or through graphics and illustrations.

One of the main tenets of early childhood education is process over product. MaryAnn Kohl (1994) stated that most young children are not concerned with the completion of an outcome but are much more interested in the process of formulating and creating. In fact, as Roc (2008) promulgated, process is valued so much by the young creators that at least a third of the materials used in the creative process are discarded. Mayesky (2009) maintained that, since young children have not yet developed the necessary skills for producing an original artifact, they need to investigate and discover the effects of varying materials. Joanne Hendrick (2003) stressed the importance of process over product to emphasize the awareness and experience of using and manipulating materials. Kathy Hirsh-Pasek, Roberta Golinkoff, and Diane Eyer (2003) used the words "stress effort, not achievement" (p. 150) to illustrate the concept of taking risks as well as the importance of procedure over outcomes.

Janice Beaty (2004) advised against the expectation of a completed project because of the nature of the creative process. Observing novices in their decisions for maneuvering artistic materials that increase their autonomy and decision-making skills can depict levels of development as well as imagination. Anticipating a finished product can backfire in its intent. Imagine a small child in the classroom who loves to paint pictures and puts a lot of effort into her work. She is proud of her work and takes it home to be put on the refrigerator. As time progresses, the child seems anxious and frustrated while trying to complete several pictures to take home. Communication with the family indicates that each family member wants a picture every day, and the child is trying to please her loved ones; this eagerness to please has decreased the creative motivation for process and increased the proclivity of production. This thwarting of creativity as a means of expression can be prolonged in later development if not remedied at its inception.

Joan Isenberg and Mary Jalongo (2001) advocated the provision of authentic construction projects that imparts meaning to the individual child so that concepts can be reinforced in the real world. The authors (2010) also maintained that creative children need to accrue substantial preparation before finalizing an acceptable achievement. This means that the child may frequently generate many inadequate efforts before attaining satisfaction and, thus, success.

For young children's learning to occur, the information presented to them must be meaningful. This means that the early childhood curriculum must incorporate elements that include developmentally appropriate practices (DAP). Too challenging an activity can lead to frustration, and an activity that is too easily accomplished can result in boredom as well as behavioral difficulties.

The commitment to be expressive is a vital characteristic of creative individuals. Barbara Taylor (2004) noted that some children are not inclined to indulge in messy activities and that this preference must be respected. Varying and alternative opportunities to express ideas, feelings, and emotions must be accommodated in order to meet developmental needs. Jerome Bruner (1972) cited play as a problem-solving mechanism that facilitates the resolution of obstacles during maturation.

Problem solving is a component of cognition that is the encompassing term for thinking, learning, remembering, reasoning, and perception. As a child plays, active thought processes continue to make connections in the brain that result in increased cognitive function. A key role in establishing a valid curriculum is the integration of cognitive development as promulgated by Jean Piaget (1969). The central concept of Piaget's cognitive research indicated that knowledge is based on reflections about the child's connections in a personal environment as well as intellectual development occurring through a series of connected stages with each being built on the attainment of the previous stage. This means that the very young child who is in the sensorimotor stage is constantly absorbing information about the world through the senses and motor skills. Until the basic elements have been understood, the child cannot progress with more advanced cognitive utility.

Lev Vygotsky's (1978) sociocultural theory expanded this context to include social interaction that augments children's development. This theory proposes that growth is contingent on connections with people and mechanisms that make the experiences of society available. In this way, the child is able to form a personal perspective of that world and his or her place in it.

The National Association for the Education of Young Children (NAEYC) is a forerunner in the edification of professionals in the field of early childhood education. The position statement of this organization exemplifies the highest standards of educational practice and contains several principles of what is considered to be developmentally appropriate based on how young children learn. One of the primary empirical doctrines for DAP includes the four closely intertwined domains of children's development—physical, social, emotional, and cognitive. Development in one domain influences and is influenced by development in other domains (Bredekamp & Copple, 1997, p. 10). To provide meaning for a culturally diverse curriculum topic, all four domains in the developing child must be addressed.

A wide-ranging tactic of supporting creativity in the classroom is Synectics (Gordon, 1961). Synectics offers a creative-thinking method that relies on observing what seem to be disparate ideas and constructing germane associations. For example, children could be asked to think of a connection between shopping and a beehive. The Synectics approach encompasses several methods of conducting creative activities, one of which is the concept of brainstorming. Alex Osborn (1957) introduced the following basic principles of brainstorming: quantity over quality of ideas, concepts that are built upon previous thoughts, outrageous and crazy impressions, and the withholding of judgment until the brainstorming session is over. Steve Rivkin (1998) added the tenet of chronicling all of the ideas in a location where the participants can see them; this can prompt the coalescing of stated ideas into new ones. Another precept of brainstorming with young children is to set a time limit because of their lack of attention span.

One of the most important considerations that a teacher can supply in the classroom is time. Allotting ten minutes for participation in an art center does not provide ample opportunity for contemplation and decision making and limits the creative process. With restrictions of No Child Left Behind, state educational standards, and local policies, creative endeavors often take a back seat to more mundane approaches, methodology, and time allotments for topics. Budget constraints and test-score accountability have all too often induced teachers to "teach to the test," and worksheets are a staple for student assessment. What many educators do not comprehend is that, since children learn through play and active participation, a creative approach to pedagogy can enhance and augment learning in a very beneficial manner. If there is time in a day for five worksheets, there is time for the exploration of concrete materials that are developmentally appropriate to reinforce the intended concept.

Another vital factor to foster creativity in the classroom is the availability of appropriate space. Making a collage of community helpers or creating a papiermâché volcano on a *single desktop* would be a factor in promoting dissatisfaction and frustration. Instead, desks can be moved and newspapers or a plastic tablecloth can cover floor space so that involvement can be encouraged. Since process over product is a fundamental principle in children's creativity, the children are able to intensify their efforts without encroaching on another child's activity.

A third critical component of promoting creativity within the classroom is the availability of developmentally appropriate materials. With the pushing down of curricula, many of the items for use by children are not developmentally appropriate. For example, gross motor skills are developed before fine motor coordination, and physical growth occurs in stages. A child can grasp a thick pencil or crayon before being able to control a thin one; however, these "fat" implements are seldom found in primary classrooms. Another learning tool that young children rarely see is called training scissors; these utensils contain a double-handled design so teachers can physically teach children how to cut by inserting both teacher and children's fingers into the tools to practice the cutting motion. Cost may be a factor in the purchase of these types of items, but the availability of them is of enormous benefit to supporting physical development.

Materials must be physically located to be accessible to children in the classroom so that they are encouraged and able to make their own selections. Enabling autonomy in this type of decision making advances the development of independence. Labeling materials with words and pictures establishes environmental print that links objects to written names. Labeling also promotes the idea of returning items to a proper location to facilitate the routine of cleanup.

Another critical element for encouraging creativity in young children is the freedom to experiment, examine, and investigate. Marilyn Segal and colleagues (2006) emphasized that the classroom ambiance must be conducive to creative stimulation. Interesting artifacts and aesthetically pleasurable surroundings that display the efforts of the students has an affective impression on the children as a class as well as on an individual basis. Jacobs and Crowley (2007) stressed that the classroom environment must incorporate stimuli for inquisitiveness, imagination, and ingenuity. Anna Craft (2002) stated that an appreciation for the child and the fostering of individual efforts are essential for appropriate pedagogy in augmenting each child's creative potential. Carol Catron and Jan Allen (2008) added that the classroom environment must promote challenges that endorse learning that is devoid of frustration and boredom. This means that the educator acts as a catalyst for individual students while supplying acceptable parameters for conduct and the encouragement of constructive communal interaction.

Misconceptions

Many educators assume that children's creative work must be naturally similar in order to be "correct." This supposition opposes the entire principle of creativity as an innovative concept. Every effort does not need to be purposeful or functional, and every endeavor does not have to result in perfection. The same precept also applies to behavior. Creative children can be disruptive because they are often bored with traditional learning methods and want to explore alternative techniques of achieving the objective of what is being taught. For example, a student teacher was teaching a kindergarten class about the family unit and how the child was assimilated into the family dynamic. One boy completed his family portrait and began to pester his friend to finish. In order to stop disruptions, the student teacher told the boy to add details to his picture that would more fully characterize each family member. The boy followed directions and proceeded to include anatomically correct features to each male member of his family. The student teacher went into shock.

Because many teachers do not wish to deviate from their customary plans or paradigms, they are unwilling to investigate novel approaches suggested by students. This type of intolerance can result in labeling a child as a trouble-maker because of nonconformist conduct. A further example of this is another observation of a student teacher in a kindergarten class. The children were studying patterns and using attribute blocks to formulate their own pattern configurations. One bright child had completed his pattern and began to disturb children at his table who were not yet finished. The boy was reprimanded twice for his distractions and did not know how to contain his energy. The observer suggested that the child try to form a pattern by placing the attribute blocks vertically instead of horizontally on the table. Since this perception of the task was totally new to the boy, he approached the task with renewed enthusiasm. The other children at the table were fascinated by this novel methodology and wanted to participate; they were told to complete the assigned task and then they could help with the vertical construction. This was rapidly done, and what had begun as boredom and disruption quickly turned into a group project with all of the children at the table offering suggestions and contributing their own blocks to the activity.

Another erroneous supposition regarding creativity is that something new or unusual denotes disturbing behavior. Too many educators are impervious to accepting a perspective that is unlike their own. Supplying a model for the children in a creative activity suppresses the original ideas of the children; they feel that the model is the desired outcome of the activity and will discard their own inclinations. This type of teacher often relies on convergent thinking with narrowly defined outcomes. Unfortunately, this style of teaching squelches inquisitiveness and curiosity and can inhibit the pursuit of lifelong learning. An example of this concept had to do with the grading of a standard test from a specific basal reading text. On the test, there was a comprehension question regarding securing the rope of the sail to the mast of the boat. The "correct" response was to wrap the rope around the hook on the mast so that it would remain fixed. Upon reviewing the test and answers with the children, the teacher had to contemplate the response from one child who stated that he was short and could not reach the hook, so he would have to take the rope and walk around the mast in order to secure it. One of the multiple-choice selections accommodated this answer and the solution made a lot of sense, so the teacher had to change her paradigm of what was actually considered "correct" from the child's perspective.

Many educators rely on extrinsic rewards to promote "correct" work. This perception encourages students to excel for transient reasons instead of for the value of learning. Many teachers assume that some kind of external accolade will stimulate the creative process when, actually, this reward distribution system sends out the message that the activity is not worth doing because of its own merit. Creativity is an internal element that can be kindled and stimulated by external forces but is not a quality to be committed to memory and made available upon request. Also, young children wish to please their role models and will subjugate their own efforts in order to satisfy the adult's expectations.

An extension of the reward format is the fostering of competition. Many teachers presume that the recognition or honor of surpassing peers in an endeavor will compel students to succeed. This viewpoint produces several difficulties when dealing with young children. The Piagetian concept of egocentrism indicates that the child, depending on the rate of cognitive development, is aware only of his or her own self in the environment (Piaget, 1954). A critical part of learning social skills and interactions is the integration of acceptable communication and understanding about others. Young children are in the coping phase of conceptualizing this capability and do not yet understand the notion of not being at the center of everything. Competition generally specifies that there is one winner or one team of winners, and everyone else is a loser. One activity that can often be found in classrooms is the game of musical chairs. When the music stops, children scramble to find an available chair so that they will not be "out" since a chair is removed every time the music plays. The continual results for each time that a child is eliminated are frustration and boredom. This activity is a contest of speed and agility that only enhances the self-esteem of one person and leaves the others with the feeling of failure. Granted, children must learn the ways of the world in order to be successful, but competition is not a developmentally appropriate practice in early childhood. Children must first learn about being productive through empowerment and the gaining of self-confidence.

Because educators are accountable for what they teach, they must be able to evaluate the progress of students. Creativity is not a usual component contained in standardized tests, so teachers are not accustomed to assessing it. Several evaluation instruments are available for the assessment of creativity such as the Torrance Test of Creative Thinking (Torrance, 1966), GIFT: Group Inventory for Finding Creative Talent (Rimm, 1976), and the Test for Creative Thinking-Drawing Production (Urban & Jellen, 1986). However, most classroom teachers are not acquainted with these types of appraisal because they are generally used with students who display exceptional capabilities.

Acknowledged as "the father of creativity," Torrance devised a methodology of measuring creative thinking, and promoted the concept that creativity is a process for the attainment of versatile information" (Maisuria, 2005). Ellis Torrance's definition is as follows:

> Creativity is a process of becoming sensitive to problems, deficiencies, gaps in knowledge, missing elements, disharmonies, and so on; identifying the difficulty; searching for solutions, making guesses, or formulating hypotheses about the deficiencies; testing and retesting these hypotheses and possibly modifying and retesting them; and finally communicating the results. (Torrance, 1974, p. 8)

Torrance (1966) and his team developed several tests based on the work of J. P. Guilford (1950), and some, such as the Circles Tests for Creativity, can be adapted to use with young children. A modified example can be seen in figure 6.1.

The scoring of this revised fluency test can be quite subjective. According to Torrance (1966), the main criteria for evaluating this type of creativity test consist of fluency, flexibility, originality, and elaboration. *Fluency* is the quantity of relevant and pertinent ideas that are produced as feedback to a specific motivating factor. In this case of circles, most students are stymied by the strict parameters of the circle without consideration of the many things in their lives that are actually based on a circle. They will draw faces and maybe a sunshine but forget about mundane everyday objects such as doorknobs, buttons, spare tires, and jar covers.

Flexibility means that the responses are adaptable and variable; an assortment of categories can be determined by the analysis of the outcomes. A noncreative child might draw a variety of faces with different expressions that would constitute one main category, while a creative student might combine three vertical circles to make a stoplight or two horizontal circles to represent a bicycle.

Originality refers to the paucity of similar outcomes or a low level of occurrence for the specific constructions. In the adapted fluency circle test, snowmen and finger rings are common, but the holes on the top view of a saltshaker or the bottom view of a spiral is much rarer.

Elaboration is the attention to detail that is used to embellish the original concept. Because of time constraints, elaboration can frequently be omitted from drawings. However, the elaboration component is often necessary. For example, illustrating a pull-tab for the top view of a soda can or the varying sized holes in the round portion of a manual pencil sharpener define the object.

Susan Besemer and Donald Treffinger (1981) used a different categorization to label the standards pertinent in evaluating creativity. These elements

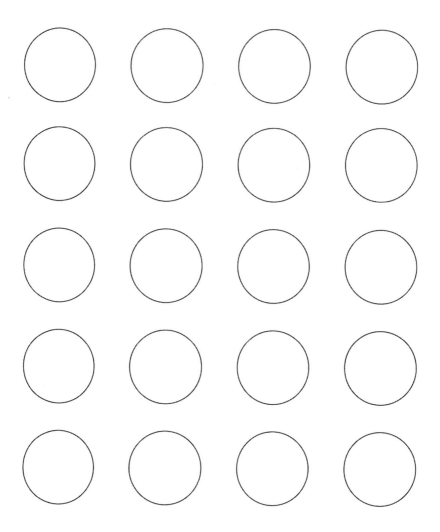

Directions: Use the circles as the basis for drawing pictures; the circles need to be the main element of what you are illustrating. You can draw fun and crazy things or serious and important things. Draw as many different pictures as possible. Try to get the main idea on paper and not take a lot of time with details. Two minutes is the allotted time, and no questions can be answered.

Figure 6.1. Modified version of the Circles Tests for Creativity

include novelty, resolution, and elaboration and synthesis. *Novelty* refers to innovative procedures, approaches, and conceptions. *Resolution* denotes a device that fulfills a necessity or determines an outcome. *Elaboration and synthesis* signifies a result that has amalgamated dissimilar components into a logical entity. Barbara Nilsen and Gini Albertalli (2001) inquired why creativity should be evaluated because it is so idiosyncratic and multifaceted.

Several broad responses can justify creative assessment such as channeling exceptional creative talents and modifying programs of study to accommodate cognitive schemata. Nevertheless, teachers often appraise work based on subjective perceptions, which may obstruct the future creative endeavors of some students. One example of this is the display of "good" art work in the classroom; children whose work is not exhibited can feel that their efforts are insignificant and that the value of these efforts has been depreciated.

One query that can cause consternation is in regard to the "cut-off point" of creativity. What is the difference between "somewhat creative" and "extremely creative"? The answer is complex and subject to interpretation. Some parents believe that every mark that their prodigy of a child makes is a masterpiece, while others are unaware or dismissive of budding creativity. In the classroom, educators must be aware that children can be creative in different ways and be able to relay this type of information to parents and families. Every child is good at something, but not every child is creative. For example, one child may excel in academic work because of good memorization skills, while another child may be able to make up an exotic story complete with illustrations that is relevant to a concept learned during the day. Clark (2002) explained that some people are not creative because

> they choose not to for fear of being thought different, strange, unusual, silly, dumb. . . . Unfortunately, being creative in a society that values rational, material gains requires taking risks. Some may not realize how creative they could be if given the opportunity and the belief in themselves. Safe places to be creative are sorely needed, both in school and at home. (p. 105)

Recommendations

Several perspectives are available for teachers to utilize in order to stimulate a creative atmosphere within which to educate young children. One of these is the quality of being open-minded and not intimidated by a student who appears to be more creative than the educator. Marjorie Kostelnik, Anne Soderman, and Alice Whiren (2007) advocate the display of authentic enthusiasm. Children are much more apt to respond positively to a suggestion or idea when it is presented with fervor and zeal. They also suggest that the creative experiences be linked to academic concepts being taught in the classroom for enjoyment as well as reinforcement. Joe Frost, Sue Wortham, and Stuart Reifel (2001) advised the limitation of teacher input in creative play activities because of the tendency to become too directive.

The provision of open-ended resources in the classroom expands the possibilities for creative activities. When materials have multiple uses, they stimulate the attraction for investigation. Lynn Hill, Andrew Stremmel, and Victoria Fu (2005) advised the use of easily available transparent storage containers to generate an interest in discovery and experimentation. Labeling these containers with words and pictures increases children's awareness of comprehension because of the environmental print and meaning introduction to reading.

Acknowledging superior ideas or achievements does not diminish the teacher's capabilities but rather enhances an environment for innovation and originality. If teachers are truly lifelong learners, they can welcome and benefit from the resourceful and innovatory impressions conveyed by children. Rosalind Charlesworth (2008) proposed that open-ended questions could stimulate the creative process. These impressions can be imaginative and delightful. For example, a teacher could ask how the children would care for a pet giraffe or what happened to Goldilocks after her adventure with the three bears. This type of question can often be relevant to curriculum topics. The pet giraffe question could be incorporated into a social studies lesson on habitats or a health lesson about the food pyramid with vocabulary including herbivore, carnivore, and omnivore. The Goldilocks question could be included in a lesson about community helpers such as police personnel or why our society has specific laws. Coming up with applicable open-ended questions may take time and effort, but the results are well worth the endeavor.

An extension of this precept is that of serving as a model for creative inspiration. If young children can observe and recognize that their teacher is flexible, tolerant, and dispassionate, they will be more eager to volunteer their perceptions and opinions. This means that they can build from the ideas of others and form a cohesive learning community. The development of this unified learning group enables children to interact in a positive way to strengthen divergent assets as well as encourage individual qualities.

Interaction and affective affirmation are crucial components in the effective educational process. When students exhibit positive feelings about what they are doing, where it is being done, who is assisting them in doing it, and how it is being accomplished, they are stimulated to pursue knowledge and endeavor to succeed. The educator who feels a firm commitment and devotion to the avocation of teaching will embody the qualities of consideration, compassion, and creativity, and will insert these dynamic attributes into the environment as well as the curriculum. Exposure to new resources and methodologies that are relevant to the students in a meaningful way will enhance the desire and inspiration to learn.

Creative children can be challenging in any classroom. They are not willing to conform to rigid policies and can become very inventive in manipulating parameters and constraints. Wise educators will abandon unnecessary power struggles and select their battles carefully. Teachers do not always have to be right; they can be accessible, accepting, and accommodating without stifling the creative processes of their students.

References

Beaty, J. (2004). *Skills for preschool teachers.* Upper Saddle River, NJ: Merrill Prentice Hall.

Besemer, S. P., & Treffinger, D. H. (1981). Analysis of creative products: Review and synthesis. *Journal of Creative Behavior, 15*(3), 158–178.

Bredekamp, S., & Copple, C. (Eds.). (1997). *Developmentally appropriate practice in early childhood programs.* Washington, DC: NAEYC.

Bronfenbrenner, U. (1979). *The ecology of human development: Experiments by nature and design.* Cambridge, MA: Harvard University Press.

Bruner, J. (1972). The nature and uses of immaturity. *American Psychologist, 27,* 687–708.

Canella, G. (1997). *Deconstructing early childhood education: Social justice and revolution.* New York: Peter Lang.

Catron, C., & Allen, J. (2008). *Early childhood curriculum: A creative-play model.* Upper Saddle River, NJ: Merrill Prentice Hall.

Center for Arts and Culture. n.d. Creativity, culture, education, and the workforce. Retrieved November 9, 2008, from www.culturalpolicy.org/pdf/education.pdf.

Charlesworth, R. (2008). *Understanding child development.* Clifton Park, NY: Delmar.

Clark, B. (2002). *Growing up gifted.* Upper Saddle River, NJ: Merrill Prentice Hall.

Craft, A. (2002). *Creativity and early years education: A lifewide foundation.* London: Continuum.

Darling-Hammond, L. (1997). *The right to learn: A blueprint for creating schools that work.* San Francisco: Jossey-Bass.

Encarta® World English Dictionary, North American Edition. Creative. Retrieved November 1, 2008, from www.askoxford.com/concise_oed/creative?view=uk.

Frost, J., Wortham, S., & Reifel, S. (2001). *Play and child development.* Upper Saddle River, NJ: Merrill Prentice Hall.

Gardner, H. (1983/1993). *Frames of mind: The theory of multiple intelligences.* New York: Basic Books.

Gardner, H., & Hatch, T. (1989). Multiple intelligences go to school: Educational implications of the theory of multiple intelligences. *Educational Researcher, 18*(8), 4–9.

Gordon, A., & Browne, K. (2008). *Beginnings and beyond: Foundations in early childhood education*. Clifton Park, NY: Delmar.

Gordon, W. (1961). *Synectics: The development of creative capacity*. New York: Harper & Row.

Guilford, J. (1950). Creativity. *American Psychologist, 5,* 444–454.

Hendrick, J. (2003). *Total learning: Developmental curriculum for the young child*. Upper Saddle River, NJ: Merrill Prentice Hall.

Hill, L., Stremmel, A., & Fu, V. (2005). *Teaching as inquiry: Rethinking curriculum in early childhood education*. Boston: Pearson.

Hirsh-Pasek, K., Golinkoff, R., & Eyer, D. (2003). *Einstein never used flash cards: How our children really learn—and why they need to play more and memorize less*. Emmaus, PA: Rodale.

Isbell, R., & Raines, S. (2003). *Creativity and the arts with young children*. Albany, NY: Delmar.

Isenberg, J. P., & Jalongo, M. R. (2001). *Creative expression and play in early childhood* (3rd ed.). Upper Saddle River, NJ: Merrill.

Isenberg, J. P., & Jalongo, M. R. (2010). *Creative thinking and arts-based learning: Preschool through fourth grade*. Upper Saddle River, NJ: Merrill.

Jacobs, G., & Crowley, K. (2007). *Play, projects, and preschool standards*. Thousand Oaks, CA: Corwin Press.

Kohl, M. (1994). *Preschool art: It's the process, not the product*. Lewisville, NC: Gryphon House.

Kostelnik, M., Soderman, A., & Whiren, A. (2007). *Developmentally appropriate curriculum: Best practices in early childhood education*. Upper Saddle River, NJ: Merrill Prentice Hall.

Libby, W. (2002). *Enriching the curriculum with art experiences*. Albany, NY: Delmar.

Maisuria, A. (2005). The turbulent times of creativity in the national curriculum. *Policy Futures in Education, 3*(2), 141–152.

Mayesky, M. (2009). *Creative activities for young children* (9th ed.). Clifton Park, NY: Delmar.

Naiman, L. (2006). What is creativity? Retrieved April 3, 2009, from www.creativityatwork.com/articlesContent/whatis.htm.

Nilsen, B., & Albertalli, G. (2001). *Introduction to learning and teaching: Infants through elementary age children*. New York: Delmar.

Osborn, A. (1957). *Applied imagination*. New York: Charles Scribner's Sons.

Piaget, J. (1954). *The construction of reality in the child*. New York: Basic Books.

Piaget, J. (1969). *The psychology of the child*. New York: Basic Books.

Piirto, J. (2004). *Understanding creativity*. Scottsdale, AZ: Great Potential Press.

Rimm, S. (1976). *GIFT: Group inventory for finding creative talent*. Watertown, WI: Educational Assessment Service.

Rivkin, S. (1998). Brainstorms and rainstorms: New ideas for the road ahead. Retrieved April 3, 2009, from www.k12.hi.us/~kealakehegt/GT_Criteria/CreativeThinkingAbstractIdeas_Rivkin.pdf.

Roc. (2008). The creative process: Over product. Retrieved April 3, 2009, from http://preschoolpunks.wordpress.com/2008/06/08/the-creative-process-over-product.

Schirrmacher, R. (2006). *Art and creative development for young children.* Albany, NY: Delmar.

Segal, M., Bardige, B., Wolka, M. J., & Leinfelder, J. (2006). *All about child care and early education: A comprehensive resource for child care professionals.* Boston: Pearson.

Seifert, K. (1999). *Constructing a psychology of teaching and learning.* Boston: Houghton Mifflin Company.

Smith, F. (1990). *To think.* New York: Teachers College Press.

Smith, M. K. (2002/2008). Howard Gardner and multiple intelligences. Retrieved November 23, 2008, from www.infed.org/thinkers/gardner.htm.

Taylor, B. (2004). *A child goes forth: A curriculum guide for preschool children.* Upper Saddle River, NJ: Pearson/Merrill Prentice Hall.

Tegano, D., Moran, J., & Sawyers, J. (1991). *Creativity in early childhood classrooms.* Washington, DC: National Education Association.

Torrance, E. P. (1966). *The Torrance tests of creative thinking.* Lexington, MA: Personnel Press.

Torrance, E. P. (1974). *Norms-technical manual: Torrance tests of creative thinking.* Lexington, MA: Ginn and Company.

Trawick-Smith, J. (2000). *Early childhood development: A multicultural perspective* (2nd ed.). Upper Saddle River, NJ: Merrill.

Urban, K. K., & Jellen, H. G. (1986). Assessing creative potential via drawing production: The Test for Creative Thinking—Drawing Production (TCT-DP). In A. J. Cropley, K. K. Urban, H. Wagner, & W. Wieczerkowski (Eds.), *Giftedness: A continuing worldwide challenge* (pp. 163–169). New York: Trillium.

Vygotsky, L. (1978). *Mind in society: Development of higher psychological processes.* Boston: Harvard University Press.

Webster's New World College Dictionary (4th ed.). (n.d.). Creativity. Retrieved November 1, 2008, from www.yourdictionary.com/creativity.

CHAPTER 7

Arts-Based Education and Creativity

Julia Cote
University of Houston, Texas

Julia Cote, M.Ed., has spent over a decade in higher education teaching developmental reading, writing, and English as a second language. Recently, she has taught and supervised preservice K–4 teachers in the University of Houston's College of Education QUEST program. Her research interests include arts-based education, narrative inquiry, and teacher as curriculum maker. Ms. Cote is presently completing a doctoral degree in curriculum and instruction at the University of Houston.

ABSTRACT

This chapter explores theories of learning and creativity that fit well with the rationale for an arts-based integrated curriculum in schools. The author seeks to show how one elementary school, the site of an ongoing research project, nurtures the creative process, develops creative productivity, and provides an environment conducive to the creative press. The purpose of this work is to offer a real-world exemplar of an alternative, arts-based approach to schooling.

Theoretical Underpinnings of Arts-Based Education

Arts-based education offers an alternative to the technical approach to learning that has been historically implemented by the public school system in the United States. Technical rationalism, which has been the prevailing U.S. educational practice since the 1800s, is based on scientific theory. It stems from the nineteenth-century philosophy of positivism, which led to a social move-

126

ment "aimed at applying the achievements of science and technology to the well-being of mankind" (Schön, 1983, p. 31). It is concerned with assessment, measurable outcomes, and external control (Eisner, 2001; Standaert, 1993). In the classroom, this traditional approach manifests itself by what educational philosopher Paulo Freire (1970) has called the "banking model" of teaching. This model views the learner as a receptacle and the teacher as an information depositor. Instruction is teacher centered with passive student involvement. In contrast, arts education and developing the creative spirit is an active learning approach supporting Freire's (1970) notions of the teacher-as-student and the student-as-teacher, with both parties seeking out reality together in the form of thematic investigation.

Elliot Eisner (1998a), art educator and curriculum theorist, provides this chapter's rationale for why the arts are so important in education. Eisner holds that the arts should not be used as a means to an end, that is, to increase student test scores or academic achievement. Instead, arts should be studied for their own sake and for the contributions art makes to human's lives. He states, "We do the arts no service when we try to make their case by touting their contributions to other fields" (Eisner, 1998a, p. 15). Eisner's four outcomes of the arts in education are as follows:

1. Students should acquire a feel for what it means to transform their ideas, images, and feelings into an art form;
2. Arts Education should refine the student's awareness of the aesthetic qualities in art and life;
3. Arts Education should enable students to understand that there is a connection between the content and form that the arts display and the culture and time in which the work was created.
4. An arts-based education produces the following dispositional outcomes:
   a. A willingness to imagine possibilities that are not now, but will become;
   b. A desire to explore ambiguity, to be willing to forestall premature closure in pursuing resolutions;
   c. The ability to recognize and accept the multiple perspectives and resolutions that work in the arts celebrate (pp. 13-15).

Three educational philosophies and literature on the four *p*'s of creativity (press, process, personality, and product) support Eisner's rationale for arts-based education as an organic, exploratory method for discovery learning and creative thinking and teaching—sadly, the converse of the type of learning environment that can be found frequently in public school settings due to the current focus on high-stakes testing.

Arts-Based Education:
Learning Theories and Creativity

DEWEY AND THE CREATIVE PRESS

Progressivism is the first educational philosophy that fits well with the concept of using an arts-based curriculum to develop creativity. This educational movement occurred in the late nineteenth and early twentieth century and was primarily concerned with the notion of the child-centered school. One of the primary leaders of this movement was John Dewey. Dewey (1938) was concerned with the notion of experiential learning. He believed that humans learn from their experiences and from interacting with their environment. He held that schools should focus on the interests of the learner. His theory explains unwanted student behavior as individuals reacting to a uniform, restrictive environment because "enforced quiet and acquiescence prevent pupils from disclosing their true natures" (p. 62). Participants must, then, be involved in forming the purposes that direct learning (p. 67). Studies must be connected to the everyday life of the learner. Not only will this enrich the quality of the learning experience, but it will also lessen the tendency of the individual to act out against the learning environment. Engaged learners will not feel the need to engage in off-task behavior.

According to Dewey (1938), schools are social settings in which all participants work together in a democratic community; subject matter cannot be learned in isolation; experiences can be "educative" and "mis-educative," and education is an "experiential continuum" (p. 28). Experiences build on one another; educative experiences, therefore, should lead to growth. Dewey (1938) believed that the *quality* of these experiences is pivotal to learning.

Thus, the learning environment, or what creative theorists call the Creative Press (Davis, 2000), must be one that supports, stimulates, and encourages learners in their pursuit of knowledge. With regard to creativity development and the school setting, Sidney Parnes (1965) and Ellis Torrance (1966) have echoed Dewey's (1938) caution against the repressive nature of educational environments, which, subsequently, represses creative growth. One of the suppositions in Parnes's (1965) theorizing is that "the individual's creative ability is frequently so repressed by his education and experiences that he cannot even recognize his full potential, let alone realize it." He indicates that education and educators should provide a creative climate and "help develop the attitudes and abilities that will enable students to meet any future problems creatively and inventively" (Parnes, 1965, p. 92).

Torrance (1966) examines the power of cultural influences in the nurture of creative development. He postulates that how creative abilities develop and function is "strongly influenced by the way the environment responds to a person's curiosity and needs" (p. 168). Torrance (1966) offered the following criticisms of the public education system in the United States in regard to stifling the creative process. His criticisms highlight five current educational practices (italics added) and the consequences of each practice. Those damaging practices are as follows: (1) *Success orientation*, where schools prepare only for success, "is detrimental to creative growth because creative learning involves experimenting, taking risks, making mistakes, and correcting them" (p. 169). Children should be given safe environments in which to experiment, without the added stress of the fear of failure. (2) *Peer orientation* relates to a culture in which students are more concerned about what their classmates think about them above all else, including parents, teachers, and other authority figures (p. 169). Peer pressure contributes to the suppression of creativity as "original ideas are common targets of pressures to conform." (p. 169). Some kids are so concerned about "fitting in" that they "give up all efforts to learn and to think" (p. 170). (3) *Sanctions against questioning and exploring* provides a climate where children learn to be afraid of asking questions, which is necessary for inquiry and excitement in the learning process (p. 170). (4) *Misplaced emphasis on sex roles* allows for the stereotyping of gender traits and behavior, such as promoting sensitivity and receptiveness in girls while praising and encouraging independence in boys. Torrance (1966) forewarned, "Creativity, by its very nature, requires both sensitivity and independent thinking" (p. 170). And (5) *divergency equated with abnormality* thinking equates "genius" with "madness" (p. 170). Teachers should not discount the child or adult who diverges from behavioral norms and look for signs of creative potential. Torrance's (1966, 1993) work strongly suggests that the current educational climate of the No Child Left Behind Act (2001) is not conducive to stimulating and nurturing creative thought. By way of contrast, an arts-based education can provide quality experiences that can nurture an individual's growth, promote learning, and enhance creativity.

PIAGET AND BRUNER AND THE CREATIVE PROCESS

Constructivism is the second learning theory upon which a creative, arts education is based. Constructivists hold that learning is an active process (Oliva, 2005). The teacher acts as a facilitator for learning, instead of as a depositor of information. According to the constructivist view, humans construct their own reality. In an educational setting, therefore, constructivists would say that learning material out of context from that reality lessens its meaning. Learners must have a vested interest in the material that they are studying. Learning through the arts addresses the individual's need for personal relevance in the curriculum.

Jean Piaget is one of several prominent constructivist learning theorists. A developmental psychologist, Piaget's (1952) hierarchical stages of learning show how intelligence increases at varying levels as humans interact with their environment. He postulated that thinking develops and enables people to learn meaningfully. Piaget believes that humans are intrinsically motivated. In a school setting, children must have a sense of competence when learning new tasks in order to achieve success. Cultivating student accomplishment is an innate function of an arts-infused curriculum and imperative for the development of creativity.

Jerome Bruner, a leading U.S. educational theorist, believes that humans can learn anything as long as the materials are organized appropriately (Eisner, 1998b). Bruner's (1966) theory of child development holds that that there are three modes of representation, or stages that children progress through as they learn. The first stage is enactive representation. This is an action stage when children learn by doing. The second stage is iconic representation, an image stage. During this stage, children begin to record their experiences visually (drawing, etc.). The third, and most advanced stage, is symbolic representation. Students at this level are able to use symbols to represent something (i.e., c-a-t = cat). Learning written language occurs during this stage. Bruner adds to constructivist theory his two "forms of knowing": the *paradigmatic* and the *narrative*, the latter fitting in with the constructivist position. The paradigmatic form represents the traditional, scientifically based approach to learning, which "seeks precision through the singular . . . tries to achieve what is definite and does this through denotation. It cherishes certainty, it embraces causality, and it defines meaning in terms of verification" (Eisner, 1998b, p. 12). The narrative form of knowing, on the other hand, resonates with the justification given for arts-based learning. This form "prizes the metaphorical, emphasizes connotation, exploits ambiguity to convey meanings that are suggested by it, and speaks of intention of purpose or agency rather than cause. What narrative provides is believability or "truth-likeness," rather than *truth* in a verified *scientific* sense" (Eisner, 1998b, p. 11). It is this sense of narrative that constructivists hold dear—the notions that human beings construct their own reality and interpret it according to their unfolding experiences and truths. The core of an arts-based curriculum is the idea that learners must deal with the context in which they live, and from within that context, learning occurs.

It is easy to see how Bruner's (1966) three stages of learning and the Piagetian idea about cultivating a sense of competence fit in nicely with the notion of the creative process. They occur in a natural progression when learning, just as creativity does. Graham Wallas (1926, as cited in Balkin, 1990, and Davis, 2000) outlines four phases in the creative process that mesh nicely with the philosophy of constructivism and developmental psychology. The first step is *preparation.* This involves thinking about the problem and gathering the materials and information needed to perform the task or solve the problem. The second step is *incubation*. Creative thoughts and ideas need time to develop and grow. Letting the unconscious mind have this time to simmer is an important part of the creative process. The third step is *illumination*, or the "aha!" or "eureka" moment. Suddenly, all the parts come together to form a new whole. There is a feeling of excitement with this phase. The fourth, and final, step is *verification*. Here, the learner-explorer double-checks his or her work to test the validity of the theory or product.

It is interesting to note that, while many differing theories about the creative process exist, several center on a series of steps or stages to be completed, and most of these stages are nonlinear in nature. It is also important to point out that by presenting the development of creativity as a process, room is left for making mistakes and returning to a previous step in the process to correct an error. Allowing room for failure helps develop a sense of competence and self-confidence in the individual. Public schools are often too centered on the end product, and make little allowances for the process, or journey, that led to that product. A failed product does not always mean that the process was flawed. In fact, failed products may be important steps on the road to discovery.

MASLOW AND THE CREATIVE PERSONALITY

The third educational philosophy that mirrors the goals for arts-based education and the development of creativity is humanism. Humanists contend that human experience is contextual. An individual's behavior is determined by his or her perceptions of self. Humanism values individual growth and enlightenment. This approach to learning is to develop the innate potential of every person. Abraham Maslow (1968), a major figure in humanist theory, developed a hierarchy of needs that is applicable to all human beings. One of the goals, if not the goal, of education is to help individuals reach Maslow's highest stage, self-actualization. At this stage, a person has reached his or her greatest potential.

Gary Davis (2000) holds that there are particular characteristics and traits of creativity. He presents the creative individual as one who is self-actualized: "a fully-functioning, mentally healthy, forward-growing human being who is using his or her talents to become what he or she is capable of becoming" (p. 54). His premise suggests that people are born with creative traits that can be nurtured.

Robert Sternberg and Todd Lubart (1993) believe that individuals share certain personality attributes, which can be nurtured in the school setting. These attributes are as follows:

- Tolerance of ambiguity
- Willingness to surmount obstacles and persevere

- Willingness to grow
- Sensible risk-taking
- Belief in oneself (Sternberg & Lubart, 1993, p. 230)

Alfred Balkin's (1990) personal definition states that creative people see connections; do something; and make a contribution to society. A creative person thinks metaphorically (Davis, 2000) and makes connections between ideas (Davis, 2000; Michalko, 2001). A person cannot fully reach his or her creative potential unless he or she has the tools to become self-actualized. This applies to the school setting in that students' individuality must be allowed to flourish in order to realize their creative potential. Teachers and administrators must recognize the creative, individual character traits of their students and educate them accordingly.

Research Study: Narrative Inquiry

As a researcher, I am aware that many who study schools have not taught in the classroom; much of their experience is derived from readings and observations; and "they are spectators, not insiders" (Atkin, 1994, p. 107). My personal teaching experience has been thirteen years at the community college level, with one year of teaching grades 7–12 in a private school before that. Despite differences in educational context, I empathize with the public school teacher who has had his or her classroom invaded by those using predetermined theoretical frameworks to make sense of teachers' realities. I keep this in mind whenever I am in a school setting. My mantra is that I am a "participant observer," there to not make judgments but rather present alongside the teacher as a learner myself. It is with this sensitivity that I approached my work with an arts-based elementary school, Armstrong Academy, in the fourth largest urban center in the United States.

The nature of my research is qualitative, with narrative inquiry (i.e., Clandinin & Connelly, 1994; Conle, 2000; Craig, 2004) being my preferred methodology. Narrative inquiry is both a method and a form (Clandinin & Connelly, 1994; Pinnegar & Daynes, 2007); it involves "rigorous inquiry into personal and collective human experience and underlying school and societal conditions" (Craig, 2004, p. 1241). It is open-ended and seeks to collect stories of personal experience, shape those stories, and retell them in order to understand people and events (Clandinin & Connelly, 1994; Conle, 2000).

The tasks for restorying a narrative inquiry are threefold, with the researcher primarily using three interpretative tools to make sense of experiences refined within context. First, the inquirer seeks to *broaden* the event (research milieu) by widening the situation and placing it within a broader context. Second, the narrative researcher concentrates on a specific event in a stage called *burrowing*, that is, focusing on the event's "emotional, moral, and aesthetic qualities" in order to ask "why the event is associated with these feelings and what their origins might be" (Connelly & Clandinin, 1990, p. 11). Finally, the third tool requires the researcher to *restory* the event by returning "to present and future considerations and ask[ing] what the meaning of the event is and how he or she might create a new story of self which changes the meaning of the event, its description, and its significance for the larger life story the person is trying to live" (Connelly & Clandinin, 1990, p. 11).

My study employs all three of these interpretative tasks, beginning with my placing of a single elementary school's arts-based curriculum within the broader landscape of No Child Left Behind; then focusing in on the particular school context as an exemplar of arts-based teaching and learning; and, finally, restorying the experiences of the teachers and students in order to create new meanings. My rationale for using narrative inquiry for this research study is that examining the personal stories of teachers and students regarding their own creative processes provides vivid exemplars of how one school has nurtured creative teaching and learning through its arts-based program that can be shared with others.

RESEARCH QUESTIONS

While narrative inquirers do not typically specify research questions, I explored the following themes as the Armstrong Academy teachers shared their experiences of their school's arts-infused program and told stories about some of the students they teach:

- Building student and teacher voice and identity
- Teacher as learner-artist
- Student as teacher-artist
- Learning *in* the arts vs. learning *through* the arts
- Arts and the "core academic subjects": math, language arts, science, and history
- Cross-disciplinary relationships
- Working with the arts partners

In this chapter, I focus on Armstrong Academy's approach to creativity and how that approach adheres to a philosophy of creativity, which is universal, active, qualitative, and developmental. I seek to show that Armstrong Academy nurtures the creative process and personalities of its students and teachers, develops creative productivity, and provides an environment conducive to the creative press.

Research Site: Arts-Based Exemplar

In the spring of 2008, I was part of a team who endeavored to create digital story as an exemplar of arts-based teaching and learning that could communicate to others what those at Armstrong Academy had learned. While my research in this school site is ongoing, the field texts (data) I gathered during my initial visits were collected mainly by sitting in the back of the art teacher's classroom listening to round-table discussions between teachers of different grade levels (sometimes whole teams) regarding their personal practices of arts-based education. The topic of these group interviews was arts-based learning and how the teachers' lives had been affected by enacting an arts-infused curriculum and how their students' lives were subsequently affected by this immersion in the arts. I kept a journal of these conversations with the first-, third-, and fourth-grade teams, which occurred on three days over a period of six weeks in April and May 2008. In addition, I was the primary photographer on this project, and it is the pictures from the students at the elementary school that truly illustrate the transformative power of an arts-based learning environment.

BACKGROUND OF RESEARCH SITE

Armstrong Academy—a school pseudonym—is a Title I urban elementary school. Students are 48 percent, African American; 46 percent, Hispanic; 4 percent, Asian; and 2 percent, white. Eighty-one percent of students receive a free or reduced lunch. The mobility rate of students is very high, around 70–80 percent, oftentimes with a turnover of almost entire grade levels of students from one year to the next (personal communication, March 1, 2008). This is not the typical setting for what, in my opinion, is one of the most promising public elementary schools that I have ever encountered, especially under the No Child Left Behind Act (2001). The three educational pillars of the campus are as follows: it is an International Baccalaureate School with a global curricular focus; it has a schoolwide arts-infused curriculum—visual, dramatic, and musical arts are integrated with the core academic subjects; and it encompasses a balanced literacy program (reading, writing, and word study workshops). In addition, the school works collaboratively with three city-based arts partners: the Museum of Fine Arts, the Alley Theater, and Writers in the Schools. These creative partners provide numerous opportunities to educate students in the arts within and outside of their school setting. In the initial three-month period that I observed in the school, I felt an overwhelming sense of awe at the astounding journeys and accomplishments of both the students and teachers alike as they embraced and excelled within an arts-based curriculum.

PHILOSOPHY

The teachers, administration, and staff are staunch believers in fostering an interdisciplinary approach that is heavily laden with the arts. They, like Joseph Schwab (1983), believe that the teacher is at the forefront of the curriculum-making process. Therefore, before the students are exposed to the arts in the classroom, the teachers must complete an "arts boot-camp," in their words, before the school year begins. The purpose of focusing intensely on arts-based instruction is to throw teachers into their own art learning and creative process. Those leading the charge believe strongly that teacher learners, just like their student counterparts, must be allowed to experiment in a safe environment. This echoes the Deweyan and Piagetian beliefs that it is imperative that students have a sense of self-competence when approaching new tasks, regardless of their age. This gives the teachers the experience of the creative process (of art making) that their students, in turn, will go through. It builds a sense of empathy and understanding and shared experience. I believe that this is a primary reason the teachers are so successful in eliciting creative work from their students.

THE ARMSTRONG ACADEMY TEACHERS

The pivotal team members are the art teacher, Bernadette Lohle, and the music teacher, Craig Richardson. Bernadette is a self-described reluctant learner with behavioral problems who grew up on the East Coast of the United States. She has an arts-based background, which was, for her, the key to understanding her world. She started out as a high school art teacher but left to teach elementary school as a challenge. Since then, she has taught all grades from pre-K through twelfth. The art on the walls in Bernadette's art classroom contains her own creative endeavors as well as those of her students. Bernadette views herself first as an artist and then as a teacher.

Craig also hailed from upstate New York, the son of two teachers. He has played the piano since the age of five. When he was fourteen, Craig toured professionally in the summer and then joined a Dixieland band as a saxophone player. He said he led two lives at that time, high school and the band. He taught high school band for a Jesuit boys school after graduating from college with a

music teaching degree. He had negative experiences with the students not practicing, so, disheartened by that experience, he moved to the elementary school
level where for the next eight years he taught interdisciplinary studies without
truly knowing what that was. In his master's program, Craig and another class-
mate basically created a degree in interdisciplinary studies. It was while he was in
this program that he snuck into an African drumming class and, noticed by the
professor, who saw him sitting in the balcony, was invited to sit in with the class.
Craig was in the process of developing a music curriculum for special education
students at the time, and this was the spark he needed to develop the program,
which ended up being his thesis. The next year he moved to Texas and started
teaching at Armstrong Academy. Motivated to use world music in his teaching
by his experiences in graduate school, Craig created a drum corps at Armstrong
Academy.

DRUM CORPS

Part of the music program at Armstrong Academy consists of a drum corps. The
drum corps is made up of third- and fourth-grade students who are invited to
audition based on their grades and behavior. During one year, Craig was sitting
in on a faculty meeting where the teachers were discussing a fourth-grade student. The teachers were talking about how the student was shutting down both
emotionally and academically with regards to reading and writing. Not having
seen such behavior from this student in his music class, Craig spoke about her
character and performance and, more specifically, how she was one of his elite
drum corps members, a natural leader. Being aware that children respond to
contextual situations, both teachers agreed to speak with this student to let her
know how much her efforts in drum corps were being noticed and appreciated.
Using the drum corp as an authentic, positive reinforcement tool, the student
spent more time working on her reading. True to theories of learning and creativity, this student showed more enthusiasm in drum corps and took a stronger leadership role, and, in addition, her attitude and academic performance
improved considerably in her grade-level teacher's class. As her concept of self
improved through her creative outlet in drum corps, so did her academic work.
On this point, all of her teachers—including her administrators—agree.

CONTEXTUAL ASSIGNMENTS

Student art is prominently displayed on every wall in every hallway at Armstrong
Academy. I especially observed assignments directly related to the children's

lives. For example, the kindergarten class created their own self-portraits after multiple art lessons on color and color layering (skin tones), lines (grass, bushes, trees), texture (roads, hair), and geometric shapes found in nature (trees, clouds). See figure 7.1.

Another social studies project assigned students to research an issue related to their neighborhood. Students created multimedia projects that included poster-board art, skits, a SMART Board presentation, and written research papers. Topics from this assignment ranged from "Living without Drugs" to "Child Abuse" to "Homelessness in America." This was a fourth-grade project (see figure 7.2). While principals in other area school may have shied away from controversial topics such as these, the principal and teachers of this school are aware of the daily reality of their students' lives and trust their students to choose topics that are meaningful to them, in true constructivist fashion.

Finally, Armstrong Academy students are given plenty of opportunities to showcase their success. Student art work is not only displayed in the school's hallways, but also, each year, the third-grade students are invited to create a work of art that is displayed in an exhibition at the Museum of Fine Arts (see figure 7.3). The lower grades look forward to the year when their art will be displayed at the museum. In the meantime, each year, Armstrong Academy holds its own

Figure 7.1.   Hallway display: "Kindergarten Self-Portraits"

Figure 7.2.   Fourth-grade project: "Stranger Danger"

schoolwide arts exhibition that is open to the families of the children. During this celebration of creativity, students showcase a piece of art of which they are particularly proud, and they teach the concept behind the piece (the art the children create is related to a curricular theme) to a mixed audience of parents, teachers, community members, and their peers (see figure 7.4).

Figure 7.3.   Third-grade Museum of Fine Arts exhibit

Together, Bernadette and Craig, with the full support of their principal and fellow educators, have helped create a school context where both teacher and student creativity flourish. The following images are samples of student work from this most remarkable school. Following the student work, I have included several quotes elicited from the teachers regarding their work at the arts-based campus. I feel these speak more for themselves than any commentary I could make about them.

TEACHER REFLECTIONS

Taken from the end-of the-year (spring 2008) portfolios teachers assemble as visual representations of the work they do, here is what Armstrong Academy teachers had to say about teaching in an arts-based school:

A bilingual first-grade teacher wrote,

> It has been a really great experience teaching through the arts. I learned that art makes teaching more interesting . . . and students enjoy the learning activities. My goal for next year is to participate in more art workshops which will give me more techniques to apply

Figure 7.4.   Student sharing work at the Spring 2008 Armstrong Academy Exhibition

in my lessons. . . . I thought that I would never be an art person; I
started to change that opinion of me.

Another teacher remarked,

> I have enjoyed incorporating art in several subject areas. It has truly
> enhanced my students' learning. I look forward to using art as a way
> of teaching in all subject areas next year. I would like to work more
> closely with the art teacher. I would also like to collaborate more with
> others on my grade level team to get their ideas. We seem to be more
> creative when we plan together.

Yet another stated, "Next year I really do want to incorporate more art into
my lessons. I believe one way to achieve this is to plan with other teachers in
order to combine creative ideas as well as work closely with the art teacher. . . . I
firmly believe that including more art means increasing learning."

Finally, an additional Armstrong Academy educator observed, "The students really enjoy the hands-on approach to learning. Also, collaborating with
the team to do more art infusion could help us as educators to step out of our
normal comfort zone." What these Armstrong teachers have shared about their
experiences teaching within an arts-based curriculum certainly reflects the literature on learning and creativity and bodes well for the further creation of schools
with similar arts-based approaches to teaching, learning, and curriculum.

Arts-Based Education: Some Thoughts

If learners are allowed to learn within the context of their daily lives and are
facilitated by educators who are aware of the developmental stages of learning,
this will enable learners to learn within a safe and supportive environment that
adapts to their needs instead of feeling forced to adapt to the learning environment, which is how the current system of education works. Fostering a creative,
nurturing learning environment is at the core of an arts-based approach to
schooling. Arts-based learning programs create learning conditions conducive
to making progress through Maslow's hierarchy of needs in order to reach the
highest stage of self-actualization.

Arts-based education innately follows the tenets of the learning theories of
developmental constructivism, humanism, and creativity. It is particularly suited
to providing experiential, meaningfully relevant, safe learning experiences that
help develop an individual's positive concept of self. It offers an alternative to
the positivistic approach to education that has become even more stifling under the oppressive school atmosphere prompted by the No Child Left Behind

Act (2001). An arts-based approach to education includes the narrative way of knowing in the public school system and supports the creative growth of the whole individual.

Reflections

Imagine the myriad of school setting encounters children experience throughout their lives as they progress through the education system, be it public or private. How important it is that the memories they create be positive ones—that the interactions they have with their teachers are constructive and confirming. The art-filled hallways of Armstrong Academy are a testament to the hard work of all who have invested their passions and energies in creating such a learning environment. It's stirring—an entire school of self-confident children who know they are good at *something* and are not afraid to take risks or share themselves with outsiders. The same applies to the teachers. What a difference it makes for educators to know that their voices are heard—to know that they have the support not only from their administrators but also from each other, the parents, and the community. Armstrong Academy gives me hope—hope that someday every child in the U.S. public school system can have an enriching, nurturing learning environment with the arts at the curricular core. It takes work to build such a program, but once built, it is easily maintained by those who have the vision to see that no child is ever left behind.

References

Atkin, J. M. (1994). Teacher research to change policy. In S. Hollingsworth & H. Hockett (Eds.), *Teacher research and educational reform, 93rd yearbook of the national society for the study of education, Part I* (pp. 103–120). Chicago: University of Chicago Press.

Balkin, A. (1990). What is creativity? And what is it not? *Music Educators Journal, 76*(9), 29–32.

Bruner, J. S. (1966). *Toward a theory of instruction.* Cambridge, MA: Belknap Press.

Clandinin, D. J., & Connelly, M. F. (1994). Personal experience methods. In N. K. Denzin & Y. S. Lincoln (Eds.), *Handbook of qualitative research* (pp. 413–427). Thousand Oaks, CA: Sage.

Conle, C. (2000). Narrative inquiry: Research tool and medium for professional development. *European Journal of Teacher Education, 23*(1), 49–63.

Connelly, M. F., & Clandinin, J. D. (1990). Stories of experience and narrative inquiry. *Educational Researcher, 19*(5), 2–14.

Craig, C. J. (2004). The dragon in school backyards: The influence of mandated testing on school contexts and educators' narrative knowing. *Teachers College Record, 106*(6), 1229–1257.

Davis, G. A. (2000). *Creativity is forever* (4th ed.). Dubuque, IA: Kendall/Hunt Publishing.

Dewey, J. (1938). *Experience and education.* New York: Touchstone.

Eisner, E. (1998a). Does experience in the arts boost academic achievement? *Art Education, 51*(1), 7–15.

Eisner, E. (1998b). *The kind of schools we need.* Portsmouth, NH: Heinemann.

Eisner, E. (2001). What does it mean to say a school is doing well? *Phi Delta Kappan, 5,* 367–372.

Freire, P. (1970). *Pedagogy of the oppressed, 30th anniversary edition.* New York: Continuum International Publishing Group.

Maslow, A. H. (1968). *Toward a psychology of being* (3rd ed.). New York: John Wiley and Sons.

Michalko, M. (2001). *Cracking creativity: The secrets of creative genius.* Berkeley, CA: Ten Speed Press.

Oliva, P. F. (2005). *Developing the curriculum* (6th ed.). Boston: Pearson Education.

Parnes, S. J. (1965). The nurture of creative talent. *Music Educators Journal, 51*(6), 32–33, 92–95.

Piaget, J. (1952). *Origins of intelligence in children.* New York: International Universities Press.

Pinnegar, S., & Daynes, G. J. (2007). Locating narrative inquiry historically: Thematics in the turn to narrative. In D. J. Clandinin (Ed.), *Handbook of narrative inquiry: Mapping a methodology* (pp. 3–34). Thousand Oaks, CA: Sage.

Schön, D. (1983). *The reflective practitioner: How professionals think in action.* New York: Basic Books.

Schwab, J. (1983). The practical 4: Something for the curriculum professors to do. *Curriculum Inquiry, 13*(3), 239–265.

Standaert, R. (1993). Technical rationality in education management: A survey covering England, France, and Germany. *European Journal of Education, 28*(2), 159–175.

Sternberg, R. J., & Lubart, T. I. (1993). Investing in creativity. *Psychological Inquiry, 4*(3), 229–232.

Torrance, E. P. (1966). Nurture of creative talents. *Theory into Practice, 5*(4), 168–202.

Torrance, E. P. (1993). Understanding creativity: Where to start? *Psychological Inquiry, 4*(3), 232–234.

U.S. Department of Education, Office of Elementary and Secondary Education. (2002). *No Child Left Behind: A desktop reference.* Washington, DC: Author.

CHAPTER 8

Labyrinths for Creativity and Peace in Schools

Sandra Wasko-Flood
Living Labyrinths for Peace, Inc.

Sandra J. Wasko-Flood received her B.A. from UCLA with a major in English and a minor in art and currently works as an artist and a teacher. She is the founder and president of Living Labyrinths for Peace, Inc., where she creates interactive labyrinths that combine art, science, technology, and nature to lead the way from inner peace to world peace. She conducts labyrinth workshops in schools, consults on new labyrinth construction, and organizes events that spotlight labyrinths as sacred spaces. Wasko-Flood lives half of the year in Baltimore and the other half in Angel Fire, New Mexico.

ABSTRACT

Labyrinth-walking programs in the D.C. metropolitan area encourage students to express creativity and peace. These labyrinth activities produce physical, psychological, and spiritual benefits. By touching each of the learning modes or intelligences posited by Howard Gardner in his theory of multiple intelligences, the labyrinth can function as a quintessential, cross-cultural symbol with potential contributions to every discipline. Labyrinths can unite all ages and races, disciplines, institutions, and cultures for peace. Creativity is stimulated through a model that emphasizes love and freedom. Knowing themselves, students can express peace wishes not only for themselves but also for their family, friends, community, and the world.

What Is a Labyrinth?

Unlike mazes with their false paths and dead ends, labyrinths have a single path that leads to the center and back (Conty, 2002; Kern, 1982/1995; Lonegren, 1996). Many people find that walking a labyrinth slows the breathing,

Figure 8.1.   "Rainbow Labyrinth of Peace"

focuses the mind, and induces a peaceful state of being (Artress, 1995; Curry, 2000; Geoffrion, 2000, 2003). In use for more than four thousand years and found in most cultures, labyrinths today are enjoying a renaissance (Lonegren, 1996; Saward, 2002; Westbury, 2001). These walkable designs can be found in churches and retreat centers, schools (see figure 8.1) and hospitals, museums and arts centers, prisons, and backyards—even the backyard of the U.S. Capitol in Washington, D.C., where in 2000, I directed a labyrinth-walking demonstration for the Labyrinth Society, an international support organization for all who create, maintain, and enjoy labyrinths.

Labyrinths have physical, psychological, and spiritual benefits (See the Labyrinth Society website at www.labyrinthsociety.org/). Physically, current research shows that a labyrinth walk can lower the blood pressure and slow the breathing. Research is under way on potential advantages for people with such ailments as dyslexia, Parkinson's disease, and autism. Psychologically, labyrinths help people process grief, make decisions, and resolve conflicts. In the conflict resolution labyrinth designed by Connie Fenty (1997), for example, each turn of the classical seven-circuit labyrinth represents a step of the conflict resolution model. Spiritually, many people find that walking a labyrinth is a fitting metaphor for the inner journey and that it expands their connection to something greater than themselves. Many have felt strong relationships with nature, with those who have died or whatever higher power in which they believe. Often, people, including children (Rosetta, 2002), express feelings of coming home to the center of themselves or the universe. One student wrote, "It [the labyrinth] told me what to do. It told me what to be."

Labyrinth Workshops in Schools

Since 2000, with grant funding and other support from the D.C. Commission on the Arts; the Washington Performing Arts Society, a program of the Kennedy Center; the Baltimore Office on Promotion in the Arts; and LLP, it has been my professional joy as a teaching artist (see *Teaching Artists Journal*) to collaborate with teachers, students, parents, and counselors on one-day and four-week artist residency programs at more than fifty schools in the Washington-Baltimore metropolitan area. Most of these workshops have taken place in the upper elementary grades (grades 3–6) and in middle schools (grades 7–9) with ethnically diverse populations, primarily African Americans and Hispanics.

The one-day workshops last three hours, while the residencies include three hours of program time per week. An initial meeting with the classroom teacher emphasizes our equality in collaboration concerning goals, classroom ethics, and the compatibility of teaching styles. My style features a loose, relaxed structure that stimulates creativity—self-discovery of the artist within. Students learn to work on any "mistake" to resolve it with their mind and heart. Having made a "mistake" myself in drawing the classic seven-circuit labyrinth (see Fenty, 1997) on the playground, one sixth-grade girl had the courage (heart) to turn the wavy line at the center into a heart. Now there exists a new seven-circuit design with a heart at the center.

Students learn the history and geography of the labyrinth and then create labyrinth books, where they pattern photocopied labyrinth designs in many media and write their labyrinth walk intentions and experiences. They enjoy my "Rainbow Labyrinth of Peace," a painted canvas that I bring to each school, and make their own guidelines for safe walking. Together, they paint permanent canvas or playground labyrinths, which they name and dedicate to their school. By making peace wishes for themselves, family, friends, community, and the world, they turn their labyrinth walks into walks for peace (see figure 8.2).

Connecting Peace and Creativity

Creativity and peace are intimately related: the student who discovers his or her creativity is more likely to find peace. If one discovers creativity is one's domi-

Figure 8.2. "Feet of Peace Labyrinth"

nant intelligence, one is more likely to find peace in activities or jobs that use this dominant intelligence. The one who discovers the inner peace that can lead to world peace also comes to know her or his creative self. Labyrinths use the forms of the circle and spiral, which are found everywhere in the universe, from our DNA to the galaxies. I believe that the universe evolves through a creative force that uses these major patterns and that there is a force for peace that strives for balance and unites such opposites as male and female, love and fear, and darkness and light.

So how does one stimulate creativity and peace in students? I begin with the idea that all people, as part of a universe that is evolving toward creativity and peace, are innately creative and peaceful. Adults and children in all religions, institutions, and cultures deserve equal rights and equal respect. I believe creativity and peace require love and freedom to blossom. A guiding love nurtures confidence, and freedom is necessary to discover oneself.

As loving guides, teachers can stimulate their students to find creativity and peace in themselves and others by communicating in ways appropriate for the students' modes of learning. Because learning is reciprocal (everyone learns from everyone else) and democratic (everyone has something to teach and something to learn), teachers need to balance their dominant mode of learning with their less dominant, while encouraging their students to do the same.

Impact of Multiple Intelligences Theory on Creativity

In a recent Washington Performing Arts Society professional development seminar, a group of teaching artists became familiar with Howard Gardner's theory of multiple intelligences (Gardner, 1983, 1993, 2000) and its practical applications in education. Rather than limit the idea of intelligence to something that can be measured with a traditional IQ test, Gardner suggests eight dimensions of human potential:

- Verbal-linguistic
- Logical-mathematical
- Spatial
- Bodily-kinesthetic
- Musical
- Naturalist
- Intrapersonal
- Interpersonal

We artists explored these with activities to determine our own dominant and less dominant intelligences and studied ways to incorporate the eight intelligences in our classroom work. It may seem obvious that, to stimulate creativity, one ideally appeals to the person's dominant intelligence. Less apparent is that developing the other intelligences can greatly assist with creative problem solving. As a practical matter, artists can collaborate with teachers who have complementary intelligences to enhance the creative classroom experience. Students also can act as guides to other students. For example, a math-dominant student may swap tutoring roles with an art-dominant one.

The Labyrinth as an Interdisciplinary Tool

A key reason to bring the labyrinth into the school environment is that it relates extraordinarily well to all traditional subject areas and to each of the eight intelligences. In drawing the labyrinth, one uses logical-math skills, whether the design expands from a seed pattern or takes shape using measured circumferences and diameters. In painting the labyrinth, spatial and interpersonal skills take precedence. Following the labyrinth path opens the door to design, visual, musical, and kinesthetic forms of learning. In making peace wishes for oneself, walking alone, and experiencing oneself at the center, students and teachers use the intrapersonal mode. In painting the labyrinth as a group, walking the labyrinth with others, and making peace wishes for family, friends, community, and the world, the interpersonal mode comes to the forefront.

To address the naturalist mode, a labyrinth walk can be considered a three-stage journey of life, death or transformation, and rebirth or reintegration, similar to the cycle followed by nature. In the first stage, one walks the path of life with an intention or goal in mind. In the second stage, one releases or "dies" to the old self and experiences transformation or change in the center of the labyrinth as one opens heart and mind to the potential realization of that goal. Finally, the transformed self returns to the world, following the same path, but in the opposite direction.

For each of the eight intelligences, the sections below relate them to the corresponding subject disciplines and highlight selected labyrinth-related activities.

VERBAL-LINGUISTIC

Subject: Language Arts

Oral Activities

- Hold up a classical seven-circuit finger labyrinth and say, "Thumbs up for those who think this is a labyrinth, and thumbs down for those who think it is a maze."
- Display posters of labyrinth designs from around the world with dates and ask, "How many of you think labyrinths are older than your parents? Raise your hands. Older than one hundred years? five hundred years? one thousand years? four thousand years?"
- After giving basic instruction on how to walk to the center of the labyrinth and back, have students walk in groups of about five people. Afterward, ask them to formulate their own "Guidelines for Peaceful Walking" that express positive qualities (e.g., "walk slowly" instead of "don't run").
- After the first labyrinth walk, ask, "Why have people all over the world walked labyrinths for more than four thousand years? Let me give you a clue. It is to celebrate important things in our lives—things that people celebrate everywhere. What kinds of celebrations can you think of?" Answers will likely include birthdays, weddings, funerals, the New Year, and so forth.
- After presenting a basic diagram of the labyrinth, point to the chart and have students say the corresponding vocabulary word, for example, entrance, path, goal, and circuits.
- Have students name the labyrinth they made for the school by soliciting suggestions and then taking a vote. Names have included "Circle of Life" (grade

6, Fort Hunt Elementary School, Alexandria, Virginia), "Fusion of Confusion" (grades 6–8, Holy Redeemer School, Washington, D.C.), and "Focused Intention" (grades 3–5, Holy Redeemer School, Washington, D.C.).

Written Activities

- Have students write their own intentions for walking the labyrinth—to express a feeling, make a decision, resolve a conflict, or make a wish for peace for themselves, family, friends, community, and the world.
- After walking the labyrinth, have students write about their experience.

For examples, see "Peace Wishes and Creative Responses" below.

LOGICAL-MATHEMATICAL

Subjects: Math, Science, and Technology

- Students learn the proportions of the labyrinth. For example, in considering the relationship between the size of the center to the size of the paths, younger students learn that the larger the center, the smaller the paths, while older students work out the actual math using circumferences and diameters.
- Using posters illustrating "How Old Are Labyrinths?" students read the dates such as 200 CE or 2500 BCE and determine how many years to add or subtract to get the current year.
- Holding their favorite poster images of labyrinths from around the world, students form a human time line from BCE to CE.
- Students learn to draw the classic seven-circuit labyrinth using a "seed pattern."
- Students use Mandala Maker and Music Maker programs on the computer to create designs and music for walking the labyrinth.

SPATIAL

Subjects: Art and Geography

- Holding an example of a classical seven-circuit finger labyrinth, tell students, "Artists use their imaginations. What does this look like? Think of something from nature or part of your body." The answers have ranged from the expected—the brain or tree rings—to the highly imaginative, such as "the waves in a lion's tail."

- Students pattern photocopied labyrinth designs from many eras and cultures, ancient and contemporary, to include in their labyrinth books.
- Invite students to design their own labyrinths, using any form and colors they want.
- Have students construct labyrinths with beads, yarn, and found objects (see figure 8.3).
- Mark a labyrinth path on a canvas labyrinth using students' hand- or footprints or symbols that are special to a particular culture. For example, in a program with the embassy of Ecuador, students used linoleum-cut designs of Inca hands with spirals and dedicated it to the embassy (see figure 8.4).
- If weather permits, create a permanent or temporary labyrinth on the school grounds. Materials have included paint, chalk, and even pine needles.
- Have students respond to each others' art works by placing them on the labyrinth and choosing the piece that has the best concept or most original idea, the best design, the most exciting color, and so on. While holding the piece and standing in the labyrinth center, students explain their choices.

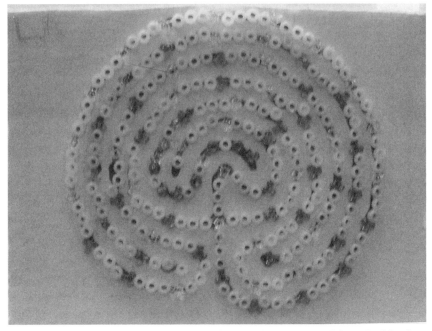

Figure 8.3. Labyrinths constructed with beads, yarn, and found objects

Figure 8.4.   "Hands of Peace Labyrinth"

BODILY-KINESTHETIC

Subjects: Physical Education and Dance

- Students use different movements to walk labyrinths.
- Students "walk" finger labyrinths.
- Students model on their faces how that felt during their first labyrinth walk: happy, confused, bored, crazy, and so forth.
- Conduct self-discovery pantomime games in the labyrinth acting out such questions as "What animal am I?" or "What am I going to be when I grow up?" One child, for example, acts out an animal's movements, and when he gets to the center, the first child who guesses the correct animal goes next.
- In larger outdoor playground labyrinths, do physical education exercises such as running or bouncing a ball through the labyrinth.

MUSICAL

Subject: Music

- Students walk the labyrinth to the sound of a drum beating like a heartbeat. Some students may join in and discover that they are excellent drummers. At

the Phillips Programs School for emotionally disturbed students in Annandale, Virginia, one child came home to himself as he did a beautiful meditative drumming that attracted even the teachers and counselors to walk the labyrinth along with the students.
• Collaborate with a music teacher who can bring other instruments for use during the labyrinth walk, for example, rattles or tambourines.
• Have students do movement in the labyrinth to a CD of meditative music.

NATURALIST

Subjects: Biology and Science

• Give students experience in categorizing labyrinth designs into the three major types—classical, concentric, and Chartres Cathedral.
• When constructing a permanent outdoor labyrinths, help students select materials that enhance the environment, mixing such materials as earth, mulch, rocks, and bricks with plants suitable to the seasons.

INTRAPERSONAL

Subjects: Psychology and Spirituality

• In their art work and writing, students express themselves, the feelings, and the ideas within.
• After blowing a whistle to signal time for a quiet prompt, the teacher says, "With your index finger, spiral in, and point to yourself. Listen to yourself first. What are you thinking about now? Your lunch? Friend? Bring yourself to the present time and task. Then spiral outwards and point to me. Listen to your teacher."
• Students' peace wishes (see Verbal-Linguistic above) may include desires related to classroom value, for example, "I wish to know myself better" (self-knowledge); "I wish to have more self-control" (self-control); and "I wish I were not afraid" (courage).
• Students walk the labyrinth to express a feeling: happiness, sadness, fear, or anger.
• Students experience the threefold path in walking: After making an intention, they follow the inward path while meditating on this life concern. At the center of the labyrinth, they listen with heart and mind to a new way of being. Upon walking out, they reintegrate their experience back into the world.

INTERPERSONAL

Subjects: Social studies, History, Psychology, and Sociology

- Have students develop their own "Guidelines for Peaceful Walking" after walking the labyrinth in a small group. Examples include "When you meet someone else on the path, step aside to let them pass. Walk silently. Keep your hands to yourself."
- When creating a canvas labyrinth, students work in small groups. Tell them that only through community cooperation will the labyrinth exist. For example, if they are not careful, spilling paint over the labyrinth will ruin it, and the school will not have one.
- To pattern the designs in their labyrinth books, have students work in four media groups: one each for watercolors, colored pencils, magic markers, and oil pastels. Within each group, they should share the materials and offer appreciation for the work of their fellow students.
- After students make their peace wishes (see Verbal-Linguistic above), they may want to announce their wishes from the center of the labyrinth, especially those that involve friends, family, community, or the world.

Peace Wishes and Creative Responses

While Gardner accepted eight intelligences, I believe that the ability to find both temporary and more lasting search for peace or spirituality functions as a ninth intelligence and touches all the others (see www.livinglabyrinthsfor peace.org/ website). In using our dominant intelligences and improving our less dominant ones, we discover our creativity. Exercising our creativity, we discover ourselves. When we know ourselves and complete our missions in the world, we become part of a greater cycle. The number 9 in many cultures represents expansion, completion, and incorporation into the larger pattern of the universe.

   Children have an innate desire for peace and creativity and express it vividly in the context of the labyrinth. A student at Holy Redeemer School in Washington, D.C., wrote peace wishes that made the full journey from inner peace to world peace: "I wish that my family will stay very close and never forget anyone. I wish my community was less noisy and violent. I wish I could better myself in school and be less worried. I wish the world was less chaotic. I wish my friends would be who they are." Here are more of the peace wishes and other responses generated by the labyrinth workshops:

FOR MYSELF

- [The labyrinth walk] told me what to do. It told me what to be.
- My peace wish is to stop worrying.
- I was walking because I was mad.
- I walked because I was sad, but I am happy now. I want to walk, because I am happy now.
- It was fun when I walked the labyrinth. As you get closer and closer to the center, it feels like you are going to tip over. I went into the labyrinth so I could find out what I will make for my mom's anniversary. I wish to walk the labyrinth every day.
- When I walked the labyrinth, I felt free and confident. I felt like the world is waiting for me. But when I walked out, I felt like I was ready for the world. To walk a labyrinth, you have to concentrate and focus. When I walked it, I just was daydreaming, and it felt like everybody in the room had disappeared. Like it was only me and the labyrinth.

FOR FAMILY

- My wish was that my uncle and aunt come safe and sound from El Salvador. Now I feel that I do not worry anymore. I feel calm. I really hope my wish comes true.
- My peace wish is for my parents to stop fighting.
- What I wish for my family is that they would be out of danger so no one would have to be killed because they were in some kind of gang.
- Let mommy be happy. Let mommy be happy. Let mommy be happy.
- I wish my father were out of jail.

FOR FRIENDS

- My wish for my friends is that they will be more friendly.
- My peace wish is about my friends. If you have friends who are mean and selfish, do not hang out with them.
- I wish my dog was alive.

FOR COMMUNITY

- My wish for my community is that we can keep it clean.
- I wish that there would be more black presidents, and I would like to campaign to make that happen.

FOR THE WORLD

- I wish that there would be no more earthquakes or floods. I wish that there would be nothing like Katrina again.
- I wish people would be more careful about how they make other people feel. I wish that everyone is careful about how other people would react to when hurt.
- I wish the poor children in the world get a home and anything they wished.
- I wish the war in Iraq would finish soon.

THANK-YOU RESPONSES

- Thank you, Ms. Sandra, for helping us make the labyrinth. If we did not have a labyrinth in our school, we would not have peace. Now we have one and our school is peaceful.
- I want to thank you for coming to Garrison. I really enjoyed you. You let me know what art is really like. It is not just colors to be coloring. It is about loving and feeling art. I had fun learning with you.

During the workshop period when students are asked to design their own labyrinths, I encourage creative confidence by telling them,

> I believe that you are all artists. Just as we all can write or do math, we can draw. Artists generally don't follow a lot of rules that other people give. They draw what's inside of them, what they want to express. Every one of you is different and has something unique to express. The only rules I can give you are:
>
> 1. Do what you feel. Just make it beautiful.
> 2. Don't copy anyone.
> 3. Don't say, "I messed up" and throw it away. Just do that "mistake" again. And that way, you will have a pattern.

The results have been marvelously creative. Many times those who do not excel in academic subjects produce great images. Recently, at a school for emotionally disturbed students, one such shy student made a complicated design with unusual metallic colors. Another with Asperger's syndrome divided her labyrinth into four quadrants representing the four elements—electricity (modern-day fire!), air, water, and earth. Other designs have included labyrinths made into animals, landscapes, paths with number sequences, and every kind of mark and color combination imaginable.

Living Labyrinths for Peace

By touching each of the learning modes or intelligences, the labyrinth functions as a quintessential symbol with potential contributions to every discipline. To make this tool more accessible, Living Labyrinths for Peace, Inc., is collaborating with counselors and teachers to produce an interdisciplinary teacher's manual with activities to stimulate creativity and peace and to appeal to all the intelligences. These activities can be easily adapted to all ages, races, and cultures.

Through school workshops and the forthcoming teacher manual, Living Labyrinths for Peace, Inc. (www.livinglabyrinthsforpeace.org/) fulfills its mission

Figure 8.5. "Labyrinths for Peace: 2000" labyrinth-walking demonstration

to create "interactive labyrinths using art, science, technology, and nature for learning programs that lead the way from inner peace to world peace." The Living Labyrinths for Peace center in Washington, D.C., also offers a unique opportunity to experience the "Dance of the Labyrinth," an interactive exhibit where visitors step on computer-programmed light boxes that lighten and darken with each pace. In a very personal experience, the visitor begins in the moonlight phase with glowing phosphorescent paint and black lights. Marking out paths of earth, air, fire, and water, the light boxes display images of mummies, icons, people, and animals that show the way to the central mirror, where one confronts one's true self. After returning along the path, back into the world, many have described this as a transformative experience embodying peace, power, and mystery.

At a speech I delivered at the U.S. House of Representatives' Rayburn Building during the Labyrinths for Peace event in 2000 (see figure 8.5), I said, "The labyrinth is an apt symbol for peace at the turn of the millennium. The labyrinth relates to many states, because it is found in most countries of the world. And it relates to many states of being, because it can bring inner peace." I have followed my bliss, as the mythologist Joseph Campbell (1988) would say, and in return have received peace and love many times over from all those with whom I've worked, especially the children. I have seen firsthand that the integration of creativity and peace within the individual human being leads to a union among human beings—their families, friends, communities, and the world. Let us live labyrinths for peace!

References

Artress, L. (1995). *Walking a sacred path: Rediscovering the labyrinth as a spiritual tool.* New York: Riverhead Books.

Campbell, J. (1988). *The power of myth.* New York: Doubleday.

Conty, P. (2002). *The genesis and geometry of the labyrinth.* Rochester, VT: Inner Traditions.

Curry, H. (2000). *The way of the labyrinth: A powerful meditation for everyday Life.* New York: Penguin Compass.

Fenty, C. (1997). *How to make a seven circuit labyrinth.* St. Louis: On Way Press.

Gardner, H. (1983). *Frames of mind: The theory of multiple intelligences.* New York: Basic Books.

Gardner, H. (1993). *Multiple intelligences: The theory in practice.* New York: Basic Books.

Gardner, H. (2000). *Intelligence reframed: Multiple intelligences for the 21st century.* New York: Basic Books.

Geoffrion, J. K. H. (2000). *Living the labyrinth: 101 paths to a deeper connection with the sacred.* Cleveland: Pilgrim Press.

Geoffrion, J. K. H. (2003). *Labyrinth and the ennegram: Circling into prayer.* Cleveland: Pilgrim Press.

Kern, H. (1982/1995). *Through the labyrinth* (3rd ed.). Munich, Germany: Prestel.

Lonegren, S. (1996). *Labyrinths. Ancient myths and modern uses.* Somerset, England: GothicImage Publications.

Robert, F., & Saward, J. (2000). Labyrinth research bibliography. Available at www .labyrinthsociety.org/.

Rosetta, L. (2002). *Labyrinths for kids.* Central Point, OR: Leihuna Enterprises.

Saward, J. (2002). *Magical paths: Labyrinths and mazes in the 21st Century.* London: Octopus Publishing.

Teaching Artists Journal. Available from Taylor & Francis, Philadelphia.

Wasko-Flood, S. Living labyrinths for peace. www.livinglabyrinthsforpeace.org/.

Westbury, V. (2001) *Labyrinths: Ancient paths of wisdom and peace.* Sydney, NSW, Australia: Landsdowne Publishing.

CHAPTER 9

A Mind with a View

EDUCATION THROUGH THE
KALEIDOSCOPIC LENSES OF THE ARTS

Beverly J. Klug
Idaho State University

Patricia T. Whitfield
Lyon College

Beverly J. Klug, Ed.D., is associate professor of education in the Department of School Psychology, Literacy, and Special Education at Idaho State University. She is coauthor of *Widening the Circle: Culturally Relevant Pedagogy for American Indian Children* (2003). Her current research focuses on American Indian education, literacy, and the arts in education.

Patricia T. Whitfield, Ph.D., is professor emerita, former Rountree Caldwell Distinguished Professor of Education, and director of teacher education at Lyon College, Batesville, Arkansas. She is coauthor of *Widening the Circle: Culturally Relevant Pedagogy for American Indian Children* (2003). Her current research interests are the role of arts in education, diversifying the teaching force, and leadership.

ABSTRACT

The arts are invaluable to the vibrancy of our societies and cultures. As such, they enhance curricula in our schools by providing alternative "languages," or semiotic systems, in which students may express themselves. Education involves teaching children to think and make connections with their worlds.

Educators are entrusted with literally shaping students' brains while providing opportunities for growth and development in classrooms (Zull, 2002). The arts, whether visual or performing arts, contribute to this growth for students.

Unfortunately, curricula offered in many schools have become those of im-poverishment rather than enrichment for children who may benefit from an arts-enhanced curriculum. The Reggio Emilia approach and curriculum adapta-tions for American Indian students provide successful examples of arts-enriched curricula developing the "whole child." "I see little of more importance to the future of our country and of civilization than full recognition of the place of the artist. If art is to nourish the roots of our culture, society must set the artist free to follow his vision wherever it takes him" (Kennedy, 1963, p. 226).

John F. Kennedy made these remarks at a tribute to Robert Frost at Amherst College in Massachusetts. Kennedy was able to situate the place of the arts in the context of life and culture: that the arts are necessary for the healthiness and survival of our world and allow us to be part of something much larger than ourselves. The arts provide us with many ways of enriching our lives, whether by attending great symphonies, visiting art museums to view the works of the masters, or being present at theater productions exploring the human condition. The arts allow one to express oneself in languages that do not rely on words to convey messages. In other words, the arts offer ways of knowing what it is to experience life in all of its complexity, to compare our own experiences with those of others who have gone before us and who are our contemporaries. They enable us to experience the feel for other times, other places, and other nations in ways that touch our hearts and minds together.

Since the 1980s, the educational system in the United States has come un-der scrutiny to determine which types of education yield the best results. These movements have led to an ever greater emphasis on viewing education through the lens of accountability systems, primarily focusing on literacy and mathemat-ics, with the arts perceived as "fringe" subject areas, nice but not necessary. This impression is inaccurate, as demonstrated by the results of arts magnet schools located throughout the country, many in large urban school districts, which have "consistently high retention rates, low absenteeism, and among the great-est number of graduates going on to further training after graduation" (Perrin, 1997, para. 7). Involvement in the arts allows students to develop motivation to do well at their given tasks, learn from their mistakes, become more flexible in their thinking, work well with others, and develop their communication skills.

The authors of "Reviewing Education and the Arts Project (REAP) Report: The Arts and Academic Achievement: What the Evidence Shows" (Hetland & Winner, 2001) concluded that, when arts are given a serious role in the cur-riculum, academic achievement increases. These conclusions are consistent with those of the *National Educational Longitudinal Study of 1988* (NELS: 88) cited by Nick Rabkin and Robin Redmond (2006). While accountability systems pro-vide some types of information, our focus as educators needs to be on successful strategies for the teaching and learning of all students. Instead of curtailing arts in our schools, we should be incorporating them across the curriculum to further enhance students' learning opportunities.

One of the misperceptions concerning the latest accountability movement is that there is no room for the arts in our educational curricula. What many fail to realize is that the arts enable students to learn how to connect with their worlds, developing "the non-cognitive aspects of experience [that] are seen as an invaluable source of qualitative, aesthetic meaning and insight" (Wong, 2007) evolving from deep learning experiences. Students learn that reading and mathematics are used for real purposes when they are engaged in activities such as music, drama, and visual literacy. The arts provide a key component omitted from the formula for making schools accountable and raising test scores: they supply motivation—a part of affective learning—for students to become involved in the very activities that we want them to demonstrate. In other words, affective development represents a critical piece of education for students (Wadsworth, 1996). This domain includes student feelings, interests, motivation, judgment, and values, all of which are addressed in the arts. Integrated with the cognitive and psychomotor domains, the arts provide a powerful formula for learning that students readily respond to in their curricula.

Former U.S. secretary of education Rod Paige reminded states and school districts that the arts were part of the core curriculum addressed in the No Child Left Behind (NCLB) legislation under Title V. His successor, Margaret Spellings, reinforced this as documented in the 2006 *Governor's Commission on the Arts in Education: Findings and Recommendations* (Education Commission on the Arts in Education, 2006):

> The importance of the arts in No Child Left Behind is clear. They're an important part of a well-rounded, complete education for every student. The knowledge and skills that learning in the arts imparts uniquely equip young persons for life. What's more, combining music, art, dance, and drama with subjects such as math, reading, and language can be highly effective, enhancing student engagement and increasing academic achievement. (p. 4)

Unfortunately, cash-strapped school districts in many urban and rural areas were forced to choose between complying with what was legislated for the 2001 Reauthorization of the Elementary and Secondary Education Act of 1965 (known as No Child Left Behind), assessment requirements, and the arts in balancing their budgets (Ashford, 2004). While positions in arts education may not have been actually cut in some districts, the amount of time required to focus on raising reading and math scores and the types of programs mandated for use by Reading First, part of the legislation, has left little space for more involvement in the arts and the ability of teachers to integrate arts across their curricula. In a study of the Chicago Public Schools' implementation of the latest accountability system, John Diamond and James Spillane (2004) found that how schools responded to the system was dependent on their status. For higher performing schools, assessment data was an important factor that assisted with providing rationale for retaining the arts "by focusing on improving the learning opportunities for all students across all grade levels" (p. 1161). However, administrators of schools placed on probationary status that were comprised of primarily low socioeconomic status (SES) African American students focused on assessment results and narrowing the curriculum to devote time to language arts, mathematics, and test-taking skills. (Latino students were not included in the analysis, as many were attending bilingual programs at the time of data collection.) Moreover, teachers in both high-performing and low-performing schools also bemoaned their abilities to teach areas such as science and social studies as they had previously because of the narrow range of subjects being tested. In many instances, these teachers had included arts activities as a way to enhance student learning.

The *Governor's Commission on the Arts in Education* (Education Commission on the Arts in Education, 2006) explored the status of arts education throughout the country. Several studies indicated that arts education did not have the same priority as reading and math in most instances across the nation and in differing school districts. The commission quoted statistics from one study that surveyed one thousand elementary and secondary principals in four states. Thirty three percent of all principals surveyed anticipated future decreases in emphasis on arts in schools, with 42 percent of principals serving highly diverse populations making those projections (Education Commission on the Arts in Education, 2006).

The purpose of this chapter is to demonstrate the integral role of the arts within our academic communities. They not only contribute to the aesthetic life of students but also enhance their learning through providing additional "languages" in which students may express themselves. In the process, the arts contribute to the growth of students' knowledge bases in all facets of their lives.

The Arts as Communication Systems

Mark Mattern (2000) examined John Dewey's position on the arts within a democratic society. According to Mattern's research, Dewey viewed the arts as a way to assist students in developing all aspects of their understandings of what it meant to be human and to participate in a world reflected by the products of their particular ethnic groups and the citizenship as a whole. He saw the arts as a window that equipped students to understand those around them, using a communication system that did not rely on words to purvey underlying perceptions, feelings, emotions, and insights. Dewey also found that the arts contrast to using oral language to express thoughts as they are imbued in the direct experience of their creators. Dewey believed, "The communicative significance of art [extended] beyond its textual meaning to include the active work that is ongoing in a social context in which its meanings are created, contested, and changed; and to include the social relationships and practices that swirl around the art piece" (Mattern, 2000, p. 58). Indeed, the arts are vital to developing students' essential understandings undergirding creation of conceptual understandings needed prior to their attaining new knowledge in different fields. The arts are essential in cultures around the world and provide second-language learners, those of underrepresented populations, and those experiencing difficulties in literacy and mathematics, with strategies for developing knowledge in ways that do not rely on verbal language alone (Haley, 2004).

Another area of concern is the difficulty of predominantly white, European American teachers to see beyond the race of their students (Watson et al., 2006). Incorporation of the arts in classroom learning permits teachers to appreciate the many nonacademic talents of all their students, undermining the counternarrative of deficit learning theory to which many teachers subscribe for underrepresented learners. Failing to recognize that the arts are also important semiotic systems representing academic achievement causes the concretization of false perceptions of students, especially across sociocultural lines. Students' abilities to produce artistic representations of their conceptual knowledge has the potential to allow them to share their understandings with their teachers, families, and members of the public who may be privy to their works in both verbal and nonverbal means whether in creative or performance arts. Students are enabled to relate their artistic productions with what they know to be culturally connected means of expression, thus enriching the world of their classrooms and schools by sharing many different types of culturally appropriate responses, enhancing their deep-thinking metacognitive skills through their efforts.

A Case for Reviving the Arts in Our Schools

There have been numerous studies that support the integration of arts across the curriculum as signifying greater academic achievement by students, especially in literacy, when done so. Information from studies of the arts as subjects unto themselves has yielded mixed results (Eisner, 1998). Nevertheless, when arts are combined with reading and other academic subjects, students appear to increase in their academic achievement (Donmoyer, 1995). In a study conducted by Allan Richards (2003), students involved in the arts and literacy activities from a low-income school district increased their achievement scores as they explored the works of great artists and cultures throughout the world. They also developed an "appreciation for art and classical music that [spilled] over into a passion for reading literature . . . providing a context for empathy, understanding, meaning, and a genuine interest for the human drama they read in selected literature" (p. 20).

Richard Deasy (2002) created a compendium of studies of the relationship between the arts and learning. These studies, as well as the synthesis of 188 research reports published as the "Reviewing Education and the Arts Project (REAP) Report: The Arts and Academic Achievement: What the Evidence Shows" (Hetland & Winner, 2001), confirm that the arts in conjunction with academic subjects do increase students' achievement in subject areas and that this finding holds for those of underrepresented populations as well as the dominant culture. It is imperative that those who serve on school boards throughout the country recognize that sacrificing the arts actually diminishes student curriculum in significant ways (Schmidt, 2001).

THE RESULTS OF RESEARCH ON LEARNING AND THE BRAIN

For the past fifteen years, or roughly since the mid-1990s, there has been a great deal of research in the area of neuropsychology and learning that has given us a different understanding of how our brains operate in order for learning to occur (Jensen, 2005). This work has been amplified significantly through the advent of brain-imaging technologies such as the computed tomography (CT) scan and functional magnetic resonance imaging (fMRI; Morgan, 2004). We now know that there are many areas of the brain involved in concept development encompassing both the left and right hemispheres, and understand more thoroughly how the brain reacts to other types of stimuli.

James Zull (2002) has provided a model of learning that is biologically based, hardwired into our brains. The estimated number of neurons in the brain that humans are born with is one hundred billion, each with the capabilities of connecting with ten thousand other neurons, creating what are known as "neuronal networks" used in the process of learning, remembering, and retrieving information. These networks connect information that we are learning both intra- and interhemispherically, usually encompassing several areas of the brain responsible for processing knowledge in the cerebral cortex.

BRAIN PROCESSING OF INFORMATION

Previously, the notion prevailed that the brain processed information differently in each hemisphere. This was supported by evidence gained on clinical posttrauma data gathered by medical professionals (Robertson, 2005). Again, through technological advances, it now appears that, while the right hemisphere is biased toward processing stimuli globally (holistically) and the left hemisphere toward local (analytical) processing, the integration of processed stimuli in both hemispheres allows humans to act more efficiently. As explained by Lynn Robertson, the white matter bundle that connects the two hemispheres, the corpus callosum, allows this integration to occur as neuronal impulses pass through this region from one side to the opposite side of the brain. Consequently, it is crucial for teachers to ensure that students are given multiple opportunities for processing what they are learning, thereby encouraging the construction of greater neuronal networks throughout the brain. Zull (2002) describes this process as "growing" or changing the brain. This supports Howard Gardner's 1983 theory of multiple intelligences, several of which involve the arts (Gardner, 1999). In addition, the affective domain is connected to the learning process through joining the arts with curricula (Peterson, 2005).

THE ROLE OF MOVEMENT AND LEARNING IN THE BRAIN

Recent studies provide strong evidence that the cerebellum, responsible for body movement, plays a critical role in acquiring and retaining information and for demonstrating automaticity (Jensen, 2005). Movement activities increase the amount of oxygen traveling to the brain, thereby enhancing students' abilities to attend to stimuli. In addition, the cerebellum appears to be involved in planning and predicting activities generated while processing information in the brain.

Movement structures of the brain are involved in the transmission of sensations between the peripheral and central nervous systems, and increase the amount of neurochemicals that support brain development and learning. Neurotransmitters such as dopamine are released in the bloodstream when the brain perceives pleasure, creating a positive association with learning, while reducing the presence of cortisol and norepinephrine, the stress hormones produced when humans perceive danger (Zull, 2002; Jensen, 2005). Too much cortisol and adrenaline lead to the probability that learning under conditions of high stress will result in decreased student retention (Bremmer, 2005).

TYPES OF MEMORIES STORED IN THE BRAIN

There are several types of memory that we associate with the brain, including short-term, long-term, and working memory (Zull, 2002). We also have information stored as semantic memories, associated with the left side of the brain, and episodic memories, associated with the right side of the brain (Jensen, 2005). Semantic memories consist of data related to names, places, events, and so forth, while episodic memories consist of stories, how things are presented in time and space, and the way events are visualized by those who perceive them and in the order they occur. The amount of information that can be stored and readily recalled as semantic memory is limited by the ability to attend to more than a few items at any one time (Marois, 2005). The opposite is true for episodic memories as information attached to a "story" is recalled more readily than isolated facts (Jensen, 2005).

Making Episodic Memory Connections through the Arts

How often have parents asked their children what they've learned in school only to be met with a vague "nothing" or "I don't know." Not surprisingly, their teachers say that they certainly have covered a lot of material over several subject areas in the course of the school day. Therefore, to be met with negative responses from children about what they learned may seem to disprove all of the learning that supposedly occurred in their classrooms. Perhaps, in our quest to relay as many facts as possible (semantic memories), too much emphasis is placed on recall of these facts in decontextualized situations. Perhaps, if we asked our children to tell us about what happened in school today, they could relay more information about what they learned in the context of telling us a story (invoking episodic memories). The use of statements followed by questions such as "Tell me about the dinosaurs. Were they scary? Do you have a favorite kind?" may yield more information and involve more discussion with students, allowing us further insight into what students really did do in the course of their day at school.

Episodic memories for students are created if knowledge is embedded in the creative or visual arts (such as storytelling, drama, music, drawing, and movement). Because episodic memories are easier to recall than decontextualized semantic memories, students are able to "demonstrate" more of the knowledge they have acquired in schools. Teachers can assist in this process by having students bring home an artifact (drawing, song, or other piece of artistic expression) relating to the concept being developed.

How does this occur? As stated previously, there is strong evidence that we do not learn with only one side of our brains. There are vigorous connections among all the parts of our brain that can be capitalized upon to increase students' understandings of the world around them. It is extremely beneficial to have students involved in fine motor (such as drawing) as well as gross motor (such as movement) activities to promote engagement with many areas of the brain. The arts enhance our lives in many ways. Louise Rosenblatt (1978) discusses the importance of having students engage in aesthetic responses toward literature. Artistic responses to literature allow them to connect aesthetically to what they are reading as they employ additional symbol systems in their learning. We experience pleasure when involved in artistic expression, enabling more of the good feeling hormones to circulate throughout our bloodstreams and into our brains. Indeed, Kathy Short, Gloria Kauffman, and Leslie Kahn (2000) demonstrated the importance of using the arts as a response to text. Children drew, engaged in drama, wrote poetry, and responded to photographs while they read and "internalized their own emotional and kinesthetic experiences with those of the character in the book and so were able to understand the character in different ways" (p. 166). Michael Schiro (2004) reports the positive results of engaging students in storytelling with related arts activities as a way to increase students' mathematical understandings.

An added benefit of engaging in artistic endeavors is that of cultivating and experiencing the concept of "beauty." Joe Winston (2006) states that developing an understanding of beauty, of what it is and is not, is essential for the fostering of students' morality. At this period of time in our society's history, when students are being bombarded with a multitude of stimuli through technological developments, creating these understandings is a much-needed addition to students' lives, assisting us as educators in our quest to "teach the whole child."

Reflections: Real Lives, Real Children

Brain research supports culturally relevant pedagogy that encourages artistic expression for all learners (Klug & Whitfield, 2003; Pewewardy, 1994; Skinner, 1992). Two approaches to incorporating visual arts and the performing arts in the educational process for students are presented below. The first focuses on Reggio Emilia, an approach originally developed for early childhood education in Italy that has been widely emulated in many countries throughout the world, including the United States (New, 2007). The second focuses on approaches incorporated in teaching American Indian students attending a public school on a reservation in the western region of the United States. Finally, it is important to stress that teachers do not have to be in a "Reggio Emilia" school or teaching on a reservation in order to adapt artistic endeavors for their classrooms and schools. In fact, unless we begin to do so in all schools, we will lose a generation—a generation that will be unable to experience the nurturing enhancements of the arts, circumventing their understandings of what it means to be a member of our diverse, democratic society, which is, after all, the goal of education.

THE USE OF VISUAL ARTS AS SYMBOLIC LANGUAGES: REGGIO EMILIA SCHOOLS

A program for early childhood education originating in the Reggio Emilia area of Italy after World War II provides powerful insight into how the arts integrated with curriculum developed around students' interests can support their conceptual development by providing another "language" in which to express themselves. The approach "fosters children's intellectual development through a systematic focus on symbolic representation" (Edwards, Gandini, & Forman, 1998, p. 3).

When the villagers of Reggio Emilia decided to use a small amount of money provided by the government after the war to build a school for their children as an investment in the future rather than a community center, Loris Malaguzzi is said to have become part of this project because it "changed the definition of the word impossible" (Wurm, 2005, p. 1). Villagers were building the school brick by brick from salvaged materials. It is important to note that these schools were not developed for the elite; indeed, this was a very poor area of Italy following the ravages of World War II. Malaguzzi believed there should be a way to provide children with relevant learning experiences combined with opportunities for development and reflection on their worlds using a variety of symbol systems. By working with young children, many of preschool age and kindergarten age, the schools could also operate as a partial solution to the need for day care in the region, as women needed to be in the workforce to provide for the needs of their families. Gradually, the schools expanded to include higher levels. So dynamic and successful in developing children's skill in using innovative symbolic and communication systems, the Reggio Emilia educational program was honored by *Newsweek* in 1991 as one of the "Ten Best Schools in the World."

Reggio schools were designed to reflect the cultural values of Italy, including building strong family-school relationships, providing experiences to develop children's understandings of the world based on their interests and inquiries about their environment, and incorporating art in all phases of children's learning, from sketching an object to completing a project reflecting what they have learned and their ideas concerning the concept (Abramson, Ankerman, & Robinson, 1995). Fundamental to the Reggio approach is a belief in "the competent child" who is (1) equipped to both construct his or her own knowledge of the world and to explore the world; (2) a "bearer of rights" to grow in experiences and contexts that create solidarity, which opens them to relationships; (3) capable of educating him- or herself, reciprocal with children of the same age; and (4) capable of empathy (Gandini, 2006). Reggio is far removed from a deficiency model in that it views children optimistically, focusing on what they can know and do, not what they lack. Malaguzzi (cited in Wurm, 2005) maintained that "what children learn does not follow as an automatic result from what is taught, rather it is in large part due to children's own doing, as a consequence of their activities and our resources" (p. 64). The schools are based on a model of socioconstructivism, in which children construct learning through relationships with others, between children and the adults in their lives, as well as the children and their peers. The curriculum incorporates constructivist philosophies based on Jean Piaget (Wadsworth, 1996), Lev Vygotsky (1978), Dewey (Mattern, 2000), and others. From the beginning of their experiences in Reggio schools, children are involved in oral communication concerning the concepts they are learning through discussions with their peers, teachers, and parents. The children's conceptual understandings are documented through teacher notes and photographs taken of the children while they are engaged in their work, whether on field trips, while walking and examining objects in their environments, while exploring secondary resources to learn about concepts, or as they ask new questions of their families. The Reggio philosophy maintains that children have an ethical right to understand what they are doing. Quality emerges from exchanges with others—not only what is learned but also how it is learned.

Aesthetics are an important element of Reggio school environments, providing a way to stimulate thought and creativity. In order to use art as a way of expressing ideas, each school has an "atelieristo"—a visual arts specialist—who works with the teachers in developing curriculum and is considered an important part of the children's educational program. This component is based on the belief that children and artists are discoverers of new ways of seeing the world. In other words, learning goes beyond words (Gandini, 2006). Schools are equipped with paper, paints, clay, recycled materials, and other necessary items to be used by students for completion of their projects. An "atelier," or studio area, is provided where students can find materials for sculpting and work on long-term projects. The "atelieristo" provides guidance and direction to children as they work on developing their understandings of concepts and on creating their final projects to show what they have learned (Schiller, 1995). The "atelier" is far more than an art studio. It is a place where children can explore various media and become "masters of . . . all the symbolic languages" (Edwards, Gandini, & Forman, 1998, p.120). It also provides a "workshop for documentation" (p. 121). The ability of the schools to communicate their approach and its effect on young learners was imperative to ensuring both community awareness and involvement, something so essential to the Reggio philosophy.

Respect for children's ideas and their capabilities to represent them is reflected in the display of students' work throughout Reggio schools. Considered a language of expression, "there is a great emphasis on children's symbolic drawing and art-making to represent their learning and implant concepts more firmly" (Schiller, 1995, p. 46). The Reggio perspective is that children are artists and discoverers of new ways of seeing the world. Representative examples of the art produced in Reggio schools have been on display as their work has toured the United States and Europe. Readers can find some of these examples captured in *The Hundred Languages of Children* (Edwards, Gandini, & Forman, 1998). Carol Seefeldt (1995) makes the following observation that reflects the importance of art as symbolic representation for children: "When art is viewed as serious, not a frill that has nothing to do with children's thoughts, ideas, or emotions, then teachers everywhere . . . offer children sufficient experiential motivation so that they will have something to express and psychological safety so that they will feel free to do so" (p. 44). Art making is making thought visible (Gandini, 2006). Children in Reggio Emilia schools work collaboratively on projects with their peers and with adults, developing their social skills. Dewey (1934) has said "art strikes below the barriers that separate human beings from each other . . . [and] renders humans aware of their union with one another in origin and destiny" (p. 272). It is not surprising that a program emerging from the ashes of World War II should place an emphasis on using a variety of symbol systems to enable children to learn, to express themselves, and to communicate through a broad repertoire of systems all designed to bring people together. The Reggio Emilia approach has crossed international borders and is used in K–8 systems around the world, including the United States, adapting to the cultures in which it resides. Consistent throughout Reggio Emilia schools is the integration of the visual arts into the curriculum for young children who are just learning to read and write as an additional symbol system rather than their being taught separately as "art." This approach enables the children to express their understanding of their worlds with a degree of fluency and eloquence that their developing reading literacy skills would preclude.

INCORPORATING VISUAL AND PERFORMING ARTS IN A PUBLIC SCHOOL SERVING AMERICAN INDIAN CHILDREN

While many American teachers have not had the privilege of experiencing Reggio schools firsthand, they have been strong supporters of the use of art within the curriculum as a way for children to express their ideas. It is the experience of both authors that allowing students to respond through the use of multiple sign systems enhances their classroom learning. While teaching underrepresented populations in many parts of the country, Klug has always found that students appear to be less threatened when allowed to use drawings to show their understandings in literacy. As part of their creations, students reflect their own ethnicities by including cultural elements such as colors and overall schematic of representations; incorporating language of their community when showing interactions of characters in drawing; and including nonverbal symbols in their representations (e.g., including a picture of a cross, bubble words, etc.).

In her work with elementary grade American Indian students living on a reservation in the western area of the United States, Klug utilizes culturally relevant pedagogy in a variety of ways. In American Indian communities, visual arts, music, storytelling, dance, and oratory all have important roles to play in cultural maintenance and instructing younger generations about their heritages (Klug & Whitfield, 2003; Pewewardy, 1994; Skinner, 1992). Fourth and fifth graders are invited to become part of a production of legends that are part of their traditional culture. By incorporating legends as their texts of choice and involving students in drama and movement activities to "feel" the legends they are preparing for presentation to the community, students increase their literacy skills, including understandings of sequencing and overall comprehension of stories. Students are also involved in blocking out scenes, needing to use intuitive mathematical abilities to estimate where scenery and action needs to take place. They are involved in deeper self-reflection as they create papier-mâché masks of the characters they will portray, estimating the amount of torn paper, glue, and water they will need for the masks, as well as the amount of different colors of paint to portray their characters. Finally, they need to create masks that reflect their character's disposition to the audience. Along with creating character representations, involving students in making scenery for the production creates new opportunities for conceptualization of "setting," not just as a word but also as a representation of space in which the action will occur.

An important part of the production as a whole is the role that these older students will play as "teachers" of the legends to their younger siblings and relatives, a tradition that heralds back to the earliest of times for this nation. Because American Indian students were not allowed to practice their traditions or speak their languages during the boarding school era, many of the stories that would have been passed down orally were forgotten or lost. Consequently, some of the students in the school have never heard their traditional stories. Taking the roles of teaching the legends to the younger students is perceived as very important.

The drum is an integral part of the students' Native traditions. Therefore, the drum is utilized as often as possible in working with the students. Students count with the drumbeat as well as moving with the beat. Using the drum has provided a way of increasing listening skills for all grade levels.

The children at the school are second-language learners, speaking American Indian English, a dialect based on their aboriginal languages (Leap, 1993). With kindergarten children, Klug has found that incorporating drama throughout the storytelling increases students' comprehension of the stories and memory for detail. By capitalizing on creating episodic memories, the children are able to relate more fully to the text being read. Therefore, words with which they may be unfamiliar may be emphasized through drama, creating linkages between story and abstract alphabetic symbols. Klug has observed that for many of these younger students, acting out the story together as it is being told, scene by scene, has improved their listening and comprehension of story events. This is reflected in the follow-up activities where the children represent their understandings through drawings or other artistic activities. Not to be forgotten are the joy and excitement evidenced by the children as they participate in these activities.

Phoneme segmentation is difficult for many of these children as many of the English phonemes differ from those present in the Native languages. Another activity strengthened through storytelling is to concentrate on phoneme-letter relationships made through words embedded in the stories, with opportunities for children to provide their own words for phonemes being emphasized. Children's words are written on large pieces of chart paper kept in the classroom for future reference. It is not uncommon for these children to produce thirty-five to forty-eight words following storytelling that contain the phoneme of the day.

For these elementary students, to demonstrate the knowledge they have of the world around them through their own representations of texts is most important. The school district requires that a scripted basal reader series be used. However, by integrating the arts with their curricula, the students have opportunities to go beyond the skill and drill activities that comprise the main menu of academic learning for many in low SES schools. When utilizing drawings as a response to literature, especially traditional legends, it is extremely revealing to see that many of the children incorporate their siblings and extended family members in their drawings, reflecting the importance of family in students' Native traditions. A prime indicator that students are interpreting the world through their cultural lenses is when they incorporate depictions of babies in cradleboards and families gathered together for celebrations—a part of their Native world that they would not readily encounter in mainstream texts. They are using the language of art to deepen their understandings of their world and their place in the larger context of society. Furthermore, stronger ties have been created between the school and the Native community as a group of people realizes that their traditions and stories are being incorporated into the education of their children, not just ignored as in days past.

The following is an illustration of students' deep thinking and interpreting the world through their own cultural lenses. This incident evolved following the storytelling-movement activity of a traditional legend in kindergarten. The story was about Coyote and his desire to visit the stars, which he was told were Indian maidens. Following the story, Klug drew a star with a stick-figure girl in the middle of it on the board as an example of one of the things they might draw, except that students could draw themselves or other people inside the star as they desired. As she went to work with the students, one of the young boys came to Klug's side and told her, "You can't have her naked!" referring to the drawing on the board. Klug agreed, and together they went to the board where the youngster watched carefully as Klug added traditional clothing to the girl's figure, including the proper decoration for her regalia. Once Klug added marks to indicate that the girl's dress was flashing (shining like a star), he was satisfied and went to work on his own drawing.

Where Do We Go from Here?

The Reggio Emilia approach has been incorporated to varying degrees in many educational systems preK–8. The incorporation of the arts across the curriculum is not difficult, but it requires active planning on the part of teachers to go beyond the restrictive curriculum that currently prevails in our schools. To have a truly educated citizenry, capable of expressing themselves with clarity, we must provide opportunities for all students to develop their deep, intuitive understanding of the world. Karen Gallas (1994) has advocated for the role of the arts in doing so:

> The arts make it possible for all children . . . to participate fully in the process of education. They transcend the limitations placed on those children . . . whose language, culture, or life experience is outside the mainstream of American schooling. . . . They confirm the perspectives of children . . . whose modes of communication do not fit in the dominant classroom. They enable all children to recognize the breadth and depth of their learning. (p. 116)

As evidenced from our discussion, it is not hard to incorporate the arts within the curriculum for American Indian children, or for that matter, children of all ethnicities, and in this way increase their opportunities for deeper learning experiences. In doing so, we are providing culturally relevant pedagogy as well as opportunities for students to utilize their multiple intelligences while strengthening and creating more neuronal networks within their brains. This will assist students in their memory of the material with which they are presented in schools.

As educators, the arts provide us with additional information we need to know to judge students' capabilities and understandings of what they have learned. Cultural anthropologists have long based their conclusions regarding the sophistication of civilization on the artifacts produced by the ethnic citizens belonging to particular civilizations. These artifacts present themselves not just in literate tomes or mathematical formulae but also in the creative and performing arts produced (Donmoyer, 1995). Policy makers and the public in general need to understand that the formation of knowledge is more than recitation of semantic knowledge related to reading and mathematics. To be truly educated, we need to provide opportunities for all students to develop their deep, intuitive understandings of the world. Instead of focusing on punishment for poor performing schools (Hoff, 2007), it is our belief that the arts provide positive innovations in curricula based on brain-based enhancement strategies that can assist students in their learning. The visual arts, including drawing, paintings, photography, filmmaking (which includes many of the elements of the visual and performing arts), and three-dimensional reproductions such as sculpture and pottery; the creative arts, including poetry, drama, and dance; music; and written expression all have a place in our curricula.

How will our nation be judged by future generations? Will we be perceived as a society that replicates social stratification that is narrowly defined by the constraints imposed on school systems by hegemonic thinking? Will our students be able to evolve into adults who will cherish their potentialities as human beings to express themselves and appreciate the eloquence of those who have gone before them? If we continue to ignore what the research results tell us about stimulating the brain through the arts, we will be making a mistake that may have ramifications for generations to come. In addition, we may be endangering the appreciation for the arts in future generations, a characteristic that has contributed to our being viewed by the world as a vibrant and valuable society. All children need to participate in stimulating learning environments, regardless of their sociocultural status and ethnicities. They deserve nothing less from us, their teachers. As President Kennedy advocated, "Let us think of education as the means of developing our greatest abilities, because in each of us . . . there is a private hope and dream which, fulfilled, can be translated into benefit for everyone and greater strength for our nation" (Kennedy, 1961).

References

Abramson, S., Ankerman, K., & Robinson, R. (1995). Project work with diverse students: Adapting curriculum based on the Reggio Emilia approach. *Childhood Education, 71*(4), 197–202.

Ashford, E. (2004). NCLB's unfunded arts programs seek refuge. *School Board News, 24*(3). Retrieved October 4, 2007, from http://www.eddigest.com/.

Bremmer, J. D. (2005). Does stress damage the brain? *Phi Kappa Phi Forum, 85*(1), 27–29.

Deasy, R. J. (2002). *Critical links: Learning in the arts and student academic and social development.* Washington, DC: Arts Education Partnership. (ERIC Document Reproduction Service No. ED466413). Retrieved August 18, 2008, from www.aep-arts.org/.

Dewey, J. (1934). *Art as experience.* New York: Perigee.

Diamond, J. B., & Spillane, J. P. (2004). High-stakes accountability in urban elementary schools: Challenging or reproducing inequality? *Teachers College Record, 106*(6), 1145–1176.

Donmoyer, R. (1995). The arts as modes of learning and methods of teaching: A (borrowed and adapted) case for integrating the arts across the curriculum. *Arts Education Policy Review, 96*(5), 14–20.

Education Commission on the Arts in Education. (2006). *Governor's commission on the arts in education: Findings and recommendations.* Denver, CO: Author.

Edwards, C., Gandini, L., & Forman, G. (Eds.). (1998). *The Hundred languages of children.* Norwood, NJ: Ablex.

Eisner, E. (1998). Does experience in the arts boost academic achievement? *Journal of Art Education, 51*(1), 7–15.

Gallas, K. (1994). *The language of learning: How children talk, write, dance, draw, and sing their understanding of the world.* New York: Teachers College Press.

Gandini, L. (2006). Reggio Emilia Infant-Toddler School study tour. Presentation, Reggio Emilia, Italy.

Gardner, H. (1999). *Intelligence reframed: Multiple Intelligences for the 21st Century.* New York: Basic Books.

' Haley, M. H. (2004). Learner-centered instruction with the theory of multiple intelligences with second language learners. *Teachers College Record, 106*(1), 163–180.

Hetland, L., & Winner, E. (2001). Reviewing Education and the Arts Project (REAP) report: The arts and academic achievement: What the evidence shows. *Arts Education Policy Review, 102*(5), 3–6.

Hoff, D. J. (2007). NCLB renewal debate launched in earnest. *Education Week, 26*(19), 21, 24.

Jensen, E. (2005). *Teaching with the brain in mind* (2nd ed.). Alexandria, VA: Association for Supervision and Curriculum Development.

Kennedy, J. F. (1961). News and trends: President urges participation in AEW. Today's education: The journal of the National Education Association, 50(7), 4.

Kennedy, J. F. (1963). In praise of Robert Frost. Tribute at Amherst College, Massachusetts, October 27. In W. Safire (Ed.), *Lend me your ears* (p. 226). New York: Norton, 2004.

Klug, B. J., & Whitfield, P. T. (2003). *Widening the circle: Culturally relevant pedagogy for American Indian children.* New York: RoutledgeFalmer.

Leap, W. L. (1993). *American Indian English.* Salt Lake City: University of Utah Press

Marois, R. (2005). Capacity limits of information processing in the brain. *Phi Kappa Phi Forum, 85*(1), 30–33.

Mattern, M. (2000). John Dewey, art, and public life. *Journal of Politics, 61*(1), 54–75.

Morgan, H. (2004). *Real learning: A bridge to cognitive neuroscience.* Lanham, MD: Rowman & Littlefield.

New, R. (2007). Excellent early education: A city in Italy has it. *Theory into Practice, 45*(6), 4–10.

Newsweek. (1991). The ten best schools in the world, and what we can learn from them. December 2.

No Child Left Behind Act of 2001: Reauthorization of the Elementary and Secondary Education Act of 1965, 20 U.S.C. § 6301 et seq. (U.S.C. 2001).

Perrin, S. (1997). Education through the arts in secondary schools. New Horizons for Learning. Retrieved March 4, 2008, from www.newhorizons.org/strategies/arts/cabc/perrin2.htm.

Peterson, R. (2005). Crossing bridges that connect the arts, cognitive development, and the brain. *Journal of Learning through the Arts: A Research Journal, 1*(1), article 2. Retrieved August 18, 2008, from http://repositories.cdlib.org/clta/lta/Vol1/iss1/art2.

Pewewardy, C. D. (1994). Culturally responsible pedagogy in action: An American Indian magnet school. In E. R. Hollins, J. E. King, & W. C. Hayman (Eds.), *Teaching diverse populations: Formulating a knowledge base* (pp. 77–92). New York: State University of New York Press.

Rabkin, N., & Redmond, R. (2006). The arts make a difference. *Educational Leadership, 63*(5), 60–64.

Richards, A. G. (2003). Arts and academic achievement in reading: Functions and implications. *Art Education, 56*(6), 19–23.

Robertson, L. C. (2005). The bilateral brain: Are two better than one? *Phi Kappa Phi, 85*(1), 19–22.

Rosenblatt, L. (1978). *The reader, the text, the poem.* Carbondale: Illinois University Press.

Schiller, M. (1995). Reggio Emilia: A focus on emergent curriculum and art. *Art Education, 48*(3), 45–49.

Schiro, M. S. (2004). *Oral storytelling and teaching mathematics: Pedagogical and multicultural perspectives.* Thousand Oaks, CA: Sage.

Schmidt, J. (2001). The school board, the keyboard, the arts, and the peaceful revolution. *Arts Education Policy Review, 102*(4), 21–26.

Seefeldt, C. (1995). Art as serious work. *Young Children, 50*(3), 39–45.

Short, K. G., Kauffman, G., & Kahn, L. H. (2000). "I just *need* to draw": Responding to literature across multiple sign systems. *Reading Teacher, 54*(2), 160–171.

Skinner, L. (1992). Teaching through traditions: Incorporating Native languages and cultures into curricula. In P. Cahape & C. B. Howley (Eds.), *Indian nations at risk: Listening to the people* (pp. 54–59). Summaries of papers commissioned by the Indian Nations at Risk Task Force of the U.S. Department of Education. (ERIC Document Reproduction Service No. ED339588)

Vygotsky, L. S. (1978). *Mind in society.* Cambridge, MA: Harvard University Press.

Wadsworth, B. J. (1996). *Piaget's theory of cognitive and affective development: Foundations of constructivism* (5th ed.). White Plains, NY: Longman.

Watson, D., Charner-Laird, M., Kirkpatrick, C. L., Szczesiul, S. A., & Gordon, P. J. (2006). Effective teaching/effective urban teaching: Grappling with definitions, grappling with difference. *Journal of Teacher Education, 57*(4), 395–409.

Winston, J. (2006). Beauty, goodness and education: The arts beyond utility. *Journal of Moral Education, 35*(3), 285–300.

Wong, D. (2007). Beyond control and rationality: Dewey, aesthetics, motivation, and educative experiences. *Teachers College Record, 109*(1), 192–220. Retrieved January 27, 2009, from www.tcrecord.org/.

Wurm, J. (2005). *Working in the Reggio way.* St. Paul, MN: Redleaf Press.

Zull, J. E. (2002). *The art of changing the brain.* Sterling, VA: Stylus.

CHAPTER 10

The First Thunder Clap of Spring

AN INVITATION INTO ABORIGINAL WAYS OF KNOWING AND THE CREATIVE POSSIBILITIES OF DIGITAL TECHNOLOGIES

Sharon Friesen
Galileo Educational Network
University of Calgary

David Jardine
University of Calgary

Brenda Gladstone
Galileo Educational Network

Sharon Friesen, Ph.D., is cofounder and director of Galileo Educational Network and associate professor in the Faculty of Education, University of Calgary. Recent work includes *Back to the Basics of Teaching and Learning* (2008) with David Jardine and Patricia Clifford. Recent papers are available at www.galileo.org/reading.html.

David Jardine, Ph.D., works in the Faculty of Education, University of Calgary. Recent work includes *Back to the Basics of Teaching and Learning* (2008) with Sharon Friesen and Patricia Clifford and online papers "On the While of Things" and "Learning Not to Speak in Tongues," with Rahat Naqvi.

Brenda Gladstone, MBA, is cofounder and chief operating officer of Galileo Educational Network. Recent papers include "Inquiry Transforms Learning Environments for Students," "Educational Reform Meets NetMedia," and "From Project within a School to Provincial Network."

ABSTRACT

In this chapter, we explore some of the affinities that can be developed between new information and communication technologies and what has become known as aboriginal ways of knowing. This work documents some of these affinities via the collaborative development of an online project entitled "Nitsitapiisini—Stories and Spaces: Exploring Kainai Plants and Culture," conducted with teachers, students, and elders of the Blood Tribe in southern Alberta. The pedagogy of this collaboration is then linked to rethinking the disciplines of knowledge entrusted to teachers and students in schools as living disciplines that make demands on the possibilities inherent in new technologies. This particular orientation rubs against instructionist practices found in many classrooms yet, once awakened, spawns curiosity and creativity.

The way we treat a thing can sometimes change its nature.

—Lewis Hyde, *The Gift: On the Erotic Life of Property*, 1983, xiii

The first thunder clap of spring tells us that the Numanska medicine bundle must be opened. Sipatsimo and Gatsomi are our most scared herbs of mind and spirit. They are used in ceremony.
The Belly Buttes is our sacred Sundance site.
It is all here. The land, the plants, our ancestors and our future.
Life is a continuing cycle of past, present and future. You cannot know the land without knowing the plants placed here by the Creator. You cannot know the Creator without knowing the plants. You cannot know the plants and their healing powers without hearing the stories from our ancestors. It is one and the same.

—Carolla Calf Robe, Blackfoot elder

The Invitation

Maria[1] lives and teaches on a First Nations reserve in southern Alberta. On a late August afternoon, she and her husband drove two and a half hours north to discuss a good idea with us.

"My mother is old. She knows the plants. I want to make a book and put the plants into the book. Would you help me?"

That's how many things begin. In the midst of all the ordinariness someone drops by to deliver a message. As Maria talked, I (Sharon Friesen) felt myself pulled backward, slowly coming into focus, running through sage and long prickly grasses under the brilliant blue prairie sky. The pungent odor of sage lingered as the wind spun the leaves about.

I, too, knew the taste of summer's first Saskatoon berries.

Maria taught a grade 4 Blackfoot immersion class at one of the schools on the reserve. Initially, she did not see how to make a place for her students in her plant project. Plant Growth and Changes is one of the topics in the grade 4 Alberta Science Program of Studies, but it seemed so distant, so flat. After several conversations with her, we worked through a way to involve her grade 4 students in the study. The way to get them involved was exactly at that point of invitation: "My mother is old. She knows the plants." Although Maria was initially unable to imagine how an inquiry into the indigenous healing plants on her ancestral land would help her meet the mandated curriculum outcomes, it was very clear to us how this could be accomplished. We had been in this place before, where curriculum mandates seem to bear no resemblance to the life one lives or the lives of one's students.

Mapping the curriculum outcomes to this inquiry study would be fairly straightforward. The *Program of Studies* states,

> Students learn about the structure and growth of plants by raising plants in the classroom and by observing plant growth within the community. They learn to recognize and describe different forms of leaves, stems, roots and flowers and learn their functions in supporting the growth and reproduction of the plant. They learn various ways of starting new plants and the plants' requirements for growth. Through hands-on activities, students learn that different plants have different needs, and they gain skills and attitudes for their care. (Alberta Education, 1996, p. B.22)

There are eleven Specific Learner Outcomes under the General Learner Outcome that requires students to "demonstrate knowledge and skills for the study, interpretation, propagation and enhancement of plant growth" (Alberta Education, 1996, p. B.22). In many classrooms the outcomes are treated in a fairly straightforward manner: plant some seeds in the classroom; water them and make observations while they grow taking careful note of the plants requirements; learn the various parts of the plants and importance of the plants to humans; and so on. All these well-meant activities are done inside the confines of the classroom, and, despite the good intentions of teachers and students, quite often our relation to these plants, and the relations of these plants to their place on earth, remains abstract.

"Hands-on" portends something somehow unfulfilled. It is precisely this abstractness that, in many ways, defines this activity as one falling within the purview of "science education." There is no pull of obligation or ancestry, no face or form of land and landscape (see Friesen & Jardine, 2009; see also Bransford, Brown, & Cocking, 2000), no knowledge carried in the body's weight and footfalls, and nothing housed in formative, intergenerational, ancestral memory (Jardine, 2006). There is little, even, of the tongue, of speaking, of the names by which plants are called (Gadamer, 1989, p. 405) and what such calling, such language, calls for in us.

In science education in particular, names are understood to be simply descriptive or taxonomic, not evocative of things or ways of life. "We"—in this program of studies—presume the great "Father of Taxonomy," Carolus Linnaeus (1707–1778), whose work, the enormous *Systema Naturae* (with its own bloodlines traceable back to the work of Aristotle before him), and his unfolding of the whole of creation into the grand typologies of kingdoms, genera, species, subspecies, and families, that are still taught, in supplemented and modified forms, in our schools. From Linnaeus's binomial naming of these typologies in the "one universal language of Latin," we have Latinate names that call back into a long colonial history that is not the one out of which this invitation had come to us. In a chilling parallel, and as was commonplace in his time, Carole Linne translated his own Swedish name to Carolus Linnaeus. Without such translation, one was not considered "a citizen of the world" (Reston, 2005, p. 127), a parallel to residential school memories where English names were given and indigenous tongues forgotten.

Entering into the invitation that Maria had sent, many things familiar to school and school knowledge and its presumed ancestries and ways had to be left behind, or at least opened up to be experienced anew, filled with curious possibility, and not simply presumed. Linnaeus's work doesn't disappear under such an invitation. In fact, now, it finally appears as a living bloodline heretofore very often simply memorized and then forgotten. He is a European *ancestor*, not just a dull name in a book.

"Not Just in the Plants"

> The healing is not just in the plants; it is in relation to the land, the animals, to the water, to us and what they communicate to us. One of the things that worries me, and I include myself, is what are we missing? What is being communicated to us that we are not hearing? Learning on the land with Elders becomes very, very important in that respect. These children are going to be brought up with this[2] and they will receive the communication from this place better than we can, the residential school generations. (N. Blood, personal communication)

How can we imagine the topics listed in the curriculum guide as rich, generous, living topics, living topographies that are full of enough room for the full range of difference and diversity that we might bring to them, including, it must be added, the full adult attention of the teacher as well? How can these topics become experienced as living topics that awaken curiosity, full of real questions and ancestries and invoking words, full of real openings and opportunities for creative exploration? It is here that the hard work begins: how can we start imagining, for example, the phenomenon of plant propagation, plant growth, uses of plants, or stories of plants as parts of a living inheritance, as part of an already ongoing conversation into which we step, as inquirers? How can the presumed familiarity of our treatment of such topics be interrupted? How can we come to experience "what we are missing?"

These matters are not solely part of the living inheritance of scientific knowledge and its bloodlines. They are matters that live in the world in all its variegated ways. Rather than separating off a cull of "plants" as if they had no place on earth, we treat them differently. Treated differently, this ordinary, all too familiar grade 4 topic would open itself to far more than a study of plants. Rather, "this inquiry weaves strong threads of connection: a web of children, Elders, plants, landscape and the stories that bind them together. These stories provide a path for our children to the future. A path that remembers and in the remembering, renews" (Kainai elder, personal communication).

In such renewal, scientific matters don't simply disappear, nor does the curriculum mandate from Alberta Education simply become ignored. Rather, such matters become remembered for what they are and what they are not. They become "placed" as a form of knowledge with their own lines of ancestry and remembrance. This is not a battle, therefore, between scientific knowledge and "indigenous knowledge" but rather a breaking of the hegemonic spell of scientific knowledge and a careful placement of this form of knowledge within the wealth of human experience. Scientific knowledge has come to lose a sense of proportion, a sense of that to which it is proper. It has lost a sense of the whole of which it is an irreplaceable part. By placing it back within the wealth of human experience, we can come to understand its uniqueness and power, an understanding that at once is an understanding of its limits. In the face of indigenous knowledge, in the face of what Maria's mother knows, science becomes renewed, revived. It regains its face, its difference.

Thus, for this invitation to be well heeded, some healing, some making hale and whole, is required in the very idea of what it means to know.

Sidestepping the New Onslaught

> Given the importance of digital information to the new knowledge economy, one of the key questions should be whether indigenous

ways-of-knowing can survive the new onslaught. (Pannekoek, 2003, p. 2)

"My mother is old. She knows the plants. I want to make a book and put the plants into the book." Bound strongly by intergenerational, ancestral knowledge and ways of knowing and being, and bound by relations to land and blood, we knew that capturing and documenting the landscape, the plants, and the stories could not be accomplished with text alone, nor could this capturing and documenting be detached, as is the wont of scientific knowledge, from the one's who know and have these tales to tell or from the one's *to whom* such telling is directed. This anonymity of knowledge, its "disinterest," will no longer do. Again, such disinterest does not disappear as a way of knowing. Rather, it is simply surrounded by its kin and held in the comfort of that surrounding. As a way of knowing, it is simply not adequate by itself and alone to the full, living existence of these plants in the life and ways of a people.

This invitation came to us just as new information technologies were breaking apart the old, fragmented, school-bound versions of knowledge that will no longer suffice. We moved carefully, having experienced full well how easily new information technologies have become simply accelerators of school-bound, traditional versions of knowledge—knowledge that was once conceived as facts and procedures, severed from the disciplines, laid out in advance on something akin to an assembly line (see Jardine, Clifford, & Friesen, 2003, 2008). But the image of these new technological prospects is consistently one of a "web." Perhaps new information technologies might not *necessarily* be an onslaught. We are struck by the prospect of a living analogue: those webs of knowledge portended by new technologies seem to bear a kinship to the webs of living into which we've been invited.

Representations of Euro-Canadian historical content in online media are evident in such online resources as *Early Canadiana Online, Our Roots/Nos Racines,* and *Historica.* However, there is a dearth of historical and cultural content created, aggregated, and placed online by First Nation peoples. Thus, while digital preservation and access is growing with regard to certain segments of the Canadian population, other segments are sorely underrepresented. The cultures not represented in online media to the broader knowledge society are, by and large, the cultures in danger of extinction. Again, the phenomenon of language and its power rears up:

> Already, material is often inaccessible because the language in which it was collected has so eroded that few understand. All except a handful of the fifty-three indigenous languages in Canada and the culture they evidence are not expected to be around within two generations. The living sources who insure the validity and transfer of this data

to community and scholars—the Elders—are also disappearing at an alarming rate. (Pannekoek, 2003)

There is, consequently, a demonstrable need for communities to claim their place in cyberspace so that generations of aboriginals may discover and remember their culture and traditions. Additionally, generations of nonaboriginal Canadians may discover and understand more about aboriginal cultures and history, leading to the development of a more informed and respectful, multicultural society.

What is at issue here, however, is not simply a replicating of the ways that cyberspace has been shaped by the dominant discourses of fragmentation and Eurocentric presumptions but rather a reshaping of those ways in light of the ways of knowing, representing, and remembering those indigenous to aboriginal culture. This is the first gesture of where the onslaught might be avoided, that new digital information technologies have lodged within them the possibility of pliability, variegatedness, responsiveness, and diversity. They are resilient; they respond to the voice and the touch if they are invited to do so. But the danger remains: they are also able to deliver old, familiar, presumptive forms of fragmented education, now at the speed of light. And, once tethered to fragmented, factory orientations of inert knowledge and delivered as facts and procedures, digital technologies lose their ability to invite students into a living landscape that requires their curiosity. Lewis Hyde's words resonate again: "The way we treat a thing can sometimes change its nature."

New technologies offer a medium where aboriginal ways of knowing can be expressed and re-created in nonlinear, oral, visual, and contextual environments—not without challenging many text-bound pedagogical practices, however. Narcisse Blood, cultural instructor from Red Crow College, suggests that it is very important for aboriginal youth to claim these technologies, so that their stories can be told, in their voice and in a way that honors their ways of knowing. Knowledge generated through structures of relationships cannot be communicated via media that privilege text and marginalize image and the voice:

> Indigenous ways of knowing share the following structure: (1) knowledge of and belief in unseen powers in the ecosystem; (2) knowledge that all things in the ecosystem are dependent on each other; (3) knowledge that reality is structured according to . . . linguistic concepts . . . ; (4) knowledge that personal relationships reinforce the bond between persons, communities and ecosystems; (5) knowledge that sacred traditions and persons who know these traditions are responsible for teaching "moral" and "ethics" to practitioners who are then given responsibility for this specialized knowledge and its dissemination; and (6) knowledge that an extended kinship passes on

teachings and social practices from generation to generation. (Crowshoe & Manneschmidt, quoted in Pannekoek, 2003, p. 4)

As is clear from any consideration of its contemporary forms *outside* of
schooling, the spell is already broken regarding how new digital information
technologies have been shaped by the familiar presumptions of the dominant
culture. Our student teachers have, in many ways, already broken down this familiarity for themselves and their friends, despite how the structures of schooling
constantly and timidly pull them back into old and worn-out ways. Advances in
new media permit new possibilities for

- creating interdependent online environments that more adequately reflect
  aboriginal structures of knowledge;
- designing geospatially and ecologically based environments that value oral and
  visual information above others (Pannekoek, 2003);
- communicating this knowledge to others in both aboriginal and nonaboriginal languages;
- providing for the use of images, voices, multiple languages, translations, and
  links; and
- providing for the possibility of the intergenerational creation and passing on
  of knowledge outside of the bounds that dominate schooling and its presumptions.

Again, we are struck by how fitting new technologies might be in taking up
Maria's invitation and in interrupting the weak patronizing of so many well-
intended aboriginal education initiatives.

Technology and the New Literacies

With the World Wide Web, the power of the oral and the visual image is now,
more than ever, an integral and significant aspect of contemporary culture
(Handa, 2004; Rose, 2005). The current emphasis on technology with the
screen becoming, along with the page, a part of the literate process, requires us
to carefully reexamine our relationship to the visual image (Illich, 1993; Illich,
cited in Cayley, 2005; Kress, 2003; Lankshear & Knobel, 2003) in terms of
our contemporary understanding of literacy. In fact, current research in new
media literacy studies challenges the contemporary understanding of literacy
and pushes the boundaries of much current textually based literacy practices in
schools (Handa, 2004; Kress, 2003; Lankshear & Knobel, 2003).

The digital environments created by new media artists offer the potential for creating and exploring nonlinear relationships among text, sound, and image:

> Approaching visual culture intertextually, incorporating the totality of images, sounds, and space that comprise the visual, rather than privileging a single strain to the exclusion of others, will allow the field to ask new questions, approach problems from unconventional intellectual angles, and, most important, unframe discussions from conventional values, histories and methodologies. (Rogoff, cited in Handa, 2004, p. 378)

"Literacy, in this sense, becomes a matter of reading different kinds of texts that integrate sound, image, text and spatial aspects" (Rogoff, cited in Handa, 2004, p. 387) as a way to enact possibilities for the simultaneously remembering (Rogoff, 2004, p. 394) of time, space, and vision. In thus doing, the dehierarchization of writing with an artist's work, rather than writing about it (Rogoff, 2004, p. 394), invites the possibility of constructing and beginning to understand places that embody real political gains (hooks, cited in Handa, 2004, p. 378).

Interdisciplinary research into literacy as new media cultural studies (Kress, 2003) in a post-typographic world (Lankshear & Knobel, 2003) sheds additional light on what it means to know in ways that are already at work in aboriginal culture. Without diminishing conventional interest in improving text-based literacy in aboriginal communities, this project suggests that there is much to be learned about digital literacy in both aboriginal and nonaboriginal environments when access to new media shapes what can be said about the world, by whom, and in what ways.

This allows, as with scientific knowledge, the resituating of text-based literacy back into the full array of literacies that actually live in the world. It "re-places" the severe European/Protestant interest in "the word" back into the world of images, oral speech, traditional knowledge, intergenerational familiarity with the land, and the like. It re-places English back into the great family of tongues. We believe that, far from diminishing the desire to improve text-based literacy, this re-placement begins to heal a wound that is long-standing in schooling and under increasing pressure in contemporary educational settings. The irreplaceable uniqueness of text-based literacies, including a deep sense of its limits, becomes visible and speakable. We even get a new glimpse of the great mongrel ancestry of English itself, all those hidden bloodlines and multifarious voices that ring through it. It becomes "experienceable," renewed into what it always was outside of the bounds of so many "English classes": a *living* language.

Stepping Outside the Factory Model

Despite the many changes that have taken place in schools over recent decades, the concern remains that too little has changed about the place called school, and the simple insertion of new digital information technologies into this locale does little more than accelerate and aggravate the structures of school. We have explored in some detail (Friesen & Jardine, 2009) the "factory model" of schooling that grew out of the industrial societies of the late nineteenth and earlier decades of the twentieth century. This is characterized—perhaps caricatured—as a school mirroring the industrial era that produced it, turning out a future workforce for the most part with basic skills and a compliant attitude. Students and teachers who worked in such settings were understood to be simply the assemblers of knowledge, with little or no investment in this process other than moving on to the next station in the assembly line (i.e., passing into the next grade).

> The question is then whether this remains the dominant model or whether instead schools have moved on to become the "learning organisations" appropriate for the knowledge-based societies of today and tomorrow. To what extent are schools and school systems willing to break the moulds of traditional classrooms and didactics? How far have they moved to become concerned with knowledge-creation as well as knowledge-transmission? (OECD, 2001, p. 62)

It is interesting to note, here, that the image of "learning organizations" still rings of the dominant model. The invitation we received had an ear toward familialness, traditions, landscapes, and learning one's way around the place. Again, language and our ability to imagine something out from under the dominant discourse is an ancient trouble.

The use of the term "learning organization" rings and resonates, and there are no innocent words that belie such resonance. We follow Hans-Georg Gadamer's (1989) invocation: "Every word breaks forth as if from a center and is related to a whole, through which alone it is a word. Every word causes the whole of the language to which it belongs to resonate" (p. 458). We therefore have found that language and its nature and limits lie at the heart of domination and also at the mainspring of innovation and change. The long history of the erasure of language in the community into which we were invited is no small matter, and its recovery lies at the core of the work we ensued.

K–12 teachers are just beginning to encounter the changes to schooling—the changes, in fact, to the langue in which their tasks are set—that creating classrooms for a knowledge society requires. Many have yet to grapple with the changes to teaching and learning that are required to engage students in the type of activity that is concerned with knowledge creation (Bereiter, 2003; Friesen &

Clifford, 2003; Hargreaves, 2003; Newmann, 2000; Scardamalia, 2005; Scardamalia & Bereiter, 2003; Seitamaa-Hakkarainen et al., 2003). This is because the knowledge-creation activity and its supporting pedagogy are not simply different activities for students and teachers to engage in. Rather, these practices embody a fundamental significant shift in the ways teachers plan and teach. Teachers come to understand themselves as working within an array of living disciplines of knowledge that form living inheritances that have been entrusted to teachers and students in schools. Understood as threads of a living discipline, the knowledge-creation activity also embodies a fundamental shift in the ways students learn and what they learn (Clifford, Friesen, & Lock, 2004).

The challenge to K–12 schooling is to find ways to develop citizens who not only possess up-to-date knowledge but also are able to participate in the creation of new knowledge as a normal part of their lives (Scardamalia & Bereiter, 2003). Here, a telling image of invitation reemerges: how are we to invite students into the living work of a living discipline of knowledge?

While finding ways to design and study learning within knowledge-creation classrooms is essential within mainstream public education, it is perhaps even more paramount that, as a Canadian society, we join with aboriginal students and their teachers to include them in the knowledge society. We face, in such "inclusiveness," the recognition that such inclusion does not leave our understanding of "the knowledge society" untouched, nor does this "our" remain the same. Inclusion, if it is to be healing, must be transformative of the very images of knowledge that are at work. Speaking in Quebec City at the 2005 CASA conference, Marlene Scardamalia made the point that we are poised to create an ingenuity gap in which inequities are magnified as we move ever more deeply toward creating a society where knowledge creation and innovation are valued. In Canada, groups at risk of being excluded from the knowledge society include the aboriginal communities.

The industrial models of schooling that present worldwide challenges to educational reform carry a particular history of oppression in aboriginal communities. Because traditional knowledge structures were systematically undermined and dismantled by residential schools, a call to eliminate an ingenuity gap must go far beyond the usual rhetoric of helping aboriginal students become "computer literate." Instead, researchers and practitioners must examine ways in which new media hold possibilities that preserve and extend aboriginal ways of knowing in ways that have never been available to us before.

Aboriginal Ways of Knowing

In aboriginal ways of knowing, "Knowledge belongs to a people and people belong to a landscape" (Peat, 2002, p. 63). Ryan Heavyhead, teacher at Red

Crow College, explains further, "Each rock is a story and when you hear the story, you have a responsibility to the story. You must live the story and pass on its essence" (personal communication). This is a reciprocal relationship between the knower and the known. True knowledge is impossible without this reciprocity. Generating knowledge is a circular process that occurs by renewing these relationships (Bastien, 2004; C. Calf Robe, personal communication; Peat, 2002).

Building knowledge in this way demands an intimacy with the landscape. Time spent on the land with elders and spiritual guides creates the milieu of possibility. Hearing the traditional language and engaging in ceremony becomes the student's preparation for receiving communication and knowledge. This coming-to-know is neither linear nor fragmented. It is embodied. It exists only within a web of relations (Bastien, 2004; Graveline, 1998; Gulliford, 2000; Horn, 2000; Peat, 2002). It is important to note, then, that the image of a "landscape" and learning your way around such landscapes is slowly emerging in the dominant discourses of educational reform (Bransford, Brown, & Cocking, 2000; Sawyer, 2006).

> An alternative to a "rutted path" curriculum is one of "learning the landscape" (Greeno, 1991). In this metaphor, learning is analogous to learning to live in an environment: learning your way around, learning what resources are available, and learning how to use those resources in conducting your activities productively and enjoyably (Greeno, 1991:175). . . . Knowing where one is in a landscape requires a network of connections that link one's present location to the larger space.
>
> Traditional curricula often fail to help students "learn their way around" a discipline. The curricula include the familiar scope and sequence charts that specify procedural objectives to be mastered by students at each grade: though an individual objective might be reasonable, it is not seen as part of a larger network. Yet it is the network, the connections among objectives, that is important. This is the kind of knowledge that characterizes expertise. (Bransford, Brown & Cocking, 2000, pp. 138–139)

In fact, our own work has examined this territory for many years. Over many years, we've explored folds of the same cloth: "family resemblances" (from Wittgenstein, 1968; see Jardine, 1992); ancestries, fields, topographies, places, and big ideas (Clifford & Friesen, 1993; Jardine, Clifford, & Friesen 2003); generative and intergenerational knowledge (Friesen, Clifford, & Jardine, 1998); living disciplines, relatedness, and interdependence (see Jardine, 1995; Jardine and Friesen, 1997); and the idea of ecopedagogy (Jardine, 1997, 2000), which explores the analogies between webs of knowledge and webs of earthly relations, including the ancestral knowledge of the topic under consideration.

To learn, children must therefore know their responsibilities to the subject, and teachings must come from the elders (Bastien, 2004). The right to knowledge must be earned. Listening to the oral stories of the elders is essential for personal development and knowledge creation. Listening to the stories of elders is very different from the Eurocentric stance of a student interviewing for information and asking questions (A. Delaney, personal communication; Bastien, 2004; Peat, 2002). To speak in aboriginal languages is to call up this web of relations. That is, the very "sound of the word is in relationship to the land, ancestors and the future" (N. Blood, personal communication). Listening to the stories of elders in their own language is necessary for attaining knowledge. "These experiences are the primary knowledge of the tribe, and they form the methods of coming to know the ways of knowing" (Bastien, 2004, p. 60).

This knowledge building is very different from what is offered up in most Eurocentric classrooms, where coming to know is often outside the context of landscape, reciprocal relationships with the subject at hand, orality, ancestral communication, time, and ceremony. David Peat (2002) writes, "When I listen to Native people I get the impression that knowledge for them is profoundly different: it is a living thing that has existence independent of human beings. A person comes to knowing by entering into a relationship with the living spirit of that knowledge" (p. 67).

Technology and Blackfoot Plant Knowledge

Digital technology has an impact on every part of our world today. It's not a passing fad. It's not another thing to add to the usual ways we think and work. And it's not just one more curriculum topic to cover, or one more thing for students to do when their "real" work is done. Technology is an integral part of our everyday world. It is, moreover, the locus of a transformation in our ability to imagine the nature of knowledge itself. *This* is what it means to live in a knowledge society: knowledge itself is becoming diversified.

Let's take a step back for a minute. The invention of the networked personal computer has and still is changing our society perhaps on the same magnitude of Johannes Gutenberg's printing press in 1455. We can just imagine some saying at that time, "It is just a tool, like a quill—a mechanical quill." And in some ways it was. Gutenberg did not invent books. "Books printed before 1501 are called *incunabula*; the word is derived from the Latin for swaddling clothes and is used to indicate that these books are the work of a technology still in its infancy (Murray, 1997, p. 28). The fifty years between 1455 and 1501 were the years of experimentation dedicated to

> establishing such conventions as legible typefaces and proof sheet corrections; page numbering and paragraphing; and title pages, prefaces, and chapter divisions, which together made the published book a coherent means of communication. The garish videogames and tangled Web sites of the current digital environment are part of a similar period of technical evolution, part of a similar struggle for the conventions of coherent communication.
>
> Similarly, new narrative traditions do not arise out of the blue. A particular technology of communication—the printing press, the movie camera, the radio—may startle us when it first arrives on the scene, but the traditions of storytelling are continuous and feed into one another both in content and in form. (Murray, 1997, p. 28)

Our plant study connecting the Creator, landscape, plants, and stories arrives during the *incunabular* days of the narrative computer. Many of the current digital media, both video and websites, strain to replicate linear narratives. However, from the outset we sought something quite different. We wanted to experiment with finding new ways of using and creating with digital media that was adequate to knowledge and was held as a web of connection.

The grade 4 students; Maria, their teacher; a number of teacher assistants; and a number of mentors and consultants from the Galileo Educational Network at the University of Calgary spent many days out on the land learning about sixty-two different indigenous healing plants through stories from several different elders. Students, equipped with digital still and video cameras recorded the treks out to various parts of the 356,755 acres that make up the Blood reserve in southern Alberta. Very little from our numerous excursions out on the land was left unrecorded. There were times that the elders spoke only in Blackfoot. The elders explained that knowledge of some plants was sacred knowledge and therefore for the Blackfoot people only.

The elders taught the children how to identify sweetgrass from the other grasses and sage from its look-a-like cousins. The children brought some plants back to the classroom. They braided sweetgrass and learned how and why it was used in ceremonies. By closely observing the various plants they created a number of detailed sketches. They even brought seeds from a number of plants back to the classroom and planted them in the classroom, observing them carefully as they grew. Oftentimes, the children pleaded to know more. They invited the elders to come into the classroom. The students designed questions to elicit more stories, more teachings, from the elders. And they carefully and thoughtfully recorded each interview.

Incunabula Days

Our challenge at the Galileo Educational Network was to experiment thought-fully with digital technologies that are still in its *incunabular* days to create an online environment. We were clear that a linear or even hyperlinked multimedia environment would not do. It was while we were drafting and designing that we came across a passage in Cervantes' Don Quixote. "Don Quixote, living 150 years after the invention of the printing press, exemplifies the dangerous power of books to create a world that is 'more real than reality'" (Murray, 1997, p. 97).

> In short, he so buried himself in his books that he spent nights read-ing from twilight 'til daybreak and the days from dawn 'til dark; and so from little sleep and much reading, his brain dried up and he lost his wits. He filled his mind with all that he read in them, with enchantments, quarrels, battles, challenges, wounds, wooings, loves, torments, and other impossible nonsense; and so deeply did he steep his imagination in the belief that all the fanciful stuff he read was true, that . . . he decided . . . to turn knight errant and travel through the world with horse and armour in search of adventures.
>
> —Don Quixote de la Mancha
> (Resnick & Pasmantier, 1994, p. 177)

Don Quixote stands for all of the part of each of us that longs to be im-mersed in a good book or great movie—getting sucked into a good story that is more real than reality. Working with this new digital media, we wanted to create forms of thought and expression, playing around with what is desirable and possible. We experimented with the representational power of the online media and these grade 4 students' actual experience out on the land, testing for the boundaries of this liminal world. We wanted to create an immersive online Web experience that honored and preserved the healing plant knowledge of Kainai elders and ancestors—a site that gathered together the students' photos, drawings, interviews, videos, and stories to create an experience for the viewer that lured them out onto the land.

We cannot, in a text only full of words, pretend to represent the work that was finally done. Rather, we invite readers to visit "Nitsitapiisini—Stories and Spaces: Exploring Kainai Plants and Culture" website, found at www.galileo org/plants/kainai.

We offer a few navigational clues so you can find your way in, so you, too, might experience the ways in which digital information and communication technologies were used to break the bounds of the *Programs of Study* and its mandated "Study of Plants" unit.

"Nitsitapiisini—Stories and Spaces: Exploring Kainai Plants and Culture" reflects Kainai ways of knowing and showcases resources for study and teaching. As you enter the site, the elders whose wisdom and experience help interpret five different landscapes of the Kainai reserve will guide you. These landscapes come alive with meaning as you hear the sounds of the animals that live there. As you scroll over each of the landscapes, the elders help you see the plants for the first time and tell you about each plant you encounter. Clicking on one of the children sitting next to the elder, you will hear a story that was told to them. Clicking on a plant will take you to further information about the plant presented in Blackfoot, English, and French that describe the botanical and cultural uses of the plants. While reading about the plants you can watch the videos the students created. Some of these videos are of times out on the land and others are their interviews with the various elders.

The medicine wheel at the top of each page acts as a navigation tool in the Web resource as it does in Native culture. Clicking on the different sections of the medicine wheel brings you to different parts of the Web resource and different kinds of knowledge. North, or white, introduces you to the elder guides. Each elder takes you to a different landscape. Yellow, or east, takes you to the medicine shelf, which is another way of accessing the information on each of the sixty-two indigenous healing plants. The red, or south, part of the wheel will take you to various elders and members of the Kainai community. By clicking on each photo you, too, can hear stories and explanations of traditional healing and ways of knowing. The blue, or west, section of the medicine wheel connects you to the classroom. Here, you will find many teaching and learning resources as well as a student art gallery, an original music composition, and an interpretative video. In each section of the medicine wheel, you will find a book icon that links you to a database to read and search forty-one completely digitized print books. You will find that some of the trails have stories told only in Blackfoot. These stories are not indiscriminately for everyone. They live in the blood and in the tongue, and trace the land to which only some are obligated. They remind us that knowledge is not always and everywhere faceless, and that the anonymity of knowledge as found in the science curriculum is itself a way of life with its own limits and consequences.

Endbit

There is a recent television commercial in which a twenty-something is showing off his new handheld gadget that has a pull-out, full keyboard. One of his friends says that this is wonderful, that she can now enter into serious and extended conversations with her friends over important issues. The others around the table look quizzical, and the owner of the new gadget looks at her condescendingly, as if she has simply missed the point, and repeats in a slower, dumbed-down voice what he has already said: "The keyboard pulls in and out," he says, with a weird sort of distain for her obvious lack of understanding.

Most of our student teachers are far more adept at new digital information and communication technologies than their elders. However, an equal number of them have become swept up into the ways in which these technologies are used to simply exaggerate fragmentation, triviality, and forms of being "in touch" that have lost bodily, ancestral, and topographical wherewithal. There is even a hint of this in the new greeting that is common with the cell phone. One used to say, first, "Hi, how are you?" and now the first greeting is often "Hi, *where* are you?"

Many new technologies have simply made the flickering of television screens seem antiquated and slow. Cascades of twittered "messages" have replaced the long and slow work of thinking, of cultivating knowledge while at once cultivating oneself. There is nothing in the new technologies themselves that requires anything new beyond the dominant ways of scattershot and ever-accelerating attention. These technologies will not ask anything of us or our students other than what we ourselves ask of them. This is the trouble with their potentiality. But when these technologies are invited into places that are allowed to speak back to what is possible, what is needed, and what is proper here, now, in this place, that potentiality can become actualized in exciting ways that interrupt.

In these *incunabular* days with our new technology, it is important to gather ourselves to seek out the appropriate medium to provide representational expression to creator and audience alike, residing in a liminal space, open to ways of knowing that don't yield themselves to sound bites. We glimpse a great parallel to the wont of scientific knowledge: that knowledge does not appear willy-nilly but is rather "won by a certain labour" (Ross & Jardine, 2009).

Coming to know the sixty-two indigenous healing plants on the lands of the Kainai people took time, with adults and children repeatedly turning and returning to the land. And with each return, the elders told yet another story, and those of us in their midst saw again, as if for the first time, what we had missed, what we had not heard. The slowness of the walks across the land, the gathering, the whiling (see Jardine, 2008; Ross & Jardine, 2009), and the waiting are all required to know this landscape, the stories, and the plants. This stands in stark contrast to the consumer marketing media hype promises of information and communication technologies—speed and indiscriminate "access." This stands in stark contrast, too, to the numerous activities delivered unconnected one to another in the name of "hands-on" science. This shows what it means to treat a thing so its nature can show.

Rather than succumbing to the hyperactivity of the marketing consumer hype that dominates so much of our culture when it comes to digital media, an inviting "return" is in order, an older memory of kinship—a "web," if you will—is required, a kinship that ignites curiosity and creativity. Even though cameras were handed to the children, entrusted into their hands quite literally, they were not simply then "abandoned to their own devices" (Arendt, 1969, pp. 192–193), as if inventiveness and enthusiasm are themselves adequate to the fullness of knowledge. The Latin root reminds us, that *invenio* is the root of inventiveness but also of "inventory" and therefore that the giddy, inventive onrush of the young takes its strength only from its relation to the cultivated wisdoms of living ancestry.

Taking seriously what this means for teaching and learning in the twenty-first century invites students and teachers alike to experience curriculum as a living landscape—an idea that presents a challenge to twentieth-century factory models of what it means to teach and learn. The knowledge for the website, just like the knowledge of the place, had to be formed, shaped, adjusted, collaboratively, and repeated; the old and young stayed firm with each other and took care of each other.

It is in this comfort, this common fortitude or strength, that we were able to accept Maria's invitation and in this place find a proper measure of new information technologies.

Notes

1. Maria is a pseudonym.
2. N. Blood is referring to the knowledge the students will gain from going out onto the land with the elders throughout this plant study.

References

Alberta Education. (1996). *Science: Program of studies*, grade 4. Edmonton, Canada: Author.

Arendt, H. (1969). The crisis in education. In *Between past and present: Eight exercises in political thought* (pp. 192–193). New York: Penguin.

Bastien, B. (2004). *Blackfoot ways of knowing: The worldview of the Siksikaitsitapi.* Calgary, Canada: University of Calgary Press.

Bereiter, C. (2003). Bringing classrooms into the knowledge age. In *Proceedings of the Reform and Initiatives in Teaching and Learning conference* (pp. 1–10). Macau, China: University of Macau.

Bransford, J., Brown, A., & Cocking, R. (Eds.). (2000). *How people learn: Brain, mind, experience and school.* Washington, DC: National Academies Press.

Cayley, D. (2005). *The rivers north of the future: The testament of Ivan Illich as told to David Cayley.* Toronto: House of Anansi Press.

Clifford, P., & Friesen, S. (1993). A curious plan: Managing on the twelfth. *Harvard Educational Review, 63*(3), 339–358.

Clifford, P., Friesen, S., & Lock, J. (2004). Coming to teaching in the 21st century: A research study conducted by the Galileo Educational Network. Retrieved April 5, 2009, from www.galileo.org/research/publications/ctt.pdf.

Crowshoe, R., & Manneschmidt, S. (2002). *Akak'stiman: A Blackfoot framework for decision-making and mediation processes.* Calgary, Canada: University of Calgary Press.

Friesen, S., & Clifford, P. (2003). Working across different spaces to create communities of practice in teacher professional development. In Proceedings of MICTE 2003 Multimedia, Information and Communication Technologies conference, Badajoz, Spain, December 3–6. Retrieved April 5, 2009, from www.galileo.org/research/publications/different_spaces.pdf.

Friesen, S., Clifford, P., & Jardine, D. (1998). Meditations on community, memory and the intergenerational character of mathematical truth. *Journal of Curriculum Theorizing, 14*(3), 6–11.

Friesen, S., & Jardine, D. (2009). On field(ing) knowledge. In S. Goodchild & B. Sriraman (Eds.), *Festschrifte in celebration of Paul Ernest's 65th birthday. The Montana monographs in mathematics education series* (pp. 149–175). Charlotte, NC: Information Age Publishing.

Gadamer, H.-G. (1989). *Truth and method* (J. Weinsheimer, Trans.). New York: Crossroads.

Graveline, F. J. (1998). *Circle works: Transforming Eurocentric consciousness.* Halifax, Canada: Fernwood.

Greeno, J. (1991). Number sense as situated knowing in a conceptual domain. *Journal for Research in Mathematics Education, 22*(3), 170–218.

Gulliford, A. (2000). *Sacred objects and sacred places: Preserving tribal traditions.* Boulder: University Press of Colorado.

Handa, C. (2004). *Visual rhetoric in a digital world: A critical sourcebook.* Boston: Bedford/St. Martin's.

Hargreaves, A. (2003). *Teaching in the knowledge society: Education in the age of insecurity.* New York: Teachers College Press.

Horn, G. (2000). *Book of ceremonies: A Native way of honoring and living the sacred.* Novato, CA: New World Library.

Illich, I. (1993). *In the vineyard of the text: A commentary to Hugh's Didascalicon.* Chicago: University of Chicago Press.

Jardine, D. (1992). The fecundity of the individual case: Considerations of the pedagogic heart of interpretive work. *British Journal of Philosophy of Education, 26*(1), 51–61.

Jardine, D. (1995). The stubborn particulars of grace. In B. Horwood (Ed.), *Experience and the curriculum: Principles and programs* (pp. 261–275). Dubuque, IA: Kendall/Hunt Publishing.

Jardine, D. (1997). Under the tough old stars: Pedagogical hyperactivity and the mood of environmental education. *Clearing: Environmental education in the Pacific Northwest, 97*, 20–23.

Jardine, D. (2000). *Under the tough old stars: Ecopedagogical essays.* Brandon, VT: Psychology Press/Holistic Education Press.

Jardine, D. (2006). Youth need images for their imaginations and for the formation of their memories. *Journal of Curriculum Theorizing, 22*(3), 3–12.

Jardine, D. (2008). On the while of things. *Journal of the American Association for the Advancement of Curriculum Studies, 4.* Retrieved October 4, 2010, from www.uwstout .edu/soe/jaaacs/vol4/Jardine.htm.

Jardine, D., Clifford, P., & Friesen, S. (2003). *Back to the basics of teaching and learning: Thinking the world together.* Mahwah, NJ: Lawrence Erlbaum.

Jardine, D., Clifford, P., & Friesen, S. (2008). *Back to the basics of teaching and learning: Thinking the world together* (2nd ed.). New York: Routledge.

Jardine, D., & Friesen, S. (1997). A play on the wickedness of undone sums, including a brief mytho-phenomenology of "x" and some speculations on the effects of its peculiar absence in elementary mathematics education. *Philosophy of Mathematics Education Journal, 10.* Retrieved October 4, 2010, from www.ex.ac.uk/~PErnest/pome10.

Kress, G. (2003). *Literacy and the new media.* London, UK: Routledge.

Lankshear, C., & Knobel, M. (2003). *New literacies: Changing knowledge and classroom learning.* Philadelphia, PA: Open University Press.

Murray, J. (1997). *Hamlet on the holodeck: The future of narrative in cyberspace.* New York: Free Press.

Newmann, F. (2000). Authentic intellectual work: What and why? *Research/Practice, 8*(1). Retrieved April 5, 2009, from http://education.umn.edu/CAREI/Reports/Rpractice/ Fall2000/newmann.htm.

OECD. (2001). *What schools for the future?* Paris: OECD Press.

Pannekoek, F. (2003). *Indigenous ways-of-knowing: A searching software proposal. Unpublished manuscript.* Calgary, Canada: University of Calgary Press.

Peat, F. D. (2002). *Blackfoot physics: A journey into the Native American universe.* Grand Rapids, MI: Phanes Press.

Resnick, S., & Pasmantier, J. (1994). *Nine centuries of Spanish literature: A dual-language anthology.* New York: Dover Publications.

Reston, J. (2005). *Dogs of God: Columbus, the inquisition and the defeat of the moors.* New York: Doubleday.

Rogoff, I. (2004). Studying visual culture. In C. Handa (Ed.), *Visual rhetoric in a digital world: A critical sourcebook* (pp. 381–394). Boston: Bedford/St. Martin's.

Rose, G. (2005). *Visual methodologies: An introduction to the interpretation of visual materials.* London: Sage.

Ross, S. M., & Jardine, D. (2009). Won by a certain labour: A conversation on the while of things. *Journal of the American Association for the Advancement of Curriculum Studies, 5.* Retrieved April 5, 2009, from www.uwstout.edu/soe/jaaacs/Vol5/Ross_Jardine .htm.

Sawyer, R. K. (Ed.). (2006). *The Cambridge handbook of the learning sciences.* New York: Cambridge University Press.

Scardamalia, M. (2005). Learning sciences and what we know about how children learn. Keynote address, CASA Annual Conference, Quebec City, October 15–17.

Scardamalia, M., & Bereiter, C. (2003). Knowledge building. In J. W. Guthrie (Ed.), *Encyclopedia of education* (2nd ed.). New York: Macmillan Reference.

Seitamaa-Hakkarainen, P., Lahti, H., Iivonen, M., Bollström-Huttunen, M., & Hakkarainen, K. (2003). Understanding cultural diversity of artifacts through collaborative knowledge building. Poster session presented at the IKIT Summer Institute 2003, Toronto, August 12.

Wittgenstein, L. (1968). *Philosophical investigations.* Cambridge, UK: Blackwell.

CHAPTER 11

Fostering Creative Minds through Problem Solving in a 3-D Visualization Design Research Program

Jacqueline Sack
University of Houston-Downtown

Jacqueline Sack, Ed.D., is assistant professor at the University of Houston–Downtown. She designed the framework and managed the development of Rice University's *Geometry Module*, which is used for mathematics teacher development in higher education institutions across the country. Her research interests include geometry, teacher leadership, and teacher development.

ABSTRACT

This chapter describes how a design research project that develops children's 3-D visualization capacity fosters creative teaching and teaching for creativity. Through the spatial operation capacity framework (Van Niekerk, 1997; Yakimanskaya, 1991) that guides the development of the mathematics in this study, children are exposed to activities that require them to act on a variety of physical and mental objects and transformations to develop spatial skills. Children use 3-D figures, 2-D representations of 3-D figures, verbal representations, and a dynamic computer interface to solve spatial problems. The project is enacted in a dual-language elementary school that serves a typical urban population.

In this chapter, the story of creativity and invention is told within an ongoing design research program to develop third graders' 3-D visualization skills. Told through the voice of the author, Jackie, this story is based on particular experiences that emerged during the study's first year of enactment.

When I considered contributing to this volume, I set about trying to understand how others defined creativity. Bob Jeffrey and Anna Craft (2004) examine distinctions and relationships between teaching creatively and teaching for creativity. Teaching creatively is about styles of pedagogy that engage and motivate children. Bill Lucas (2001) believes that creativity is "a state of mind" (p. 40) and not necessarily something inborn in a teacher as others have argued (e.g., Gardner, 1999). In an exemplar for creative teaching, Lucas attends to a social environment in which everyone is respectful; each child is treated as an individual; teachers leave space for thought; and, when appropriate, they provide the structure to help children learn. There is one more caveat: such an environment is possible only with the right kind of leadership at the helm. The principal of Lucas's exemplar school has gathered an extraordinary teaching staff, individuals who are innovative risk-takers.

Jeffrey and Craft (2004) consider teaching for creativity as a vehicle for fostering empowerment. They argue that, in order to survive in the twenty-first century and in a global economy, people will need to be more creative about the way they manage their careers in order to maintain expected incomes and standards of living. In this context, "the relationship between creativity and work has become more symbiotic" (p. 5). I agree that creative teachers and teaching for creativity are essential components in today's schools if we are to empower children to face the challenges of living competitively as adults in our contemporary global society.

As I wrestled with these broad ideas, conversations with colleagues arose about creativity and problem solving within the content sphere of mathematics education. Stephen Krulik and Jesse Rudnick (1987) examine instructional strategies to promote problem-solving environments. These include involving one's students in the problem, requiring students to create their own problems, and having students work in pairs or small groups. In particular, to develop children's capacity to share and become proficient at defending their own positions while considering the positions of others, they believe children should be encouraged to allow their imaginations to "run rampant," "put forth as many ideas as possible," and "build upon the ideas or modify the ideas of others" (p. 50). Open-ended problem-solving tasks that result in multirepresentational solution pathways lend themselves to these strategies.

Further reading provided Lucas's (2001) definition of creativity as involving "seeing, thinking and innovating" (p. 38). He believes creativity engages "all of our intelligences working together" (p. 38), something that is possible in any school course or subject. I hope to show, through carefully articulated examples, how our design research program, now in its second year of enactment, fosters creativity through our belief in and attention to differentiated instructional strategies that encourage learners of all kinds to learn creatively about three-dimensional figures.

Project Rationale and Theoretical Frameworks

Why did we embark on this particular study? The National Research Council's report, *Learning to Think Spatially* (NRC, 2006), notes that the teaching of spatial thinking in the K–12 curriculum is not formally and systematically taught. The report notes that spatial thinking *is* the start of successful thinking and problem solving, an integral part of mathematical and scientific literacy. From a purely academic perspective, the importance of visual processing has been documented by researchers who have examined student performance in higher-level mathematics. For example, David Tall and colleagues (2001) found that, to be successful in abstract axiomatic mathematics, students should be proficient in both symbolic and visual cognition; Tommy Dreyfus (1991) calls for integration across algebraic, visual, and verbal abilities; and Norma Presmeg (1992) believes that imagistic processing is an essential component in one's development of abstraction and generalization.

The National Council of Teachers of Mathematics' *Principles and Standards for School Mathematics* (NCTM, 2000) supports this view. In their early years of schooling, students should develop visualization skills through hands-on experiences with a variety of geometric objects and use technology to dynamically transform simulations of two- and three-dimensional objects. Later, they should analyze and draw perspective views, count component parts, and describe attributes that cannot be seen but can be inferred. Students need to learn to physically and mentally transform objects in systematic ways as they develop spatial knowledge.

The spatial operation capacity (SOC) framework that guides the development of the mathematics in our study aligns with these views and is based on the research work of I. S. Yakimanskaya (1991) and Retha van Niekerk (1997). Children are exposed to activities that require them to act on a variety of physical and mental objects and transformations to develop the skills necessary for solving spatial problems (Yakimanskaya, 1991). The instructional design based on the SOC model (see figure 11.1) uses *full-scale* models (or scaled-down models) of large objects that can be handled by the child; *conventional-graphic* models that are two-dimensional graphic representations that resemble real three-dimensional objects; and *semiotic* models that are abstract, symbolic representations that usually do not bear any resemblance to the actual objects. Examples include view and numeric top-view diagrams.

We also utilize a *dynamic computer interface*, Geocadabra (Lecluse, 2005), a tool that was not available when the SOC framework was originally developed. Through the Geocadabra Construction Box module, complex, multicube structures can be viewed as two-dimensional conventional representations or in symbolic ways, for example, as top, side, and front views or numeric top-view diagrams (see figure 11.2). Whereas one can move around a three-dimensional model to see it from different vantage points, one may see various views of a computer-generated figure through its ability to be rotated in real time (see figure 11.3). The computer interface serves as a mediator of knowledge (Borba & Villarreal, 2005) rather than as a unique form of representation.

We believe that children should develop competence using all visual representation modes in addition to *verbal* descriptions regardless of the representation given in any particular problem using physical and mental processes. Our instructional activities provide children with opportunities to move among these different representations initially using loose wooden cubes and Soma figures (see figure 11.4; Weisstein, 1999), progressing to two-dimensional conventional graphic and semiotic models (Freudenthal, 1991) and verbal representations integrated with Geocadabra.

The seven Soma figures are made from twenty-seven unit cubes glued together in different three-cube or four-cube arrangements. Transformations are implicitly and explicitly used in our activities while children move among the SOC framework's representations. Our introductory activities rely on materials of our own creation, such as task cards and the activities in the Geocadabra manual (van Niekerk, 2006), to help children develop beginning competency in moving among these representations. However, very early in the program, we challenge children to use Geocadabra to create their own two-dimensional figures that we print as task cards and coding puzzles. These later become important materials for use in a variety of activities. When children create puzzles and problems for others to solve, their motivation and interest heightens. Furthermore, they self-select within these creative activities according to their own abilities, interests, and learning profiles (Tomlinson & McTighe, 2006).

Our instructional decisions are guided by the design research methodology of Paul Cobb and colleagues (2003) that calls for iterations of experiment preparation, teaching phase, and retrospective analysis. Our intent is to support and give an account of young children's development of spatial reasoning and ultimately to create curricular resources that may be integrated into the elementary-level mathematics curriculum. Each lesson we enact is part of a design experiment in which the research team hypothesizes learning outcomes, designs instructional activities to support that outcome, and enacts the lesson. During the retrospective analysis following the lesson, the research team determines the actual outcomes and then plans the next lesson, which may be an iteration of the last lesson to improve the outcome, a rejection of the last lesson if it failed to produce adequate progress toward the desired outcome, or a change in direction if unexpected, but interesting, outcomes arose that are deemed worthy of more attention.

The ongoing study is conducted in a dual-language urban elementary school within one of the largest public school districts in the midsouthwestern United States. During the 2007–2008 academic year, teacher-researcher, Irma, and coteacher, Raquel, joined me to form the research team that worked with a third-grade and then a fourth-grade group of children weekly (one hour per group) in Irma's classroom during an after-school program. At the beginning of the fall semester, English and Spanish parent/guardian and student consent-to-participate forms were sent home to parents of all after-school third and fourth graders. All respondents were accepted into the program.

With respect to the classroom ecology, Irma had taught mathematics and science to all fourth-grade participants during their entire third-grade year. Due to staffing changes for the third-grade class, she taught all core subjects to half of the school's third-grade students. Consequently, some of the third-grade participants in the after-school SOC program were not her students during the school day. However, all participants became attuned to her behavioral and communal expectations very quickly during the first month of the research program. She expected all students to develop independence by asking each other for help or support before asking the teacher and to treat each other respectfully.

We developed and supported a dominant social constructivist approach. This supportive environment allowed students to express their understandings, confusions, or frustrations safely in front of their peers. They were expected to explain and provide justifications for their mathematical conclusions. We rarely gave away answers or explanations. Students constructed meaning and representations for themselves. Furthermore, our design incorporated learning experiences that challenged each child according to particular readiness, interest, and learning profile. Our strong attention to differentiated instruction ensured "processes and procedures that ensure effective learning for varied individuals" (Tomlinson & McTighe, 2006, p. 3). This environment supported problem solving and fostered creativity in our participants while as researchers we were able to make sense of student understanding of 3-D structures. In particular, we encouraged students to share their ideas and solutions to each other or to the whole class. This resulted in deeper understanding and further development of key concepts.

Lucas (2001) presents a list of fifteen ways in which the teacher-student relationship may foster an individual's creativity. I realized that our program embodied every single bullet in this list:

• Being respectful rather than dismissive;
• Encouraging active not passive learning;
• Supporting individual interests rather than standardized curriculums;
• Engaging many learning styles not one;

- Encouraging and exploring emotional responses;
- Posing questions not statements;
- Offering ambiguity rather than certainties;
- Being open-ended rather than closing down;
- Being known as surprising rather than predictable;
- Offering many patterns rather than a standardized model;
- Moving the "classroom" to varied environments;
- Recognizing multiple intelligences;
- Including visual representations as well as auditory ones;
- Including tactile and experience-based activity; and
- Stimulating social as well as private learning. (p. 40)

Our classroom environment fostered curiosity and creativity in ways that surpassed our expectations. Our data sources include formal and informal interviews, video-recordings and transcriptions, field notes, student products, and lesson notes. I now provide example lessons to illustrate how our program builds students' curiosity and creativity. I invite the reader to consider Lucas's list of ways to be creative as each story is told.

Example Research Lessons

EXAMPLE 1: NONCONVENTIONAL TOP-VIEW CODING

Over the course of six lessons spanning November–December 2007, students worked with the Geocadabra Construction Box to master numeric top-view coding of 2-D conventional images. For example, students rebuilt the figures shown in a customized manual using blocks and a mirror and then created the complete structure on the computer using Geocadabra (for example, see figure 11.5). Finally, they recorded the numbers displayed on the screen's top view. Based on students' readiness, subsequent activities focused on mastery of top-view coding.

Using task cards with different levels of complexity (examples shown in figure 11.6), students identified the two Soma pieces required to build the illustrated conventional graphic figures. Then they coded the figures' top-view plans. Some students were capable of drawing freehand grids; others needed a printed grid. In addition, they decoded each others' codings by building the figures using loose cubes or combinations of Soma pieces. They checked their three-dimensional figures using the original task cards. They worked independently or in self-selected groups. The seamless implementation of flexible grouping and differentiated levels of difficulty allowed students to make choices, maintaining their motivation and interest on the tasks presented. These approaches, early in the year, encouraged active learning that supported individual interests and learning styles. This work laid the foundation for the creativity that ensued.

The creation of about four hundred different task cards representing two connected Soma figures had been daunting for me. Instead of continuing to provide teacher-created task cards, we realized that our students could create their own. The existing Geocadabra Construction Box module limited users to constructions that grew from a base layer and could have no spaces or overhangs. Within days, the developer, Ton Lecluse, customized the software with a new module, the Extended Construction Box, which allowed students to construct figures with spaces and overhangs (see figure 11.7). This new module does not use top-view numeric coding. Instead, one places individual cubes or linked combinations of cubes along axial lines in a three-dimensional octant. At this point, the children competently moved among top-view numeric codings and corresponding 3-D models or 2-D conventional pictures for relatively simple structures.

We challenged them to create a numeric top-view coding system that included holes and overhangs since we were not aware of a conventional coding system of this nature. In this problem setting, students blind tested each other's invented codings to see if they could re-create the corresponding 3-D figures; challenged each other and offered suggestions for improvement; and compared and rated their invented codings. If a student challenged another's coding, we asked him or her to write an explanation describing the concern. A written response was expected. In this way, the verbal representation came into play, further developing students' descriptive spatial language base. Since Irma used this communication strategy in her general studies classroom across all content areas, this particular activity helped students make connections globally across the curriculum. Nonconventional activities like these provided the children with opportunities to think about and try to solve open-ended problems without specific or predictable solutions and to build on each other's ideas and interpretations.

Previously, we had discovered that our students ascribed to two different but conceptually appropriate interpretations of the conventional top-view coding system (as in the original Construction Box). For example, in figure 11.8, some children said the "2" in the front left position represented a stack of two cubes. Others said the "2" represented a cube on the second level, implicitly knowing that there is a cube (or a stack of cubes) supporting that cube from below. These interpretations came into conflict when students tried to decode someone else's invented coding for structures with empty spaces or overhangs. This was especially problematic if one's initial interpretation of a grid number was different from the coder's interpretation. For example, one student used ($\uparrow$2), where the arrow meant one empty space and two cubes above the empty space, which aligns with the first interpretation described above. Another used (**3) to mean two empty spaces and one cube on the third level. His coding sprang from the second interpretation of the conventional coding described above. The plethora of invented codings created classwide confusion.

Irma called a class meeting to discuss the need for a classwide coding system that would continue to honor the conventional system but would also include a way to denote holes or overhangs. She invited them to share or create ways to solve this dilemma. Using Sarah's task card and a 3-D model, each student drew his or her own way of coding the spaces on the left side of the figure. For examples, see figure 11.9. During the negotiation stage, each child who wished to present a coding system was videotaped while the others respectfully attended. Finally, each student was invited to defend his or her choice. They agreed to use third-grader Sarah's coding system (see figure 11.9c) with a class-negotiated modification: the use of a circle instead of a square to denote the number of empty spaces. The coding in figure 11.7 uses this class-created convention. This open-ended task presented students with an opportunity to be creative, to judge each other's work respectfully, and to come to a consensus over a new convention that all would use. The items in Lucas's (2001) list were fully engaged in this activity.

EXAMPLE 2: THE CAKE DESIGN

We had originally intended to address the SOC framework's representations in a relatively balanced way. However, we expected the semiotic and 2-D conventional representations to be the most challenging for students to produce. Both groups became very successful at numeric top-view coding through the Construction Box as a mediator, and students continued to use that representation for the rest of the year. Even upon returning for their second year with us, they reverted to this representation when asked to show a record of their work. For the class's end-of-year party, we challenged the children to design a cake using all seven Soma figures. Our mathematics objectives were for children to apply knowledge of multiplication facts in array form and to use the Soma figures to create the array. Their work was to be recorded using the class' conventional top-view coding system.

Excerpts from Field Notes, Lesson 26, April 16, 2008

> Both classes [recognize that, to use all seven Soma figures,] the cake [must] have a minimum of 3 "candles" (layer-2 cubes). If they use the remaining 24 cubes for the base layer, how many ways can a rectangle be created? (This problem involves finding factor pairs.) Both classes explained [that] only three Somas [#5, #6, and #7] cannot lie flat.

Grade 3 students noticed that the three candle Soma [figures] have the same [L-shaped] "footprint" as the #1 piece. Dina created and coded a 3 × 8 cake [see figure 11.10] and helped Gary. Sarah created a 4 × 6 cake with #5, #6, and #7 having the same footprint orientation. We asked how many ways she could arrange the three candles. She successfully found all six translational permutations of #5, #6, and #7, and listed them, using a vertical F (front), M (middle) and B (back) format [see figure 11.11]. She then transferred the knowledge to arrange three randomly selected digits in decreasing order (she had struggled with this in class that day). The language of FRONT and BACK was reinforced. Also, formal use of [the terms] "translation" and "rotation" was introduced [and] reinforced.

Retrospective Reflections

• Sarah struggles academically and stays for after-school tutoring regularly. During the school day she rarely volunteers and often slumps in her chair. The SOC program has provided her with a place to shine. In this nonthreatening environment, safely separated from the test-focused stress that pervades in-school hours, Sarah has opportunities to savor a taste of the empowerment she will need to succeed in later years. She confidently contributes to discussions and relishes the opportunities Irma offers her to explain her thinking to the whole group, as in example 1 above. Irma shared with me that she offers children like Sarah opportunities to shine and express themselves in front of the group in order to build their self-esteem and motivation that is so often absent during the regular instructional day where the curricular focus is on analytical development, for example, numeration and reading comprehension. In this counting activity, taking advantage of Sarah's observation of the particular arrangement of the numbers 5, 6, and 7 Soma figures in the rectangle, Irma was able to help her make connections to aspects of her development in mathematics that were problematic during the academic day. Sarah's ability to draw and complete the tabular listing was a huge accomplishment for both teacher and learner. Is this creative teaching or learner creativity? Providing any level of empowerment to students qualifies the event as creative teaching. Even if Sarah's counting activity seems routine to the average mathematics educator, for Sarah it was an exciting discovery, a problem to explore and emotionally very satisfying to solve.

• Both classes created several cake designs using 3 × 8 and 4 × 6 rectangles. Vena (third grade) was convinced she could create a long, narrow 2 ×12 pattern and worked with the Soma figures for most of the class period. She eventually gave up, believing she had exhausted all possibilities. I encouraged her to explain why this was not possible. She simply shrugged. Of note, when she returned the following year, she immediately began to create new cake patterns, and tried again to build her long, narrow 2 × 12 pattern. Vena had invested in a problem of her own creation, one we knew had no solution but that continued to fascinate her. The motivation and interest she displays in this personally generated problem qualifies it as a creative-learning experience.

The cake-designing activity captured student interest in various ways. Dina created more than ten different designs, quietly working independently, and then stunned the class with her originality. We selected one of her patterns for the class's cake. We challenged students to create assembly diagrams to show how to form a cake pattern using all seven Soma figures. This activity developed students' capacities to work fluently with this semiotic representation.

Irma offered a new challenge to the class, with an eye on those who had become proficient at coding. Third graders were to decode the assembly diagrams created by fourth graders and vice versa. Further, if they found errors, they were to describe the errors carefully on Post-it® notes and await a response. This format challenged students to look for coding and assembly errors carefully and to respond respectfully. Activities of this nature address several of the items on Lucas's list, in particular, active rather than passive learning, supporting individual interests, engaging multiple learning styles, encouraging emotional responses, posing questions rather than stating facts, offering ambiguity, being open-ended, and creating many patterns and extending these through permutations (a learning objective for much older children), including visual representations through tactile, experience-based activity, and stimulating social and private learning.

The following field note excerpt illustrates how students actively assessed each other's work in constructive ways.

> Maddie (3rd grade) corrected Mylie's (4th grade) coding—language usage again! Maddie first used "top" and "bottom" in describing positions on the coding grid (on paper). Irma redirected her to use "front" or "forward" and "back" or "backward" in her explanation. (Mylie accepted the critique, but found a shorter way to correct her work using a diagonal translation.) (field notes, April 16, 2008)

The next excerpt shows how students related others' creations to their own. With respect to the SOC framework, this example illustrates students' developing capacity to mentally transform figures. We believe that by creating their own figures students build stronger mental imaging capacity than when provided teacher-made figures.

> Carolyn and Vena (3rd grade) checked "cake" patterns and found Vena's pattern to be almost a reflection of the [4th grade] one she

> was checking. They were very excited but the critical learning with this experience was their recognition of the mirror image [see figure 11.12]. (field notes, lesson 29, May 7, 2008)

Emotions were addressed positively as the children learned that they had the capacity to be critical without being hurtful. Mylie's response to Maddie's critique resulted in a minor modification of her original assembly plan. Mathematically she recognized the validity of a diagonal translation where most of the other students had only used horizontal or vertical translations. We did not realize the extent to which the children had memorized their own cake patterns until Carolyn and Vena noticed a particular pattern among a large number of patterns. That the children had extended their knowledge beyond the immediate requirements of the task was surprising and exciting.

EXAMPLE 3: JAMIE'S BULL

Fourth-grader Jamie had presented Irma with interesting challenges for almost two years. He was a very bright child with very advanced visual capacity. Irma grasped every opportunity to help the class recognize Jamie's talents and to help Jamie respond in socially acceptable ways. Many of our activities were too simple for Jamie. The cake caught his attention for a short time. He quickly produced a pattern and then, in his usual way, he began to explore this cake challenge in new ways:

> Jamie created something amazing. His "cake" had more than 3 cubes on the upper level. I think the base level was a 3 × 7 rectangle. Lengthwise, his figure had a plane of mirror symmetry. He showed that he could tilt both ends of the rectangle up to interlink and form the 27 cube! [See figure 11.13.] (field notes, lesson 29, May 7, 2008)

An Internet search using keywords "Soma" and "puzzle" yielded the information that there are 240 distinct ways to build the 3 × 3 × 3 cube using all seven Soma figures. Jamie had produced several versions of the cube. However, this particular construction, stemming from the cake problem, stunned all of us. Over the course of the year, Jamie had frequently strayed from the tasks that occupied the others in the fourth-grade group. He often extended our tasks into problems of his own creation. We always encouraged him to push his own limits. He was constantly challenged to verbalize his findings, especially to the whole group. On one hand, they might have gained some insight into his way of thinking; on the other, he grew in ways that will empower him as he meets social challenges in the future.

Educational Importance of the Study

I now reflect on our work from two perspectives: first, as a researcher and, second, as a teacher. Our study began with the SOC framework and fragmented activities (van Niekerk, 1997). We designed activities to allow students to move among the SOC representations based on hypothetical concept-development trajectories. Through retrospective reflection, we proceeded along or revised our trajectories, influenced by student interest. Both groups of children were fascinated by numeric top-view coding, which became the focus of much of our work for the year.

Our activities allowed students to progress at their own paces and create personal contributions to the bank of tasks for other students to use. Students became self-directed and maintained their engagement throughout. They were comfortable expressing their understandings or misconceptions in front of their peers. Mistakes were seen as opportunities to learn. They enjoyed watching reruns of themselves on our video clips. These became instructional tools in themselves as students reviewed their work critically, and this provided us further insights into their thinking. Since a primary research goal was to clarify a range of levels of understanding, differentiating according to individual needs and interest was an implicit requirement. Many times during debriefing conversations, we asked, "What if . . . ?" or "What can we change to help . . . ?" We were not limited by constraints that classroom teachers in public schools face daily since our program took place after the regular school day.

I now turn to our teacher perspective. For about eighteen years, I taught secondary-level mathematics, and Irma continues to teach elementary children, sometimes as a mathematics-science specialist, other times as a general studies teacher. We believe in providing mathematical experiences through which students discover rules or principles. In this learning environment, through small group and whole class discussion, students formalize, or reinvent, concepts that later become the foundation for further mathematization.

Although these concepts may be new to students, they generally constitute age-old mathematics that form the basis of school mathematics curricula. Hans Freudenthal (1973) uses the term "re-invention" (p. 120), sometimes known as discovery-based instruction, for this approach to learning mathematics. Teachers rarely have opportunities to experience mathematics in this way. However, in a teacher development program in which I recently participated (MLI, 2006, 2008), high school mathematics teachers engaged in several sessions of problem solving with this approach as an explicit goal.

The research mathematician leading the sessions provided the participants with packets of problems divided into *essential, interesting,* and *challenging* sets. They were expected to engage in these problems in any order and to select those that they found interesting and appropriately challenging. When participants complained that they needed to know if they were on the right track by checking the answers to the problems, the mathematician explained that mathematicians problem solve every day without answers to guide them. He assured them that the best check is through dialog with somewhat knowledgeable peers. Answers were not forthcoming. At the end of this problem-solving experience, many participating teachers commented that they had never experienced mathematics in this way, and they had a better sense of how their struggling students might feel. They also left with a good sense of how to adjust their instruction to provide their students with the necessary support to empower them to become creative problem solvers in mathematics. Although we did not provide prepared sets of problems with known answers to our students, we emulated this approach to problem solving and mathematical reinvention.

Freudenthal (1973) further describes the process of learning mathematics to be "structured by levels. The activity of the lower level . . . becomes an object of analysis on the higher level; the operational matter of the lower level becomes a subject matter on the next level" (p. 125). Thus, the conventional top-view coding system mastered by our students became the basis for the new coding system that they developed for figures with holes and overhangs.

More than reinventing mathematics, our students invented a new mathematical representation. We expected our students to negotiate and debate over various invented representations. Our confidence in managing such an approach comes from cumulative years of giving our students opportunities to share problem-solving strategies and solutions with their peers in order to deepen their knowledge of the concepts at hand. Indeed, providing problem-solving opportunities has resulted in creative thinking, reinvention, and invention. Turning to Peter Woods's framework (Jeffrey & Craft, 2004) on creative teaching, our design research method allowed us to maintain relevance in all activities that we developed, gave our students ownership of their own developing knowledge through the communication styles that we foster, allowed students to manage their own learning through differentiated levels of difficulty of their own choice, and lastly, fostered innovation in encouraging students to create and negotiate among most of the SOC representations.

Personal Reflections on Curriculum

Some years ago, in a curriculum theory class, I was introduced to a view of curriculum (Aoki, 1989) as seen through one's experiences in life where personal experience meshed with professional experience. As a teacher, my beliefs about curriculum and its enactment in the classroom are shaped by multiple experiences, as a student, a member of society, a teacher of young children and teenagers, a professional developer, a parent, and in numerous other roles.

Through this lens, I contend that, if teachers believe in letting students flow with the currents that drive their interests and imaginations, then reinvention and invention will occur.

Searching more deeply into my orientation toward curriculum, I think about John Dewey's (1938/1997) views on the continuity of experience that "takes up something from those which have gone before and modifies in some way the quality of those which come after" (p. 35). Is this about past experiences informing present or future practice? Or, is it about how one's personal experiences are shaped by the experiences provided by others, in this case, teachers? I believe that teachers should ask the questions, provide the interesting problems to solve, but should not always hold the keys to the answers. We empower our students to become confident problem solvers and therefore more flexible thinkers by withholding these keys and encouraging them to convince themselves of the correct answers.

Creative teachers can foster creativity in their students through problem-solving approaches to learning. Our students created experiences (and products) as a result of our own belief that learning best occurs through problem solving and reinvention. As researchers we carefully document student understanding. As teachers, we also assess student understanding in real time and may document it in different ways. During our reflection meetings following each lesson, we wear both hats: considering how to improve what has just transpired or how to provide further experiences to deepen and extend students' understanding and development. As we think about next steps, one week at a time, our minds always turn toward ideas that will be exciting and will encourage our students to develop their mathematical understanding in interesting but substantial ways.

Final Thoughts

Given the current top-down performance-driven climate that pervades public education, I wonder how the classroom teacher can consider creative approaches and still retain faith that this will tide students over the state-mandated assessment. In some regions, teachers emphasize topics that are covered heavily by the state assessment at the expense of other topics, thereby robbing children of a comprehensive educational experience. How can three-dimensional spatial reasoning be tested thoroughly on paper, a two-dimensional medium? This aspect of official mathematics curricula is not represented on tests in significant ways and is often overlooked in the classroom.

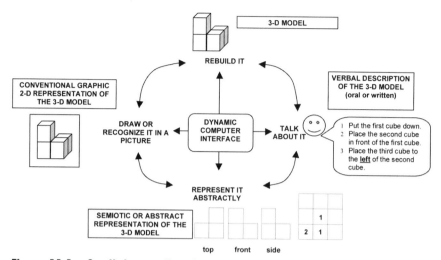

Figure 11.1. Spatial operational capacity (SOC) framework

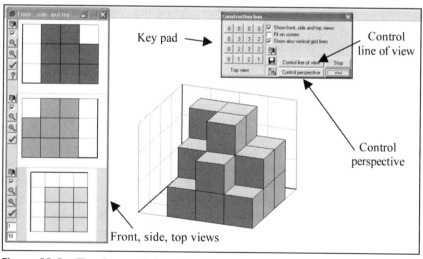

Figure 11.2. The Geocadabra Construction Box

Figure 11.3. The same figure viewed using the Construction Box View Control option

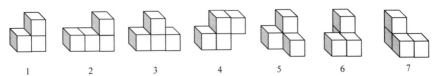

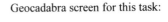

1   2   3   4   5   6   7

Figure 11.4. The Complete Set of Soma figures

Build the following figure and its mirror image on your screen. Write the correct numbers in the grid next to the figure.

Geocadabra screen for this task:

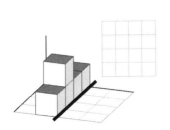

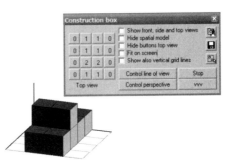

Figure 11.5. Mirror Image Task

(a)   (b)

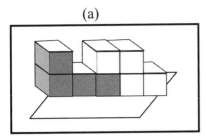

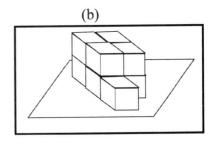

Figure 11.6. Examples of task cards

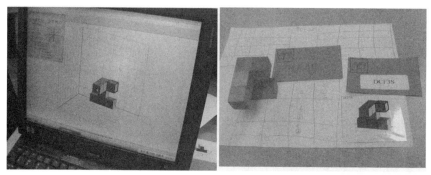

Figure 11.7. Student-created task Card, coding and 3-D figure

Figure 11.8. Conventional coding system developed through the Construction Box

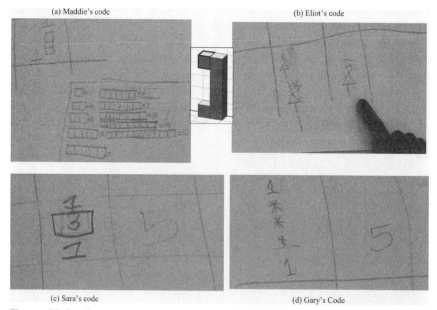

Figure 11.9. Top-view numeric coding systems to represent holes in cube figures

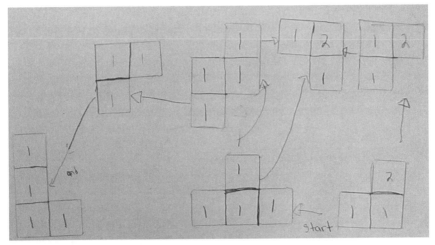

Figure 11.10. Dina's cake assembly code

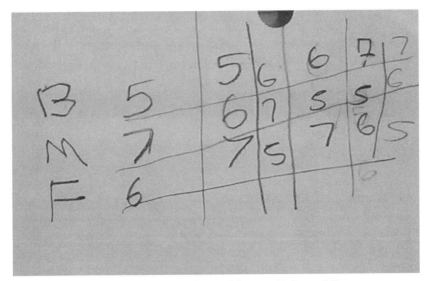

Figure 11.11. Sarah's permutations of Somas 5, 6, and 7

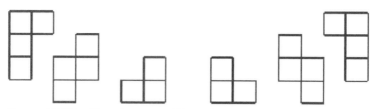

Figure 11.12.   Vena's recognition of the reflection

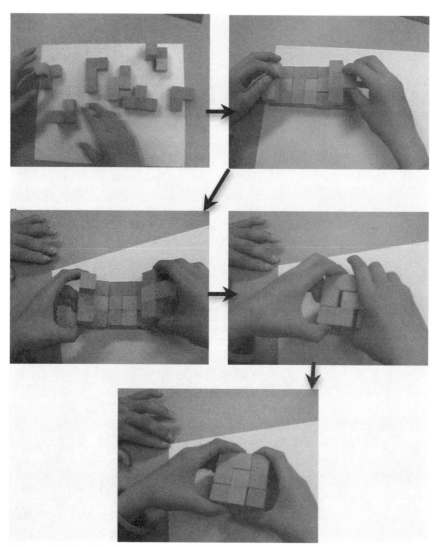

Figure 11.13.   Jamie's "Bull"

References

Aoki, T. (1989). *Beyond the half-life of curriculum and pedagogy.* Alberta Teachers' Association Specialist Council Seminar, Barnett House, Edmonton, Alberta, Canada, September.

Borba, M. C., & Villarreal, M. E. (2005). *Humans-with-media and the reorganization of mathematical thinking.* New York: Springer.

Cobb, P., Confrey, J., diSessa, A., Lehrer, R., & Schauble, L. (2003). Design experiments in educational research. *Educational Researcher, 32*(1), 9–13.

Dewey, J. (1938/1997). *Experience and education.* New York: Touchstone.

Dreyfus, T. (1991). On the status of visual reasoning in mathematics and mathematics education. In F. Furinghetti (Ed.), *Proceedings of the 15th P.M.E. Conference* (pp. 1, 33–48). Genoa, Italy: University of Genoa.

Freudenthal, H. (1973). *Mathematics as an educational task.* Dordrecht, The Netherlands: Kluwer.

Freudenthal, H. (1991). *Revisiting mathematics education: China lectures.* Dordrecht, The Netherlands: Kluwer.

Gardner, H. (1999). *Intelligences reframed: Multiple intelligences for the 21st century.* New York: Basic Books.

Jeffrey, B., & Craft, A. (2004). Teaching creatively and teaching for creativity: Distinctions and relationships. *Educational Studies, 30*(1), 77–87.

Krulik, S., & Rudnick, J. A. (1987). The pedagogy of problem solving. In *Problem solving: A handbook for teachers* (2nd ed.) (pp. 37–74). Boston: Allyn and Bacon.

Lecluse, T. (2005). Geocadabra [computer software]. Retrieved October 4, 2010, from http://home.casema.nl/alecluse/setupeng.exe.

Lucas, B. (2001). Creative teaching, teaching creativity and creative learning. In A. Craft, B. Jeffrey, & M. Leibling (Eds.), *Creativity in education* (pp. 35–44). London: Continuum.

Mathematics Leadership Institute (MLI). (2006, 2008). Rice University, Houston, TX. http://nsfmli.rice.edu/.

National Council of Teachers of Mathematics (NCTM). (2000). *Principles and standards for school mathematics.* Reston, VA: Author.

National Research Council (NRC). (2006). *Learning to think spatially: GIS as a support system in the K–12 curriculum.* Washington, DC: Author.

Presmeg, N. C. (1992). Metaphors, metonymies and imaginative reality in high school mathematics. *Educational Studies in Mathematics, 23*(6), 595–610.

Tall, D., Gray, E., Bin Ali, M., Crowley, L., DeMarois, P., McGowen, M., Pitta, D., Pinto, M., Thomas, M., & Yusof, Y. (2001). Symbols and the bifurcation between procedural and conceptual thinking. *Canadian Journal of Science, Mathematics and Technology Education, 1*(1), 81–84.

Tomlinson, C. A., & McTighe, J. (2006). *Integrating differentiated instruction and understanding by design: Connecting content and kids.* Alexandria, VA: Association for Supervision and Curriculum Development.

van Niekerk, (Retha) H. M. (1997). *A subject didactical analysis of the development of the spatial knowledge of young children through a problem-centered approach to mathematics teaching and learning.* Ph.D. diss., Potchefstroom University for CHE, South Africa.

van Niekerk, R. (2006). Build and explore with Geocadabra (J. J. Sack, Trans.). Retrieved October 4, 2010, from http://nsfmli.rice.edu/curriculum/Lecluse/GeocadabraGeobuddyConstructionBoxEnglishTranslation.pdf.

Weisstein, E. W. (1999). Soma cube. From MathWorld, a Wolfram Web Resource. Retrieved November 7, 2006, from http://mathworld.wolfram.com/SomaCube.html.

Yakimanskaya, I. S. (1991). *The development of spatial thinking in school children* (P. S. Wilson & E. J. Davis, Trans.). Soviet Studies in Mathematics Education 5. Reston, VA: NCTM.

CHAPTER 12

A Report on the Introduction and Resulting Effects of Novel Teaching Strategies in Increasing Creativity and Independent Thought

Teresa Leavitt
Brigham Young University

Madalina Tanase
University of North Florida

Teresa Leavitt, Ph.D., is assistant professor in the Department of Teacher Education, College of Education, Brigham Young University. Her teaching and research interests are in the areas of comparative and international education, teacher knowledge, teacher education, and classroom management.

Madalina Tanase, Ph.D., is assistant professor in the Department of Foundations and Secondary Education, College of Education and Human Services, University of North Florida. Her teaching and research interests are in the areas of comparative and international education (literacy and mathematics), teacher education, classroom assessment, and classroom management.

ABSTRACT

This chapter discusses a report on the results of the introduction of novel teaching strategies to an otherwise rigid and nonconstructivist approach to teaching. The novel teaching strategies are aimed to foster creativity as well as independent thought in both teaching and learning among elementary school students and their teachers. As part of a larger team, the authors taught English at a summer camp in China using methods based initially on the reader's and writer's workshop approach in the United States, which, in itself, is assumed to spur the development of creative minds. Obstacles and difficulties discussed include initial resistance, tremendous need for structure on the part of the students, and lack of exposure to using independent thought. Attention is also paid to successes. Data arose from the authors' periodic reflections throughout the camp as well as on samples of student work. Student work was analyzed for skill of English use, as well as for independent and creative content. Assessment tools included a set of rubrics developed by the researchers to determine level of English proficiency and degree of creativity and independent thought contained in each assignment. Researchers initially coded assignments together to ensure interrater reliability, then coded separately; once complete, researchers met to discuss and compare coding of the data. This field-based research study could serve as a valuable beginning for further research comparing a more constructivist approach, including learning environments where students are creatively at work and teachers facilitate an environment conducive to learning through discovery, with more traditional, structured approaches, where teacher and students follow preestablished patterns for teaching and learning, which may stifle creativity and curiosity in learning.

In an attempt to address the realities of today's diverse classrooms with an ever-increasing number of students whose first language is not English (National Clearinghouse for Bilingual Education, 2008), teachers need to create rich educational contexts to support their students' second-language acquisition (Furr, 2003; Mohr, 2004; Piro, 2002; Ranker, 2007). In this respect, teachers need to develop and use those strategies that enable students to use their first language as a scaffold in order to learn how to read and write in English.

Despite very rich literature in the field, with researchers and studies advocating for an integrated reading-writing approach, which would promote creativity in students through the use of their past and present experiences to communicate both orally and in writing, as well as to learn to write while learning to read (Cochran-Smith, 1984; Cook-Gumperz & Gumperz, 1981; Enright & McCloskey, 1988; Ernst & Richard, 1995; Scarborough, 2001), the current tendency is still to focus on oral language acquisition prior to learning how to write (Mohr, 2004; Perrotta, 1994). This linear approach to teaching English as a second language or as a foreign language emphasizes, therefore, the development of listening and speaking skills in young students before exposing them to reading and writing (Krashen & Terrell, 1983; Mohr, 2004). Consequently,

English as a Foreign Language/English Language Learner (EFL/ELL) students are expected to listen to the teacher, yet they are oftentimes excluded from classroom discussions and creative writing assignments on the grounds these might be too challenging for them (Franklin, 1986; Mohr, 2004).

Opponents of this linear approach argue for the need to modify this traditional approach to second-language acquisition and, moreover, give up reading basal stories and filling out worksheets, as even very young students can be exposed to creative writing opportunities while at the same time acquiring the basic skills (Mohr, 2004; Perrotta, 1994; Rigg, 1981). Second-language acquisition, very similar to first-language acquisition (Gersten & Geva, 2003; Krashen, 1993; Krashen, 1996, 1999; Perrotta, 1994), should be based, therefore, on an integrated approach, where reading, writing, speaking, and listening are interrelated and interdependent in an attempt to develop these skills through creative approaches (Clay, 1982, 1998; Cochran-Smith, 1984; Ernst & Richard, 1995; Mohr, 2004; Perrotta, 1994). In alignment with the Association of Teacher Educators' (ATE)' Yearbook theme, cultivating curious and creative minds, the above studies advocate that, in order to reach our EFL/ELL students, we need to expose them to reading and writing along with the acquisition of basic vocabulary, speaking, and listening skills. If literacy transfers across language and if, moreover, we acquire the ability to read and write the same way we acquire a second language (Krashen, 1996), it is therefore important to investigate what might be good practices to use when teaching reading and writing along with speaking and listening to young students in environments that foster creativity. This chapter will address the following questions posed in this issue of ATE's Yearbook: What practices and strategies spur the development of curious and creative minds? What does curious and creative teaching, learning, and assessment look like? How does curious and creative teaching and learning rub against current practices in schools and teacher education settings? The first two questions will be approached in the literature review as well as the report of the findings, while the third question will be discussed in the analysis section of this chapter.

Literature Review

Numerous researchers (Gersten & Geva, 2003; Kamps et al., 2007; Perrotta, 1994; Rudden & Nedeff, 1998) have analyzed the best practices to teach reading and writing to young nonnative English speakers, and a great variety of studies have produced important findings that may provide a more in-depth understanding about how EFL/ELL students learn English (Baker, 2000; Ernst & Richard, 1995; Liu, 2004; Mohr, 2004). In the context of this literature, reader's and writer's workshops were accounted for as a successful integrated approach to teach students multiple skills at the same time in an environment that fosters creativity and curiosity. The idea behind reader's and writer's workshop is to acknowledge the content understanding developed in the reading, learning, and speaking stages of the lesson and to transfer this understanding into writing, with the help of the teacher (Atwell, 1987; Calkins, 1983; Clay, 1991, 1998; Freeman & Freeman, 2000; Sowers, 1985; Tompkins, 2000).

In order for teachers to help their students become good readers and writers when conducting reading and writing workshops, they need to provide them with ample opportunities to do both while at the same time enabling students to be creative in their writing. Moreover, encouraging young readers to be curious, to choose what books to read, and young writers to be creative with the topics to write on seems to enhance student acquisition of oral and written skills (Atwell, 1987; Graves, 1994; Krashen, 1996). Reading is a part of writing (the input comes from written language [Krashen, 1996] to the extent to which writing is a part of reading), and while composing, children read continuously and draw on their reading (Calkins, 1983; Freeman & Freeman, 2000). Researchers recommend, then, to couple good reading programs with good writing programs, as "it is hard to become a good writer without doing a lot of reading" (Freeman & Freeman, 2000, p. 105).

Research findings reveal that some of the most encountered practices for teaching reading are read-alouds/choral reading, thematic units, and a combination of text and visuals (using comic books or comic strips to enhance reading understanding; Ernst & Richard, 1995; Liu, 2004; Mohr, 2004; Ranker, 2007). On the other hand, the following creative writing practices are deemed as essential by teachers in teaching successful writing: using texts as writing models, publishing books, and writing letters (Furr, 2003; Perrotta, 1994; Vos, 2003). In other words, exposing students to a variety of strategies that address various learning styles may be beneficial to developing both reading and writing skills, while at the same time spurring the development of curious and creative minds (Freeman & Freeman, 2000; Mohr, 2004; Taberski, 2000; U.K. National Curriculum in Action, n.d.). Authentic assessment tools, such as portfolios, books, and journals, have the goal to increase student learning (Gronlund & Waugh, 2008), prompting increased creativity in the learning process.

A closer analysis of the reading practices deemed successful for EFL/ELL students shows that being exposed to read-alouds of books can develop students' oral language (Cochran-Smith, 1984; Mohr, 2004; Piro, 2002). An extension of the read-aloud, reading bilingual versions of books may also enable students to understand the content more clearly (Schirmer, Casbon, & Twiss, 1996). Using read-alouds can be especially beneficial to EFL/ELL students, as they can listen to the language and make connections between oral and written text and make meaning from reading (Ernst & Richard, 1995). Read-alouds may be prefaced with a discussion of the textbook, an opportunity during which the teacher introduces the book and activates students' prior knowledge. Following the read-alouds, and before students are given the chance to be involved in writing (to ensure students understood what the book was about), the teacher can create opportunities for students to engage in independent reading or partner reading (Ranker, 2007).

Employing thematic units during a reader's and writer's workshop is also considered an instructional approach that fosters creativity, as students have a chance to read and write about meaningful content while spending enough time on a particular topic to allow students to develop conceptual and linguistic knowledge (Ernst & Richard, 1995; Enright & McCloskey, 1988; Freeman & Freeman, 1998, 2000; Mohr, 2004). The main advantage of using thematic units is the fact that teachers develop the topics around their students' backgrounds, sparking student curiosity and interest and, hence, engaging them in collaborative activities meant to increase their speaking, listening, and writing skills in conjunction with students' independent thought (Ernst & Richard, 1995).

Using visuals to accompany text in teaching reading and writing to EFL/ELL students is also considered a good way to make reading more enjoyable and has long been a preoccupation of researchers (Ernst & Richard, 1995; Levie & Lentz, 1982; Levin, Anglin, & Carney, 1987; Liu, 2004; Piro, 2002; Ranker, 2007). From this perspective, researchers advocated for the use of text and visual together in an attempt to improve student comprehension (Hadley, 2001; Tang, 1992). Among the various visual supports that may be used with this goal, Jun Liu (2004) stated that the attention of researchers was captivated by the use of comic strips, as they are "communicative, popular, accessible, [and] readable" (p. 229). Deemed as a good way to enhance students' literacy skills, comic strips use both words and images, providing the students with an additional support to understand the written text (Bitz, 2004; Liu, 2004; Schwartz, 2002).

Liu (2004) describes the benefits of using comic strips in teaching reading, while investigating the retention of text both accompanied and not accompanied by visual support with the English as a Second Language (ESL) population of a southwestern university registered for ESL courses in a summer language program. Students were provided with the text and then asked to write an essay based on what they could remember from the text. Findings showed that not only young learners but also college students could benefit from the exposure to the visual accompanying the written text, although to a different extent. As such, low-level students who received a higher-level text along with a comic strip scored higher than low-level students who only received the high-level text. No such correlation of text and visual support was found to be true for the high-level group. That comic books that accompany texts are likely to enhance understanding is also shown in the study conducted by Jason Ranker (2007). Gathering data from his observations of an ELL teacher who used comics as read-alouds in her classroom, he found that, while using comic strips, the teacher created opportunities for her students to be engaged in reading, writing, speaking, and listening activities at the same time.

Although looking at the teaching of reading from different perspectives, all these studies share one characteristic, namely, that reading was taught from the perspective of an integrated approach, with the teacher creating opportunities for students to engage in meaningful listening, speaking, and writing activities that came as a continuation of the classroom readings. The fact that writing should be an extension of reading, and not an activity in itself, in order to help EFL/ELL students learn to read and write in English is supported by further research that analyzed how writing practices came about as natural extensions of the reading process (Ammon, 1985; Edelsky & Jilbert, 1985; Rudden & Nedeff, 1998).

Using texts as writing models, making writing personal, and publishing books are only a few of the strategies deemed essential in teaching writing skills that also happen to promote creativity (Ernst & Richard, 1995; Furr, 2003; Rudden & Nedeff, 1998; Graves, 1994; Vos, 2003). If writing is not made personal, and if it is considered a mere school assignment, students will not develop authorial voices (Macrorie, 1985). Teachers can develop creative and curious young minds by making writing personal, by allowing students to choose a topic to write on, and by tying information to their experience in a unique way (Graves, 1994; Furr, 2003; Morris, 2006; Starko, 2004). Genuine writing occurs when the writing product is new and original, but to be able to become independent writers, students need to be allowed to be creative in their classrooms.

In addition, if "individual teachers can have a huge influence on encouraging students to be creative" (Morris, 2006, p. 6), then they must develop a safe learning environment in which students are allowed to make mistakes, take risks, and make connections between reading and writing, while being given ample time to reflect and being provided with materials and resources meant to help them become independent readers and writers (Morris, 2006; Starko, 2004; U.K. National Curriculum in Action, n.d.).

In an attempt to develop both reading and writing skills, while at the same time encouraging creativity in writing, Vos (2003) encouraged her students to write letters to the authors whose books they had recently read and enjoyed and ask them meaningful questions. Through this creative writing workshop, Vos used teacher-student conferences to prompt her students to draft, revise, and publish their letters. Findings showed the impact letter writing made not only on students' writing skills as their writing improved as a result of the conferences but also on students' further reading, as they became more inquisitive and eager to read other books by the same author and compare similarities. This is another strategy of fostering curiosity in reading and encouraging creativity in workshops that have reading and writing interconnected.

Another example of how to develop good writing skills, in conjunction with reading, is discussed by Rudden and Nedeff (1998) in a study of ELL students attending an elementary school in a Mid-Atlantic state. Third-grade students attending this school authored at least one book every year pertaining to a different genre (information books, fiction books, storytelling books, and fantasies). The school's writing program focused on the combination of a pull-out approach (where students are removed from the classroom for intensive English instruction) and a push-in approach (in which the reading specialist visits each classroom each day to help ELL students). Findings revealed an adherence to criteria for literary genre, which may be the result of this particular's program using literature and writing in combination to teach ESL students.

As the above studies show, even in the cases where only acquiring reading or writing skills were targeted, reading and writing are never seen as separate from one another, but they are shown as interrelated and interdependent. Successful EFL/ELL teachers know how to creatively engage their students in reading and writing activities that promote English-language learning by enabling their students to make connections in the oral and written language (Clay, 1991), as well as to make connections with their daily lives (Morris, 2006). That this is the case is further shown by the following studies, in which the teachers incorporated reading and writing in the daily schedule, offering their EFL/ELL students, along with their American students, opportunities to make connections between reading and writing.

In a study spanning over two years, Russell Gersten and Esther Geva (2003) observed thirty-four first-grade classrooms where three-fourths of the classroom students were ELLs, in an attempt to observe the impact a combination of learning new words and using them both orally and in writing would have on student comprehension. Researchers found that there were six facets of instruction contributing to the reading growth over two years: explicit teaching, English learning, phonemic awareness and decoding, vocabulary development, interactive teaching, and instruction geared toward low performers. Findings revealed that teachers who had more success with their students shared the six characteristics of instruction discussed above. Teachers used a visual support to teach reading; moreover, all these teachers placed a strong emphasis on writing, using writing in conjunction with reading in order to reinforce basic reading skills.

Some of the writing activities these teachers exposed their students to were taking dictation, using new vocabulary in workbooks, and generating stories about their personal lives. This shows again that, when teaching reading and writing together, rather than in isolation (Cook-Gumperz & Gumperz, 1981;

Enright & McCloskey, 1988), and fostering creativity in class, by allowing students to have input in their topic selection, as well as what books to read (Furr, 2003; Morris, 2006; Vos, 2003), teachers have a better chance of developing successful readers and creative writers.

In another study of elementary students, Ernst and Richard (1995) drew data from student sample writings and conversations collected across one year in an attempt to show student growth in reading and writing as a result of their participation in a conversational ESL program. The second-grade ESL classroom teacher, similar to the teachers in the above study, created many opportunities for her students to be engaged in reading and writing activities as she read aloud stories and then had students draw pictures of a particular topic covered in the book and write short sentences about their drawing. The teacher gave her students a chance to practice their new vocabulary in context as they discussed their drawings, understanding the significance to link oral and written language in order to develop the reading and writing skills in her ESL students, the result of such an endeavor being students who could read, talk, and write better.

To further show the connection between oral and written language, Askew and Frasier (1999) observed thirty-two Reading Recovery first-grade students in eight states working daily with a specialized teacher in reading and writing texts. Drawing data from student writing records (vocabulary chart and book) as well as reading records (teacher record of text reading), findings indicated that, by being exposed to writing daily, low-progress students acquire knowledge about words and letter sounds and can move toward becoming independent writers.

Developing creative and curious young minds as part of a reader's and writer's workshop can, therefore, occur if teachers provide their students with countless opportunities to engage in reading (choral, independent, and pair), speaking, and writing (creating books or writing sentences in relation to the book the teacher read to them).

Are students engaged in enough opportunities to use oral and written language? While some of the above studies show opportunities created by teachers to engage their students in both oral and written language, how much of the class time is spent in having students talk and be active? A study conducted by Arreaga-Mayer and Perdomo-Rivera (1996) shows that ELL students were only engaged in using oral or written language 21 percent of the classroom time. Have times changed? Do teachers engage students more in oral and written language? In an attempt to fill the gap in the literature identified by Baker (2000) and gain more insights into the types of oral and written opportunities EFL/ELL students are exposed to in the classrooms, and in alignment with ATE's Yearbook theme, this current study focuses on developing creativity in young students from the perspective of a reader's and writer's workshop in an experimental summer school in a major city in southwestern China.

Experimental Summer School in China

Possessing a more traditionalist education environment, China has undergone various degrees of reform at the curriculum level. Following the issue of the English Language Curriculum Standards in 2001 by the Ministry of Education, EFL teachers were expected to adopt novel teaching strategies focusing more on oral communication, while, at the same time, relying less on memorization and practice (Ministry of Education, 2001). A recent study (Zhan, 2008) shows, however, a dependency of some teachers on transmitting knowledge to students as part of a very structured environment (lectures and drill). This may be the cause of the teachers' weak knowledge of theories about language learning and child development that would enable them to teach English from a more constructivist approach, engaging their students in talking, reading, and writing activities of a more personal nature (Zhan, 2008).

CONTEXT

As part of a group of teachers traveling as a group sponsored through the College of Education of the University of Nevada, Las Vegas, the researchers prepared for and traveled to China to teach at an English summer camp. The primary curriculum adopted by the organizers was a modified version of the reader's and writer's workshop (Atwell, 1987; Calkins, 1983; Clay, 1982). The researchers gathered data throughout the three-week summer camp to track the effects of the implementation of not only the reader's and writer's workshop but also a novel approach in teaching to which the students were not accustomed. In order to answer another one of ATE Yearbook's questions, namely, how does curious and creative teaching and learning rub against current practices in schools, results of the implemented teaching strategies are analyzed and discussed.

BACKGROUND

In order to improve the conversational skills of elementary-age students in China, in alignment with the requirements of the Ministry of Education's English Language Curriculum Standards (2001), an agreement was reached for foreign teachers, including Ms. T and Ms. M, from the United States, to travel to a large city in southwestern China to teach at an English summer camp. The summer camp was six days a week for three weeks at a local, but private, school. Prior to departing for China, the teachers (including researchers) met weekly for two months to not only plan for the camp but also develop and share curriculum and lesson plans. Although the group of teachers had reviewed the Chinese standards for the grade levels of students they would be targeting, the lesson plans were forwarded to the school ahead of time for feedback to ensure that levels of difficulties were congruent with expectations and abilities for the level of students for whom they were intended. Some feedback was given from some of the corresponding teachers from the school in China, but overall the lesson plans were left intact as planned by the group from the United States.

The primary schedule for a typical day was planned to include reading, writing, conversation, cultural studies (i.e., social studies geared around U.S. geography, customs, cultures, etc.), and extracurricular activities (rotating through drama, dance, music, sports, and arts and crafts) followed in the evening by English movies, review, and homework. Days were scheduled to begin at 8:30 a.m. and to end at 8:40 p.m. (with breaks for lunch and dinner). Novel teaching strategies focused primarily on the reading and writing portion of the day and also extended into conversation and cultural studies. Upon arrival, each foreign teacher was paired with a Chinese counterpart, Ms. T with Teacher S and Ms. M with Teacher J. The Chinese teachers were regular classroom teachers who worked in conjunction with the foreign teachers to help facilitate the lessons presented by the foreign teachers (i.e., help with translation, etc.).

METHODS AND TECHNIQUES

In order to implement reader's and writer's workshop type of instruction, deemed as essential not only in acquiring language acquisition but also for fostering creativity and developing independent readers and writers (Freeman & Freeman, 2000; Mohr, 2004; Scarborough, 2001), the group of teachers was briefly introduced to the methods, strategies, and intents of the goals of a reader's and writer's workshop by both a university professor whose focus is literacy and also by classroom teachers who had previously implemented reader's and writer's workshops in their classrooms in the United States. After a short workshop, teachers coordinated with one another seeking out advice from those in the group who had had more experience with reader's and writer's as classroom teachers in the United States; however, no further formal training was offered.

Despite this limited amount of training, both of the researchers had a combined number of nine years experience as classroom teachers and were able to plan and design what they viewed as engaging, informative, and effective lessons for the classes they were to teach. Lessons included books to be read by students with accompanying writing activities to fulfill the reading and writing portion of the day. Conversation lessons were usually connected to what was read earlier in the day and included active learning activities designed to engage students in conversations geared around various topics such as going shopping, visiting a restaurant, and so forth. Initially, one researcher prepared to teach fifth and sixth grade while the other prepared for kindergarten and first-grade students. Once enrollment for the summer camp was finalized, both researchers were moved to the second-third-grade level in adjacent classrooms. The researchers planned and implemented identical lessons allowing for collaboration, reflection, and modifications as needed throughout the day. This also allowed for a more standardized, though not directly replicable, form of data collection.

A significant difference in the approach to every lesson, as compared with the traditional Chinese lesson, was that the researchers worked to provide an environment that would foster creativity and uniqueness in students' work and thought. The challenge that this posed was clearly evident from the outset. How students responded to a more constructivist and less structured learning environment in which students were encouraged and expected to complete assignments uniquely individual to the student, although the content was based on reading and class discussion, was of utmost interest. The following scenario was fairly typical of the start of the summer camp:

The first writing assignment followed brief introductions with the students. After introducing themselves to the class, the researchers asked students to write a short autobiography about themselves that included things such as name, age, hobbies, what they enjoyed about school, and so on. A very short list was written on the board of items for students to include. It was apparent that students were still unsure of what to do. Teacher S, the Chinese teacher counterpart to Ms. T suggested a more structured example be given.

Although hesitant, Ms. T filled in some outlines of her autobiographical information including name, age, and hometown. Ms. T explained that this was her information and that students were to use their own information and to include other details Ms. T had not listed on the board. Ms. T began monitoring the room as students started working. After just a couple minutes, it was evident that students were for the most part simply copying the information from the board as it appeared. Both Ms. T and Teacher S explained once again in both English and Chinese, respectively, that the students were to complete this narrative and accompanying picture with information that would tell about them and not to use the sample information on the board.

Teacher S felt that more definitive examples must be put on the board and proceeded to write statements such as "My name is _____. I am __ years old." This was more structured than what Ms. T had planned, but students were struggling, and Teacher S was rather insistent. Students seemed more at ease copying information off the board than developing their own information. With further clarification both to the class and then to some individuals after the explanation, students were able to complete their introductory autobiographies to varying lengths and details. Even those students who were able to extend beyond the samples from the board did tend to start by copying the sample sentences and filling in the blanks with their information.

The situation was quite similar in Ms. M's class, as students felt more comfortable following a certain established pattern of copying sentences from the board and only filling in the blanks. In the third written assignment, for example, students had to talk about their day. This activity was initially developed to enable students to freely discuss what they do throughout the day, but students felt lost when Ms. M only provided them with a few activities on the board. In Ms. M's case, like in Ms. T's case, the Chinese teacher asked Ms. M to provide students with more structure, so Ms. M decided to write on the board a few sentences that might help children in their writing: "My name is . . . . In the morning, I . . . . In the afternoon, I . . . . In the evening, I . . . . " Ms. M wrote down her few activities on the board, asking students to come up with their own activities. Students proceeded to fill in the missing information, but both Ms. M and Teacher J, the Chinese teacher, had to reexplain in both Chinese and English that they were not to copy Ms. M's information from the board but develop their own answers.

The need for such structure and rigidity slowly began to fade as students were encouraged, expected, and supported in developing their own work. Using a modified version of reader's and writer's workshop, the researchers' connected the various parts of the day's lessons to one another. The books that were read in the morning transitioned into the writing activity, which, in turn, influenced the oral component of the day as well as creating minithematic units from day to day.

As the researchers were able to work more closely with their Chinese counterparts to explain their approach and confidence in students' abilities to complete assignments with less structure, both Chinese teachers provided more support to the approach and helped to encourage students to use independent thought. Students became more familiar with the routine and expectation that they would not be copying work from the board but would instead develop their own work based on guidelines, suggestions, and some required elements for each assignment.

Due to the nature of the summer camp, particularly its brevity, along with the fact that students were accustomed to more rigid and structured learning approaches, it was evident that, with the goal in mind to increase student creativity and independent thought, the researchers' ability to implement a more conventional approach to reader's and writer's workshops was limited. Rather, researchers provided a topic each day that aligned with the book read as a class. It was intended that reading the book along with class discussion about the topic would pique their curiosity in the subject and would lead to increased creativity when completing the writing assignments. Although a topic with some prompts and examples were provided for each assignment, students were then encouraged to be as creative and original as possible. To aid students' pursuit of creativity and originality, researchers avoided writing structured examples on the board that might then be copied by the students.

Student samples from throughout the summer camp were collected by the researchers in order for a careful examination of what, if any, changes were evidenced throughout the time students were encouraged and supported to increase their own creativity from each of the researchers' classes. Students were occasionally absent from the summer camp for a variety of reasons; to allow for a more comparable analysis, researchers included only those students from the two classes who were present and completed all of the selected samples. This resulted in a combined total of thirty-two students. Each student sample was evaluated using rubrics that included categories for English use and to examine creativity and required elements. The English rubric included the use of grammar and mechanics; the creativity rubric included attractiveness of the visuals and use of time as an indication of whether students were able to use their time creatively and uniquely to address the given topic. Each rubric item was based on a scale of one to four, for a total of twenty possible points per sample. Scores for each student's sample were further broken into English and creativity scores and then compared—both in total and total average format as well as segregated into English and English average and creativity and creativity average format—to other students.

RESULTS AND DISCUSSION

During the three-week summer camp, fostering creativity and independence in both writing and conversation was a major focus. Based on the writing sample data collected during these three weeks, the majority of students improved only slightly or remained the same in terms of writing (see table 12.1). Changes in student work, either increases or decreases, were deemed measurable if the change to students' score was greater than 25 percent, in either a positive or negative manner. The possible number of points in the English component categories for each assignment was eight, while creativity accounted for twelve points per assignment. One-time variances in scores were furthered analyzed, but it was determined by the researchers that the presence of only one score, whether

Table 12.1. Table of Student Data

Student	Total Point Average	Total Points Ranking	English Average (out of 8)	Total English Ranking	Creativity Average (out of 12)	Total Creativity Ranking
Amy	15.5-	4	3.75-	9	11.75	1
Charlie	15	6	3.5	10	11.5	2
Susan	17.5	1	6.25	1	11.25	3
June	14.5	8	3.5	10	11	4
Sam	14.75	7	4.25	7	11	4
Lucy	15	5	4	8	11	4
Ada	16	3	4+	8	11	4
Amilia	13.75	10	3	12	10.75	5
Amie	15.25	5	4.5	6	10.75	5
Lindsay	15.25	5	4.5	6	10.75	5
Jerry	15	6	4.5	6	10.5	6
Jim	16	3	4.5	6	10.5	6
Polly	16.5	2	6	2	10.5+	6
Tony	12.5	14	2.25	14	10.25	7
Simon	12.25	15	2.25	14	10	8
Ana	13	12	3	12	10	8
Linda	14.5	8	4.25	7	10-	8
Peter	14.75	7	4.75	5	10	8
Jack-+	14.5	8	4.75-	5	9.75+	9
Mike	14.75	7	5	4	9.75	9
Alice	14.75	7	4.5	6	9.75	9
John	15.5	4	5.75	3	9.75	9
Christina	12.75	13	3.25	11	9.5	10
Bruce++	14+	9	6+	2	9.5	10
Lily	11.25	17	2	15	9.25-	11
Andy	12.25	15	2.5	13	9.25	11
Mikey-+	12.5	14	3.5-	10	9+	12
Candy	10.75	18	3.5	10	8.25	13
Leo	11.5	16	3.25	11	8.25	13
David	12.5	14	4	8	8.25	13
Dennis	13.25	11	6	2	7.5	14
Bobby++	8.5+	19	2.25+	14	6.25+	15

Note: Student's average scores and rankings in terms of total points, English scores, and creativity scores: a - denotes a measurably negative change in score while a + denotes a measurably positive change in score. Students with a -+ next to their name indicates a measurably negative change in English but a measurably positive change in creativity. Those with ++ by their name indicates a measurably positive change in both English and creativity.

significantly higher or lower, did not merit the conclusion that there was sufficient change in the student's overall progress.

Cumulative point totals for each sample were analyzed prior to breaking the scores into separate English and creativity categories. Only 9 percent of students (three students) exhibited a change of 25 percent or greater for total scores. Of these students, 3 percent (or one student) decreased in total points when comparing total points of individual assignments, while 6 percent (or two students) showed an increase. These three students ranked fourth, ninth, and nineteenth respectively in terms of total points. Thus, one of the highest ranked students overall actually had a measurable decline over time. On the other hand, a midranked and the lowest ranked student both showed measurable increase during the summer camp. Looking only at overall point totals, these results might indicate that an approach such as this, implemented in a short amount of time, might be more beneficial in increasing scores of lower achieving students; however, overall there was not a measurable impact for the majority of students either positively or negatively for high-, mid- or low-achieving students.

Despite a short amount of time with the students, 22 percent of the students (or seven of thirty-two students) exhibited measurable changes in their creativity scores. This group of students was comprised of 13 percent of students (four students) who exhibited change in both English and creativity, as well as 9 percent (three students) who only had measurable change in creativity. In this category, 6 percent of students had negative changes in their creativity scores, while the remainder (16 percent) had positive changes in their scores. Students in this category when ranked in overall creativity scores ranged from sixth highest overall to fifteenth (equivalent to lowest score achieved in the creativity category). It is evident that the initial level was not a consideration in the development of creativity and independent thought, although it does seem to have favored those students who scored in the bottom two-thirds of the overall rankings.

Although not linked directly to increasing creativity and independent thought in students, a brief explanation of changes in English proficiency is included. In this area, 19 percent (or six out of thirty-two students) had measurable changes in their use of English in their writing assignments. Half of these students (three), or 9 percent of the overall sample population, actually decreased by the established 25 percent or greater margin. These students were ranked fifth, ninth, and tenth for overall English scores. The other half of this group (again, 9 percent overall) increased their English scores. These students were ranked second, eighth, and fourteenth in English scores. The remaining students remained fairly consistent in their use of English, regardless of whether they scored high or low in this area. Unlike the total point analysis, students who had measurable changes in their English scores included a wide range of students' rankings for both positive and negative changes. This might be attributed to the fact that, although proper use of English was discussed and checked for, the focus of the camp was on improving conversational skills with an underlying focus on increasing creativity and independent thought. Thus, no grammar or spelling lessons were incorporated into the camp and could have affected these scores.

Of these students, 13 percent (or four students) showed measurable change in both English and creativity scores. These students fell into two, equal categories of 6 percent (two students) each. The first category included students whose English rankings were fifth and tenth accompanied by creativity rankings of ninth and twelfth, respectively. Changes for these two students were measurably negative in English but measurably positive in creativity. In contrast, the second category included students whose English rankings were second and fourteenth with creativity rankings of tenth and fifteenth respectively. Both students had measurably positive changes in both English and creativity.

It must be noted that, although it is a small percent of the overall sample population who showed measurable increase, 69 percent of the students (twenty-two of thirty-two students) had creativity scores of 81 percent or higher. This included three of the students who showed measurable change in their creativity scores. Of the remaining 21 percent of students, four students showed improvement. This is equal to 31 percent of the total sample but is 40 percent of the subgroup who had creativity scores of less than 81 percent. Three of these students, (9 percent overall, 30 percent subgroup) had measurably positive changes in their creativity score. From this, it is evident that students who had the greatest room for improvement benefited at a much larger scale. The student who underwent the most change in both English and creativity was Bobby, one of the low-achieving students participating in the summer camp. Improvement is obvious when looking at Bobby's first and third work samples (see figures 12.1 and 12.2): in the first sample, students had to write an autobiography in which they had to talk about themselves as well as draw a picture. Even with suggested topics provided, Bobby's first assignment only shows a drawing of him and his name written next to him. In the third assignment, students had to talk about their day (what they usually do in the morning, afternoon, evening, and at night). The third assignment shows improvement in creativity, as Bobby wrote both short and longer sentences discussing activities from various times of a typical day for him.

The change in Bobby's work is similar to that seen in work of other students who exhibited measurable change throughout the course of the short summer camp. Students in this category increased their writing both in terms of quantity and quality. With comparatively fewer prompts and examples, students were able to develop independent and creative written work on the given topic. How these students performed under the more traditional and structured learning

BoBY

Figure 12.1.   Bobby's autobiography

environment is unknown; however, it is evident that the modified reader's and writer's workshop approach not only fostered creativity and independent thought but also resulted in lengthier written work from these students.

In contrast to Bobby and those students who were grouped into the initially lower achieving category for both English and creativity, Amy scored comparatively higher in both areas. Her overall total point average and her English average both ranked fifth, and her creativity average ranked sixth overall. As stated above, Amy and most of the students had initial creativity scores above 81 percent; however, even with higher initial scores, and less dramatic improvements, even higher achieving students seemed to benefit from instruction focused on increasing creative and independent thought. As with Bobby's first assignment, Amy was also asked to write a brief autobiography. Unlike Bobby, Amy was able to describe herself and family, as well as other interesting facts (see figure 12.3).

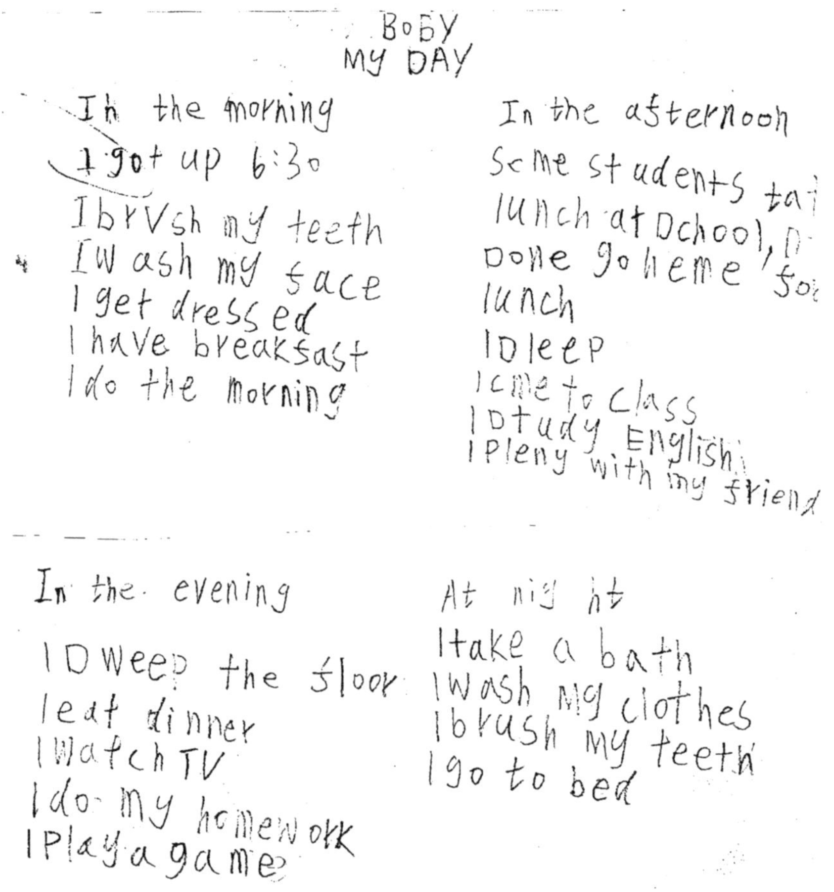
BoBY
MY DAY

In the morning
I got up 6:30
Ibrvsh my teeth
IWash my face
I get dressed
I have breakfast
I do the morning

In the afternoon
Seme students ta
lunch at Dchool, n
Done go heme fo
lunch
IDleep
Icme to Class
IDtudy English
IPleny with my friend

In the evening
IDweep the floor
leat dinner
IWatch TV
Ido my homework
IPlay a game

At nig ht
Itake a bath
IWash My clothes
Ibrush My teeth
Igo to bed

Figure 12.2. Bobby's "My Day"

This was a big difference from Bobby's picture and no text; however, the narrative in Amy's first assignment did not stray far from the prompts and suggestions given. Amy's third assignment was not deemed to show measurable difference (25 percent or greater change) in comparison to her first assignment, but it is evident that an improvement was made (see figure 12.4). Unlike her first assignment, when describing her day, Amy provided information from the prompts and ideas discussed but extended her thinking to include descriptions and information uniquely and independently her own. Not only did Amy include descriptions of whether or not she enjoyed her various activities throughout the day, but she also presented her work in a dialogue format.

It would have been much more difficult, if not impossible, for students such as Amy, who started at a higher overall creativity score than lower performing

My name is Amy, I like swimming. I don't like big pig.
My family has a me father and mother. My mother has long hair,
She like rabbit I like too. My father is theacher, he is short and
ft. I have a little rabbit, it's black.

Figure 12.3. Amy's autobiography

students such as Bobby, to increase by 25 percent to be deemed measurable. Despite this fact, even higher achieving students, such as Amy, were able to demonstrate an increase in creativity and independent thought. Thus, while the implemented strategies seemed to have made a larger impact for mid- to lower performing students, such strategies also seem to have made an impact on higher achieving students.

Only 6 percent (or two students) had measurable changes across all three areas. The first of these students ranked the lowest in each of the categories: fourteenth for English, fifteenth for creativity, and nineteenth for total points. That this student had measurable increase in all three areas seems to indicate that this modified reader's and writer's approach was an effective method of helping this lower achieving student in all three areas. The second student in this

Morning

"Good morning dad, good morning mom. I go to the play ground OK? Where? I go to the play ground to do morning exercise. OK!

Afteroom

Afteroom. I don't like shopping. But, I like draw. Look I draw a sun It's beautif

Evening

Oh, mom! where's my book? It's on the desk? No. It's on the table? Yes, I to read a book.

Night

Night, I go to bed. Good night mom dad. Good night daughter. Amy

Figure 12.4. Amy's "My Day"

category had high to middle ranking in each category: 2nd for English, 10th for Creativity, and 9th for total points. This student also realized positive gains in each area indicating this approach was also effective for mid- to high-achieving students. Again, it should be noted that although this may seem like a small number to improve across all three areas, what these students had in common was a lower achievement in the area of Creativity, which in turn affected their comprehensive scores as well. Regardless of their English rankings, one being quite high and the other quite low, both showed measurable gains. Had the camp been longer, it is possible similar results may have been evidenced in a greater number of students.

LIMITATIONS

Limitations of this study include both the small number of students and the limited numbers of student samples. A larger sample size both in terms of number of students and, perhaps, even across grade levels might yield more significant data that would help describe the effects of this approach on increasing student creativity and independent thought. Another limitation of this study is the short length of time in which the researchers had to work. Given that the summer camp was only three weeks long, the research was necessarily limited to this amount of time. Extending the data by returning to summer camps in successive years or working to implement such an approach on a more long-term basis would also add to the data set, with the possibility that a longer term implementation could provide different results.

Conclusion

Results from the short time students were in the summer camp indicate that even a modified version of reader's and writer's workshop is an effective teaching method and approach in increasing creativity and independent thought among students. Although measurable changes were limited to a small percentage of the students, it is evident that change did occur, and this was particularly evident in the area of creativity for students of varying levels of achievement. Despite the differences in approach from what was implemented and how this contrasted with what students and Chinese teachers were accustomed to (since it was less structured by allowing, encouraging, and supporting independent thought and creativity), students were able to adjust and increase creativity while Chinese teachers were able to see some benefits of this type of instruction. Further research must be conducted to more fully understand the impact of this approach on increasing student creativity. A longer period of time would be necessary; however, it is the conclusion of this study that, given the brief amount of time, change and progress was obtained in helping students increase creativity and independent thought.

References

Ammon, P. (1985). Helping children learn to write in ESL: Some observations and some hypotheses. In S. W. Freedman (Ed.), *The acquisition of written language: Response and revision* (pp. 65–84). Norwood, NJ: Ablex.

Arreaga-Mayer, C., & Perdomo-Rivera, C. (1996). Ecobehavioral analysis of instruction for at-risk language-minority students. *Elementary School Journal, 96*, 245–258.

Askew, B. J., & Frasier, D. (1999). Early writing: An exploration of literacy opportunities. *Literacy Teaching and Learning, 4*(1), 43–65.

Atwell, N. (1987). *In the middle: Writing, reading and learning with adolescents.* Portsmouth, NH: Heinemann.

Baker, S. (2000). What we know about effective instructional practices for English-language learners. *Exceptional Children, 22*(6), 1–22.

Bitz, M. (2004). The comic book project: Forging alternative pathways to literacy. *Journal of Adolescent and Adult Literacy, 47*, 574–587.

Calkins, M. (1983). *Lessons from a child: On the teaching and learning of writing.* Portsmouth, NH: Heinemann.

Clay, M. M. (1982). *Observing young readers.* Portsmouth, NH: Heinemann.

Clay, M. M. (1991). *Becoming literate: The construction of inner control.* Portsmouth, NH: Heinemann.

Clay, M. M. (1998). *By different paths to common outcomes.* York, ME: Stenhouse.

Cochran-Smith, M. (1984). *The making of a reader.* Norwood, NJ: Ablex.

Cook-Gumperz, J., & Gumperz, J. (1981). From oral to written culture: the transition to Literacy. In M. F. Whiteman (Ed.), *Variation in writing: Functional and linguistic-cultural differences* (pp. 89–109). Norwood, NJ: Ablex.

Edelsky, C., & Jilbert, K., (1985). Bilingual children and writing: Lessons for all of us. *Volta Review, 87*(5), 57–72.

Enright, D. S., & McCloskey, M. L. (1988). *Integrating English: Developing English and literacy in the multilingual classroom.* Reading, MA: Addison-Wesley.

Ernst, G., & Richard, K. L. (1995). Reading and writing pathways to conversation in the ESL classroom. *Reading Teacher, 48*(4), 320–326.

Franklin, E. A. (1986). Literacy instruction for ESL children. *Language Arts, 63*(1), 51–60.

Freeman, D., & Freeman, Y. (1998). *ESL/EFL teaching: Principles for success.* Portsmouth, NH: Heinemann.

Freeman, D., & Freeman, Y. (2000). *Teaching reading in multilingual classrooms.* Portsmouth, NH: Heinemann.

Furr, D. (2003). Struggling readers get hooked on writing. *Reading Teacher, 56*(6), 518–525.

Gersten, R., & Geva, E. (2003). Teaching reading to early language learners. *Educational Leadership, 60*(8), 44–49.

Graves, D. H. (1994). *A fresh look at writing.* Portsmouth, NH: Heinemann.

Gronlund, N. E., & Waugh, C. K. (2008). *Assessment of student achievement* (9th ed.). New Jersey, NJ: Pearson.

Hadley, A. O. (2001). *Teaching language in context* (3rd ed.). Boston: Heinle & Heinle.

Kamps, D., Abbott, M., Greenwood, C., Arreaga-Mayer, C., Wills, H., Longstaff, J., Culpepper, M., & Walton, C. (2007). Use of evidence-based, small-group reading instruction for English language learners in elementary grades: Secondary-tier intervention. *Learning Disability Quarterly, 30,* 153–168.

Krashen, S. (1993). *The power of reading.* Englewood, CO: Libraries Unlimited.

Krashen, S. (1996). *Every person a reader: An alternative to the California task force report on reading.* Culver City, CA: Language Education Associates.

Krashen, S. (1999). *Condemned without a trial: Bogus arguments against bilingual education.* Portsmouth, NH: Heinemann.

Krashen, S. D., & Terrell, T. D. (1983). *The natural approach: Language acquisition in the classroom.* Englewood Cliffs, NJ: Alemany Press.

Levie, W. H., & Lentz, R. (1982). Effects of text illustrations: A review of research. *Education Communication and Technology Journal, 30,* 195–232.

Levin, J. R., Anglin, G. J., & Carney, R. N. (1987). On empirically validating functions on pictures in prose. In D. M. Willows & H. A. Houghton (Eds.), *The psychology of illustration: Volume I. Basic research* (pp. 51–86). New York: Springer-Verlag.

Liu, J. (2004). Effects of comic strips on L2 learners, reading comprehension. *TESOL Quarterly, 38*(2), 225–243.

Macrorie, K. (1985). *Telling writing.* Upper Montclair, NJ: Boynton/Cook.

Ministry of Education, P.R.C. (2001). *English language curriculum standards.* Beijing, China: Beijing Normal University.

Mohr, K. A. J. (2004). English as an accelerated language: A call to action for reading teachers. *Reading Teacher, 58*(1), 18–26.

Morris, W. (2006). Creativity—Its place in education. Retrieved November 23, 2008, from http://74.125.45.132/search?q=cache:8SGkBHSd_OAJ:www.amcreativityassoc.org/Articles/MorrisCreativity%2520in%2520Education.doc+creativity+in+education,+wayne+morris&hl=en&ct=clnk&cd=5&gl=us&client=firefox-a.

National Clearinghouse for Bilingual Education. (2008). Rate of LEP student growth in the United States. Retrieved November 1, 2008, from www.ncbe.gwu.edu/.

Perrotta, B. (1994). Writing development and second language acquisition in young children. *Childhood Education, 70,* 237–241.

Piro, J. M. (2002). The picture of reading: Deriving meaning in literacy through image. *Reading Teacher, 56*(2), 126–134.

Ranker, J. (2007). Using comic books as read-alouds: Insights n reading instruction from an English as a second language classroom. *Reading Teacher, 61*(4), 296–305.

Rigg, P. (1981). Beginning to read in English the LEA way. In C. W. Twyford, W. Diehl, & K. Feathers (Eds.), *Reading English as a second language: Moving from theory* (pp. 81–90). Monographs in Teaching and Learning 4. Bloomington, IN: University of Indiana.

Rudden, J. F., & Nedeff, A. R. (1998). ESL learners: Process writing and publishing good literature. *Reading Horizons, 38*(3), 181–202.

Scarborough, H. (2001). Connecting early language and literacy to later reading (dis) abilities. In S. B. Neuman & D. K. Dickinson (Eds.), *Handbook of early literacy research* (pp. 97–110). New York: Guilford.

Schirmer, B. R., Casbon, J., & Twiss, L. L. (1996). Innovative literacy practices for ESL learners. *Reading Teacher, 49*, 412–414.

Schwartz, G. (2002). Graphic novels for multiple literacies. Reading Online. Retrieved October 5, 2006, from www.readingonline.org/newliteracies/lit_index.asp?HREF= jall/11-02_column/index.html.

Sowers, S. (1985). Learning to write in a workshop: A study in grades one through four. In M. Farr (Ed.), *Advances in writing research: Vol. 1. Children's early writing development*. Norwood, NJ: Ablex.

Starko, A. J. (2004). *Creativity in the classroom: Schools of curious delight* (3rd. ed.). Mahwah, NJ: Routledge.

Taberski, S. (2000). *On solid ground: Strategies for teaching reading K–3*. Portsmouth, NH: Heinemann.

Tang, G. (1992). The effect of graphic representation of knowledge structures on ESL reading comprehension. *Studies in Second Language Acquisition, 14*(2), 177–195.

Tompkins, G. (2000). *Teaching writing: Balancing process and product* (3rd ed.). New York: Prentice Hall.

U.K. National Curriculum in Action. (n.d.). Retrieved November 23, 2008, from http:// curriculum.qca.org.uk.

Vos, M. (2003). Author to author: Extending literacy through letters. *Reading Teacher, 56*(4), 340–342.

Zhan, S. (2008). Changes to a Chinese preservice language teacher education program: Analysis, results, and implications. *Asia-Pacific Journal of Teacher Education, 36*(1), 53–70.

CHAPTER 13

Poetry from Report Cards

CHILDREN'S UNDERSTANDING OF THEMSELVES IN RELATIONSHIP TO THEIR TEACHERS

Shaun Murphy
University of Saskatchewan

Shaun Murphy, Ph.D., is currently assistant professor at the University of Saskatchewan in curriculum studies. He worked alongside children in elementary classrooms for over twenty years. His research interests include curriculum, assessment, and identity using narrative inquiry.

ABSTRACT

This chapter describes how children wrote poetry to represent their understanding of themselves in relation to their teacher's comments on their report cards. The children were asked to find phrases or fragments that were personally significant and then creatively place them in order to shape poems as representations of themselves. They used these phrases and fragments to create poetry that helped the researcher and their teacher understand the ways their knowing of themselves was influenced by their teacher's knowing of them. Nona Lyons's (1990) concept of "nested knowledge" helped the researcher understand this relational aspect of knowing and curriculum making between the children and their teacher. This highlighted the ways the children's "stories to live by," a narrative concept referring to identity, were shaped in a knowledge relationship and creatively represented in the children's work.

In November, the children at Ravine Elementary received their report cards. As I watched Lian, the year 5/6 classroom teacher, work on them, I was reminded of writing report cards myself, the hours they took, the need to understand the children, and my concern about what sense the children and their families would make with them. Lian was overwhelmed with the report cards and felt as though her focus had shifted from teaching to writing reports cards. She was looking forward to being done so she could return to the rhythms of teaching.

Watching Lian write her report cards about the children I, as a collaborative researcher, wondered how the children made sense of what was written about them in the reports. I have often wondered as I wrote my own report cards how children and their families will interpret what I write. Will the report cards provide a coherent sense of them in relation to their work in school over time? Do the report cards match how parents understand their children, both in and out of school? What tensions do children have as they read what is written about them? Certainly, I know that some children have tension around their report cards because it interrupts their story of school and in some instances their relationship with a teacher.

In this chapter, I take up these questions and wonders in relation to forms of representation made by the children. In order to do this, the classroom teacher and I asked the children to write found poems using their report cards. Maxine Greene (1995) wrote,

> Aesthetic experiences require conscious participation in a work, a going out of energy, an ability to notice what is there to be noticed in the play, the poem, the quartet. Knowing "about," even in the most formal academic manner, is entirely different from constituting a fictive world imaginatively and entering it perceptually, affectively, and cognitively. To introduce students to the manner of such engagement is to strike a delicate balance between helping learners to pay heed—to attend to shapes, patterns, sounds, rhythms, figures of speech, contours, and lines—and help liberate them to achieve particular works as meaningful. (p. 124)

Lian and I hoped that the children would take up the work of representing themselves based on their report cards. This bumps up against an institutional story of report cards being written about children, and as the children in the inquiry took up the task of writing poems, it gave them authorial voice. Two questions from the call for submissions for this edition of the Yearbook are particularly salient to this chapter: What does curious and creative teaching, learning, and assessment look like? How does curious and creative teaching and learning rub against current practices in schools and teacher education settings? I would add a further wonder: what does relationship shaped in artful representation look like, and what does it allow children to say about themselves?

Situating the Inquiry

This narrative inquiry (Clandinin & Connelly, 2000) took place over eighteen months in an ethnically and economically diverse urban school in a western

Canadian city. I negotiated entry into Ravine Elementary along with a group of researchers who were part of a larger inquiry.[1] A group of interested teachers met with us and I began to work with Lian Elliot[2] and the children in the year 5/6 classroom.[3] The school was organized in multiaged grade groupings, which facilitated teachers and children working together over a two-year period. Throughout the first months of the inquiry, my field notes focused on the life of the classroom and conversations with Lian. During this time, I began the work of negotiating a research relationship with the children in the classroom. I did some coteaching with Lian, helped children, interacted with parents, and observed in the classroom and various locations throughout the school.

Narrative inquiry supported our research as a methodology because it attends to the storied experience of people and is deeply relational in the ways it invited me to live alongside the research participants. The three narrative inquiry commonplaces of temporality, sociality, and place (Connelly & Clandinin, 2006) focused my attention on the particulars, the contexts, and the people I was in research relationships with in this year 5/6 classroom (Clandinin & Connelly, 2000). These understandings of experience and the use of the commonplaces as a way to attend to storied experience resonated with how I understood experience.

I wanted to understand the ways children use various kinds of knowledge to understand and story their lives in school (Murphy, 2004). Clandinin and Connelly's (1995, 1999) work on school landscapes and identity shaped my inquiry into the experiences of children in school. The use of landscape as a metaphor provided a way of talking "about space, time and place. Furthermore, it has a sense of expansiveness and the possibility of being filled with diverse people, things, and events in different relationships" (Clandinin & Connelly, 1995, p. 4).

I drew upon the metaphor of landscape to think about the lives of children and the knowledge they hold and make in schools. Children's knowledge is diverse and influenced by relationships among people, places, and things. My research puzzle was to understand how the children were influenced and how their knowledge was shaped in these relationships.

In order to maintain my focus on understanding children's knowledge as it was shaped and reshaped in relation with their teacher, Lian, I attended to their stories to live by, a narrative term conceptualized by Michael Connelly and Jean Clandinin (1999) "[that] helps us understand how knowledge, context, and identity are linked and can be understood narratively" (p. 4). Teachers and children, in their work together in schools, shape their stories to live by in relationships. Nested knowing (Lyons, 1990) unpacked this relational aspect of knowing by considering the influence knowers have on each other. Lyons's focus on the relationship of teachers and children in knowledge creation was of particular importance in my inquiry into children's understanding of themselves in the reports written by their teacher. As a teacher who lived alongside children in classrooms in both Canada and Australia prior to engaging in doctoral study, I understood the importance of relationships. This understanding was foundational in the development of my narrative inquiry and my curiosity concerning how children made sense in schools in relation to their teacher.

COMING TO FOUND POETRY

As my earlier described wonders in relation with the children's report cards emerged, I became interested in understanding how the children's stories to live by were being shaped by the report cards. I wanted a clear sense of the children's sense-making relation with their report cards and therefore did not want to analyze the report cards on my own. I wanted the context of the children's understanding. I also wanted a distillation of the children's experience of the report card so this precluded lengthy interviews. Poetic response seemed to be the direction toward which I was inclining, but I still wanted the teacher's voice to be evident in the written work of the children. I decided on found poetry as the medium for the children's representation.

Found poetry is a poetic form that borrows from other texts. In the process of writing a found poem the writer uses the original text as a source for phrases and words. The writer pieces together words and phrases to create their poem. While the poem may highlight a sense of the original text, it also conveys its own meanings, sometimes in contradiction to the original text.

In her book *Mornings Like This*, Annie Dillard (1995) wrote a collection of found poetry based on a variety of texts. In her author's note, Dillard wrote, "By entering a found text as a poem, the poet doubles its context. The original meaning remains intact, but now it swings between two poles. The poet adds, or at any rate increases, the element of delight. . . . It serves up whole texts, or uninterrupted fragments of texts" (p. ix). Dillard's words helped me understand the possibility of found poetry. The idea of doubling context was appropriate to understanding the nested knowing of the children and their teacher.

In her work on nested knowing, Lyons (1990) considered the ways teachers' epistemologies were influenced by their work with children. I was interested in how the children's stories to live by were shaped by their teacher. By using fragments from the report cards, some of the original meaning created by the teacher would remain intact. However, the children might increase this meaning or use it to demonstrate a different way of understanding the words and, of understanding themselves, their stories to live by. While Dillard might consider this "the element of delight," I wondered if, for some children, this might show tensions they experienced in relation with report cards.

The poetry activity was one of the ways I thought of to accomplish understanding this aspect of their lives in school, and in this context, their experience of the report cards with a focus on the relationship they had with their teacher. As a classroom teacher myself, I understood my own teaching in relation to the children with whom I worked. I had a sense this was the same for the children. The children's work in the inquiry with the report cards gave me the opportunity to more clearly understand the ways they perceived how their teacher knew them in relation to the report cards.

The children's experience of the report cards occurred in the situated relationship they shared with their teacher and understood in the relational context of the classroom. By situated, I refer to the context of being in school. The report cards are about experience in school and therefore are situated in this context. John Dewey (1938) described experience when he wrote,

> Individuals live in a world . . . in the concrete . . . in a series of situations. . . . It means, once more, that interaction is going on between an individual and objects and other persons. The conceptions of *situation* and of *interaction* are inseparable from each other. An experience is always what it is because of a transaction taking place between an individual and what, at the time, constitutes his environment, whether the latter consists of persons with whom he is talking about some topic or event, the subject talked about being also a part of the situation. (pp. 43–44)

I drew on Dewey's conception of experience to understand children's experiences of school. I used the ideas of situation and interaction as I endeavored to understand children's knowledge of school, particularly when considering Lyon's (1990) concept of nested knowing. In the context of the children's work with the report cards, it was helpful to think about the continuity of relationship with their teacher and assessment over the school year. In order to do this, the children wrote poems after both the November and March report cards.

Lyons (1990) wrote about how teachers' knowledge of students shaped their epistemological understanding of themselves, one side of the teacher-student relationship. In this way, teachers as knowers were shaped by the knowing of the children with whom they worked. The idea of knowers knowing knowers is complex and multiperspectival, and in conversation with Lyons (personal communication, April 20, 2003), we began to wonder how the children's epistemological understanding was also shaped by the ways the teacher knew them. This was further complicated as the inquiry progressed by understanding how, like a spider's web of connected strands, children's nested knowledge was entwined with the ways their classmates knew them as well. Nested knowledge was not only a two-way dialogue between the teacher and the child in the context of the classroom but also a conversation among all members.

The children's poetry became an important interim text in my inquiry into the children's knowledge. With only the report cards, I could not understand how the children experienced Lian's assessment of them. However, by writing the poems the children shaped my understanding of how their stories to live by were being shaped by their teacher.

We asked the children to do this by repeating lines from the report card that were important to them, using phrases from the report card that they thought showed who they might be in school with or who resonated with them and words that captured or did not capture their work in school. In this sense, the children created interim texts for me and helped me understand the field texts of the report cards. Interim texts are defined by Clandinin and Connelly (2000) as "texts situated in the spaces between field texts and final, published research texts . . . these interim texts are built into the inquiry that is, they are built into the negotiations that bring the researcher to the field" (p. 133). As interim texts, the poems were situated in this middle space of the inquiry and supported a negotiation of understanding with the earlier field texts represented by the report cards.

CREATING THE POETRY

In order to understand the process of found poetry before we began to work with the report cards, Lian and I taught a found poetry lesson based on the book *An Angel for Solomon Singer* (Rylant, 1992). On a subsequent day, Lian retaught the lesson using a different book, in order to give the children experience across diverse texts. We followed this by asking the children to choose a folk tale or fairytale from which to create a found poem. As part of my field texts, I wrote that

> the children had chosen books of interest to them. For some children I returned to the library to find other books that interested them and in some cases matched more appropriately their reading levels. The depth and quality of the poems varied greatly. In some, children wrote lines that did not seem to have any aesthetic quality. In others, powerful images were conjured by the words and phrases they chose. (field note, December 5, 2002)

Now that the children had a sense of what a found poem was, we handed out copies of their report cards. We explained they were going to create found poetry using the text of their report cards in the same way they created poetry using the folk tales and fairytales from the library.

When we returned the report cards to the children as working documents, they took them and read through them. By this time, they had taken the reports home, and some of them had returned their copies to the school. After they read through the report cards, they highlighted phrases that were important to them or resonated somehow. The focus of the activity was to create a poem that showed how they felt about their report cards while at the same time demonstrating what the report card and, therefore their teacher, was saying about them.

The poems the children created were diverse in form, structure, and content and are included later in this chapter. The children found creating poetry based on the report cards more difficult than creating poems based on the fairytales because the language was not as full of images. However, the poems they created were successful in communicating how they saw themselves through the report cards.

In some poems, the children focused on positive comments; in others, the focus was on areas for growth. In some, the focus was on the grades they received. Some were positive, and others focused more on what might be seen as negative comments. What was significant to me was how the children saw themselves in a situated way, given the report cards were written by their teacher about them. The children had never before been offered the opportunity to play with the words of their report cards and, in a sense, to own them. I use the word "situated" to describe this because it suggests the layered nature of knowing, the back and forth movement that added texture to the work with the report cards. The work of writing the poems was also an intentional act that gave power (Cook-Sather, 2002) to the children in the form of being able to shape statements about themselves with someone else's words, in this case, their teacher's, Lian's, words. The children became involved in curriculum making with their teacher (Clandinin et al., 2006) as they explored ways of representing identity.

At Ravine Elementary, the report cards did not have letter grades. Instead, the report cards used the phrases "work meets acceptable standard, work exceeds acceptable standard, and work meets standard of excellence" to grade the children. Some of the children used these comments in their poems. Others translated these comments into letter grades and made this the focus of the found poems based on their report cards. Christa's poem is an example of this interpretation. On her report card, she wrote the letter grades beside the phrases. Christa was not the only student who wrote letter grades beside the assessment phrases. Other children's marked-up report cards and poems made reference to this interpretation of the assessment phrases.

Christa: Editing Her Report Card, Editing Her Stories to Live By

Christa was absent when the first report card went home. Therefore, she had less practice with creating found poetry. She and I had a brief conversation about the intention of the activity. Interestingly, her poem provided me with a perspective different from the other children. In her poem, she did more editing and shaped it to fit her interpretation. Christa worked hard to make sense of her life in school. This poem is an example of sense making in relation to the report card Lian wrote about her.

> Progress report and Me
> Out of effort I
> Got three excellent
> Out of A's, B's, and C's,
> I got one A, three B's
> And four C's
> I was upset
> I was upset
> But one A to rise my
> Fallen hopes
> One A to please me
> I am glad
> I am glad
> My hope rises and my thirst
> Becomes stronger for another A
> I am eager
> I am eager (student work, April 2003)

In this poem, Christa highlighted that one of the ways she saw herself in school was shaped by the words Lian wrote about her. Lian did not use letter grades, but Christa easily translated them. Just as found poetry distills the essence of a text to what the writer wishes, Christa's poem distilled how she saw herself in the report card. Her poem gave her an opportunity to retell. In her poem, she writes of the tensions she felt by not doing well in the marking scheme. However, while she did avoid naming the three Cs, she focuses our attention on the one A and her desire to do better.

It is important to note that Christa did not use the form of found poetry in her writing. She did not use fragments from the report card to create her poem. In that way, there is no doubling of context between the teacher's words and Christa's. However, the poignant use of letter grades along with her own words makes it clear how her story to live by is influenced by the report card. The interplay between the representations she saw in the letter grades and her desire to do better is evident. When I looked at the report card copy from which she worked, I saw that she highlighted the phrase "effort excellent" three times and "work meets standard of excellence," which occurred only once in the area of art. Beside all the phrases for achievement and effort, she had written the corresponding letter grades, which comprise the main theme of her poem. It would seem that Christa understood report cards in this manner. For Christa, report cards are a judgment of her ability according to a scale. Christa did not have a smooth experience of school. She had difficulty negotiating relationships with other students and struggled with concepts in her schoolwork.

In this poem, Christa's drew my attention to the ways her identity making, the making (or remaking) of her stories to live by, took place in the nested relationship she had with Lian. Her emotions were tied to the ways her teacher represented her, supporting an understanding of the place of nested knowledge (Lyons, 1990) in the classroom and the social commonplace of narrative inquiry. This illustrated how Christa's story can be understood socially within the relationship she has with her teacher. Both Lian and I read Christa's poem with a deeper sense of the tensions she held. Dewey (1980) wrote, "The career and destiny of a living being are bound up with its interchanges with its environment, not externally but in the most intimate way" (p. 13). With her poem, Christa highlighted the internal, intimate response her report card engendered and exposed these thoughts to her audience. In this way, she creatively stories herself forward as a successful child in school.

Serena: Maintaining Narrative Coherence in Knowledge and Identity Making

Poems written by some of the other children were composed by lifting fragments from the report cards and writing them in the order they appeared in the original text. Others played with the structure of their poems and manipulated the fragments they used from the report cards often repeating phrases they saw as important. Serena, a child with quite a smooth story of life in school, composed the following,

> Serena
> Helpful and cooperative,
>   respectful
> Completes assignments
>   on time
> Strong role model
> She is a willing writer who is able to:
>   jot down ideas,
>   observations,
> memories,
>   and reflections in her writer's notebook
> Strong role model
> Helps readers visualize the piece

> Communicated effectively with group members,
>   sharing ideas,
>   cooperating,
> Strong role model
> She was able to select pertinent:
>   information,
>   create treasure notes,
>   and write paragraphs,
> Worked very hard on this project
> Strong role model
> Showed an interest in and enjoyment of our
>   cooperative games,
>   positive attitude
> Cared for and put good effort into her projects
> Strong role model (student work, December 2002)

In all subject matter areas on her report card, Lian assessed that Serena's "work meets the standard of excellence." The narratives written by the teacher in each subject matter section began with "Serena is able . . . " then gave examples of how she is able and finished with a goal or an area to work on. Serena's poem shows a similar sense, that is, she also perceives herself as able. My observations of her in class working or interacting with her classmates confirmed how her poem mirrors who she was in school. The sense of delight for Serena in this poem is evident. The fragments Serena chose are intact phrases from her report card.

Dewey's (1938) understanding of experience points to the ways poems are transactions between the text and the children, with the teacher in the background as the creator of the text. In the continuous making and remaking of identity on school landscapes, Serena highlights the ways she is a strong role model. Naming herself as a strong role model, she notes the transaction she has within the environment of her classroom. Choosing these words from her teacher's representation in the report card underscores the element of transaction. She has chosen not words like good student, which might be understood privately, but rather the more public and possibly transactional identity of being a role model.

Catrina: Interpreting Her and Retelling Her Stories to Live By

In another poem, Catrina, a girl who lived life in the year 5/6 classroom on the margins of the social space created by the children, played with the structure of her poem and combined elements that are present in both Christa and Serena's poems.

Grade 5

Never late
Responsible
Organization
neatness
fighting less
standard of excellence
enjoyment in reading
willing writer
acceptable
quality skills
recorder playing
willingly participates
good effort
A
A
A
A
A
B
B
B
acceptable
willingly participates
recorder playing
standard of excellence (student work, April 2003)

Alongside her poem, Catrina had used a red felt pen to write, "A+, 100%, and 'Good job, Catrina!'" In the previous report card poem she wrote in December, she had filled the page around the poem with As and Bs. Beside each A she put a ✓, and beside each B, an X. Like Christa, she converted the reporting phrases into letter grades and used them in her report card. In the poem above, she manipulated both word meaning and context. For example, "never late" comes from the documentation at the top of the report card about attendance: "Times late: None"; nowhere in the poem does it say never late. She also played with the words "fighting less" because Lian had written, "One goal of Catrina's will be to work on fighting less and staying organized." Catrina clearly and creatively edited her report card to shape the poem she wanted to craft in order to represent herself to us. This creative reconstruction highlights the way imagination and shifted representations can maintain narrative unity (Clandinin & Connelly, 1988).

As an added dimension, Catrina was a girl who saw ghosts at school and at home, dealt with witches, and described some of her reality using paranormal references. She was able to bend reality to describe her experience, and I see this in the way she manipulated the report card words to shape her poem. While she was influenced by Lian's comments, she also asserted authorship and interpretive stance on the wording of the report card. Catrina's poem is more about who she is in relation to her own work and not the social life of the classroom.

Layers of Assessment: Doubling Nested Knowledge

An important part of the nested knowing in this piece of the inquiry was that before each report card was written by Lian the children did a writing piece about their lives and work in school. In October, they completed a sheet titled "Skills for School Success." On the sheet, they were asked to finish leading sentences or answer questions about their experiences in school related to their work and relationships with others. In March, the children kept a journal for a week and then used the journal entries to create poems.

These poems were not found poems but rather research-based poems, although in some of the children's work, elements of found poetry were evident. The children used these journal entries to create a research-based poem about their experiences in school. Lian's intent was to use these student-generated reflections to help her write the report cards. A careful examination shows the influence of the student writing in Lian's report cards. I chose Kerry to demonstrate this recursive assessment writing in more depth across the school year. Using the poetry of Kerry over the time period of the two assessments attends to the ways temporality shaped Kerry's representations of the ways he was composing his story to live by in the year 5/6 classroom.

On Kerry's October skills for school success sheet, he wrote he was a learner and funny. He also wrote, in response to a question about whether or not he is respectful, "Yes I'm [respectful] because I play with them [other students] and we . . . have fun" (student work, October 24, 2002). On his report card, Lian wrote, "He shows respect to classmates and teachers" (student report card, November 15, 2003). Throughout his skills for school success writing, Kerry wrote about how he was distracted easily by other interests and children. In his response to the questions "Do you stay on task? Do you stay focused?" he responded, "I stay on task most of the time. I get distracted reall[y] easy so I'm sometimes focused" (student work, October 24, 2003). In the report card Lian wrote, "He tries his best to stay focused but finds it easy to get distracted" (student report card, November 15, 2003).

KERRY: MAKING SHIFTS IN HIS STORIES TO LIVE BY

Here is how Kerry constructed his poem based on the November report card. In it I saw how his poem was situated within his skills for school success writing and the report card written about him.

> Kerry
> Able to jot down ideas, observations,
> memories and reflection.
> Easy to get distracted.
> Compare experimental and theoretical
> results.
> Easy to get distracted.
> Sharing ideas and cooperating while
> Working.
> Easy to get distracted.
> Gather notes affectively.
> Easy to get distracted.
> Enjoyment of our cooperative
> games and volleyball units.
> Easy to get distracted.
> Recognize, analyze and create abstract
> works of art. (student work, December 2002)

In this first poem, it is interesting how Kerry repeated the line "easy to get distracted" when all the other lines indicate a student with good skills who is doing well in all of his subjects. What he chose to ignore was Lian's comment about his "trying to stay focused," a line he wrote himself on the skills for school success sheet. He was successful in his work and his relationships. As an observer in the class, I found that Kerry was, at times, distracted from his work. He did visit with other children, he drew when he was supposed to be working on other projects, and sometimes, as I watched, he was obviously not paying attention. However, none of this was a significant part of how I knew Kerry within the context of the classroom. He was not unlike some of the other children in his level of distractibility.

What intrigued me most about this activity was the obvious nested nature of what was occurring. Kerry saw himself as a distracted individual within the context of being a student in a class. He wrote twice on his skills for school success sheet that he "goofs off" and he listens "sometimes because I usually talk to Leo" (student work, October 24, 2003). This knowledge is reflective of knowing how he should behave in class and his perceived ideas of how he is seen as a student. He wrote he preferred to work independently: "[Because] I sometimes say to myself and say, 'Oh no I have to do my best work because somebody is watching me'" (student work, October 24, 2003). In a classroom, students learn quickly that someone is watching them. Lian wrote in his report card in the skills for school success section,

> Kerry is a contributing learner in our classroom. He tries his best to stay focused but finds it easy to get distracted. He consistently completes assignments on time and takes pride and care in his work. He shows respect to classmates and teachers. One goal of Kerry's will be to try and make better use of class time. I will be encouraging Kerry to volunteer in our Ravine School community. It is a pleasure to have Kerry in our classroom. (student report card, November 15, 2002)

These words reflected what Lian knew about Kerry but also what Kerry had written about himself on his personal assessment. This is how Lian and Kerry demonstrated their nested knowledge. But in a classroom, nested knowledge is not only found in the relationship of the teacher and student. It also is a part of children's relationships with each other.

In a situated relationship with Leo, Kerry might say he is good at talking. Leo, who sat beside him and also liked to draw, might tell us Kerry is a good artist. Kerry knew, however, the skills for school success was communication with his teacher. Lian knows her reports are about communicating with parents and children. For Kerry and the other children, the report cards are about achievement and behavior within a nested relationship with their teacher bound by the expectations of school.

Kerry's April poem based on the March report card had a different tone to it. This may be attributed to a deeper relationship with his teacher, a greater understanding of himself as a student, or perhaps more trust in his relationship with me. It might also indicate Kerry had settled into the rhythms and expectations of school. He might be, as Patrick Chamoiseau (1997) would see it, more domesticated as a student. There is also a more relaxed tone to this poem that I attribute to the opening line. School skills still factor in this poem, but there is a more personal tone.

> Funny member of our classroom
> and is responsible for his choices
> Enjoys reading
> Finds multiples and factors and
> still working on problem solving
> Enjoys reading
> Can record observations accurately with good detail

Enjoys reading
We have an artist in the room
and puts good effort into his pro-
jects
Enjoys reading
Participates in dance and on his
Skills in basketball
Enjoys reading (student work, April 2003)

This poem demonstrated Kerry had developed a smoother story of school. He enjoyed reading, and for him this was a shift, obviously a significant one. Instead of being easily distracted, now he is responsible for his choices. There is a sense from the shift in Kerry's poems that he may be intentionally reforming his identity at school. His poems highlight a difference in his identity at school, and his journal entries demonstrate a desire to step out of older plotlines and create new ones.

Concluding Thoughts

Methodologically, the found poems gave me insight into how the children understood themselves in relationship to their teacher's assessment by creating their own texts based on the report cards. Writing the poems also allowed them to shape an understanding of their identities around the report cards and exert some control over the words that were written about them, a shaping of a life curriculum (Clandinin et al., 2006) in relation to their identities. As a researcher, it allowed me to look at how they saw themselves represented. When I read the report cards, I did not have the same sense of them the children captured in their writing. They are report cards, respectful in tone, but written in the jargon of reporting.

Christa, Serena, Catrina, and Kerry, and the other children, regardless of whether their poems were smooth or tension filled, reflected a knowing of self, based on their report cards. The nested knowledge demonstrated by the children is evident in the way they wrote, the words they chose, and the phrases they highlighted in the report cards. It was evident the report cards' comments shaped the children's understanding of themselves in school. Greene (1995) wrote, "Others determine 'exactly' what 'you are' and use fixed names. To be yourself is to be in process of creating a self, and identity" (p. 20).

Thinking about how the children's stories to live by were shaped by the report cards highlighted the authority of the teacher's voice in the nested knowledge relationships of a classroom. It was easy to understand how the children responded to the report cards, and the words they selected show how they are known in the document. I am left to wonder what is absent from the report cards in how these children might know themselves. This draws my attention to what is excluded when we assess children, given the constraints of assessment and its representation in report cards. However, what is absent was brought back imaginatively and creatively in the children's representations. Places of tension, delight, desire, and levels of interpretation all became part of the poems. Dewey (1980) reminds me that "experience enacted is human and conscious only as that which is given here and now is extended by meanings and values drawn from what is absent in fact and present only in imagination" (p. 272).

The children's found poetry helped me understand more about the children and how their stories to live by in school were shaped by the nested knowledge relationship they had with their teacher. The poems were a fundamental way for me to consider the nested knowledge of the children, to understand the connection between the ways their teacher knew them and how this shaped their school stories to live by. As a teacher, this work helped me understand that, "to learn and to teach, one must have an awareness of leaving something behind while reaching toward something new, and this kind of awareness must be linked to imagination" (Greene, 1995, p. 20). We asked the children to imagine what they might write about themselves in their poems, but as teachers we also challenged ourselves imaginatively to live alongside the children in a different way in relation to their report cards.

This work with the children and their found poems also drew me to new questions and deeper understandings of the ways in which report cards can shape the identity making and, therefore, the life curricula of children and how children can creatively bump up against this and through their own work hold open spaces for identity making, even in places of tension. One aspect that might be otherwise is that Lian's and the children's negotiations and nested knowing in relation with their report card making is so evidently relational. If we attend to what the children showed through their found poetry making over time, they are, I think, trying to push back against sole teacher authority in report cards. They want to have, and can have, as the report cards show, agency and voice in the process, which can then shape whole new layers or threads in their identity making, in their life curriculum making.[4]

Notes

1. This study, "School Landscapes in Transition: Negotiating Diverse Narratives of Experience," was supported by a Social Sciences and Humanities Research Council grant held by F. M. Connelly and D. J. Clandinin.

2. Pseudonyms are used for the teacher, children, and school.

3. Year 5/6 refers to a diverse group of ten- to twelve-year-old children. At Ravine Elementary School, "year" was used in place of grade.

4. Special thanks to Janice Huber; her careful reading and ideas strengthened this chapter.

References

Chamoiseau, P. (1997). *School days*. Lincoln: University of Nebraska Press.

Clandinin, D. J., & Connelly, F. M. (1988). Studying teachers' knowledge of classrooms: Collaborative research, ethics, and the negotiation of narrative. *Journal of Educational Thought, 22*(2A), 269–282.

Clandinin, D. J., & Connelly, F. M. (1995). *Teachers' professional knowledge landscapes*. New York: Teachers College Press.

Clandinin, D. J., & Connelly, F. M. (2000). *Narrative inquiry: Experience and story in qualitative research*. San Francisco: Jossey-Bass.

Clandinin, D. J., Huber, J., Huber, M., Murphy, M. S., Pearce, M., Murray-Orr, A., et al. (2006). *Composing diverse identities: Narrative inquiries into the interwoven lives of children and teachers*. London: Routledge.

Connelly, F. M., & Clandinin, D. J. (1999). *Shaping a professional identity: Stories of educational practice*. New York: Teachers College Press.

Connelly, F. M., & Clandinin, D. J. (2006). Narrative inquiry. In J. Green, G. Camilli, & P. Elmore (Eds.), *Handbook of complementary methods in education research* (pp. 375–385). Mahwah, NJ: Lawrence Erlbaum.

Cook-Sather, A. (2002). Authorizing students' perspectives: Toward trust, dialogue, and change in education. *Educational Researcher, 31*(4), 3–14.

Dewey, J. (1938). *Experience and education*. New York: Simon and Schuster.

Dewey, J. (1980). *Art as experience*. New York: Perigee Books.

Dillard, A. (1995). *Mornings like this: Found poems*. New York: HarperCollins.

Greene, M. (1995). *Releasing the imagination: Essays on education, the arts, and social change*. San Francisco: Jossey-Bass.

Lyons, N. (1990). Dilemmas of knowing: Ethical and epistemological dimensions of teachers' work and development. *Harvard Educational Review, 60*(2), 159–180.

Murphy, M. S. (2004). Understanding children's knowledge: A narrative inquiry into school experiences. Unpublished Ph.D. diss., University of Alberta, Edmonton, Canada.

Rylant, C. (1992). *An angel for Solomon Singer*. New York: Orchard Books.

Summary and Implications

Cheryl J. Craig

Louise F. Deretchin

Division 2, "Students, Programs, and Schools," began with Ginny Esch's chapter, "Young Children: Creativity in the Classroom." Through carefully chosen story fragments, Esch reminded readers of how young children's minds work. She additionally underlined the importance of process over product, offered approaches that have met with success in the past, and addressed misconceptions about how creativity is expressed in youth.

Following Esch's chapter 6 came Julia Cote's chapter 7, "Arts-Based Education and Creativity." Whereas the former chapter dealt with arts-based learning strategies within a classroom, the latter chapter took up the topic of cultivating arts-based instruction in a school and how that might be fruitfully accomplished, particularly with a faculty whose members who were not uniformly arts oriented.

Chapter 8 centers on Sandra Wasko-Flood's idea of "Labyrinths for Creativity and Peace in Schools." The work informs readers that labyrinths are universal symbols with deep cross-cultural roots. In addition to this, labyrinths can be used to pedagogically mingle multiple intelligences. Walking the labyrinth, students have the opportunity to become transformed. Then, they return to the beginning via the same pathway, albeit in a different direction. Students' peace wishes and responses included in chapter 8 attest to the fact that the experience of the labyrinth is powerful and potentially life altering.

Chapters 9 and 10 addressed creativity as cultivated in programs in which aboriginal children participated. Authored by Beverly Klug and Patricia Whitfield, chapter 9 was titled "A Mind with a View: Education through the Kaleidoscopic Lenses of the Arts" and involved American Indian children. Meanwhile, chapter 10, "The First Thunder Clap of Spring: An Invitation into Aboriginal

Ways of Knowing," dealt with First Nations children in Canada and was written by Sharon Friesen, David Jardine, and Brenda Gladstone.

In chapter 9, Klug and Whitfield outlined programs that had been successfully adapted for American Indian children. At the same time, they maintained that strategies and foci could be borrowed from these programs and used in ways that would resonate with the cultural uniqueness of the youngest members of what has been a historically underserved group.

From educating a historically underserved group in the United States, we moved on to the teaching and learning of the same historically underserved group, albeit in Canada. In chapter 10, authors Friesen, Jardine, and Gladstone demonstrated how the aboriginal view of knowledge as something living was honored in curriculum offerings. Moreover, affinities between new information and communication technologies and aboriginal epistemology were tapped in ways that spawned curiosity and creativity while challenging conventional approaches to teaching social studies curriculum.

Exemplars were also integral to Jacqueline Sack's chapter 11, "Fostering Creative Minds through Problem Solving in a 3-D Visualization Design Research Program." In that work, students created experiences and products through the deliberate use of problem solving and reinvention. Sack appropriately used nine figures to chart the understanding of how diverse children were educated in an after-school program in a major urban center in the United States.

In chapter 12, readers travelled to China, another culturally distinctive place, alongside Teresa Leavitt and Madalina Tanase, authors of "A Report of the Introduction and Resulting Effects of Novel Teaching Strategies in Increasing Creativity and Independent Thought." With the authors, readers came to know both the possibilities and paradoxes associated with increasing students' English proficiencies and creative and independent thought. As with so many of the other chapters in the divisions, this one included powerful exemplars that both depicted and illuminated growth, albeit in a camp setting.

In chapter 13, we moved to Canada once again and the chapter "Poetry from Report Cards: Children's Understanding of Themselves in Relationship to Their Teachers," which asserted the primacy of relationship between teachers and students and how student identity is shaped by it. Written by Shaun Murphy, the work particularly pointed to tensions in students' identities and how teachers' report card responses to them influenced how students "identify" themselves. As with other chapters in this division and volume, this chapter was filled to the brim with creative thought as lived and expressed by children, teachers—and researchers.

Like the chapters in division 1, the eight chapters that comprised division 2 did not disappoint. They cajoled us, tantalized us, and left us in a state of perpetual wonder: why is something so critical as the development of curious and creative minds being left to the fringes (one program, one school, one camp, one after-school activity, and one creative research project, for example) when the opportunities it affords deny limits?

Afterword

Cheryl J. Craig

Louise F. Deretchin

In *Cultivating Curious and Creative Minds: The Role of Teachers and Teacher Educators, Part II,* readers have experienced how the topic plays out in the teacher education arena (division 1) and with students, programs, and schools (division 2). Part II added to insights gained from the companion publication *Cultivating Curious and Creative Minds: The Role of Teachers and Teacher Educators, Part I,* which focused on teaching. Once again, we thank the authors in the two-part series for allowing readers to get inside the rich experiences that have been shared and to understand curiosity and creativity and the fundamental human need for both from the perspectives of preservice and in-service teachers, teacher educators, and students in schools.

Despite the palpable constraints placed on educators and youth who meet face-to-face in the contested classroom space (Craig, 2009), it is comforting to know that, even amid the narrowing of the stated curriculum, some are still finding and making wiggle room to explore creative possibility. Their maneuvering and their ongoing willingness to maneuver—sometimes at considerable personal risk—enables us to end this volume on an optimistic note.

Reference

Craig, C. (2009). The contested classroom space: A decade of lived educational policy in Texas schools. *American Educational Research Journal, 46*(4), 1034–1058.